Two Years
Before the Mast

G·K
Hall
&Cº

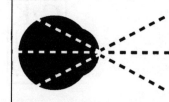

This Large Print Book carries the
Seal of Approval of N.A.V.H.

Two Years Before the Mast

A Personal Narrative of Life at Sea

R. H. DANA

G.K. Hall & Co. • Thorndike, Maine

G.K. Hall Large Print Perennial Bestseller Series.

This Large Print edition was produced from the 1909 Famous Fiction Library edition.

Set in 16 pt. Plantin by Juanita Macdonald.

Printed in the United States on permanent paper.

Library of Congress Cataloging in Publication Data

Dana, Richard Henry, 1815–1882.
   Two years before the mast : a personal narrative of life at sea / by R.H. Dana.
      p. (large print) cm.
   ISBN 0-7838-8453-2 (lg. print : hc : alk. paper)
   1. Voyages and travels. 2. Seafaring life. 3. Large-type books — Specimens.   I. Title.
   [G540.D2 1998]
   910.4′5—dc21   98-5398

ALL'S WELL.

Deserted by the waning moon,
Then skies proclaim night's cheerless noon,
On tower, or fort, or tented ground
The sentry walks his lonely round;
And should a footstep haply stray
Where caution marks the guarded way,
"Who goes there? Stranger, quickly tell!"
"A friend!" "The word?"
   "Good-night"; all's well.

Or sailing on the midnight deep,
When weary messmates soundly sleep,
The careful watch patrols the deck,
To guard the ship from foes or wreck;
And while his thoughts oft homewards veer,
Some friendly voice salutes his ear —
"What cheer? brother, quickly tell;
Above — below."
   "Good-night"; all's well.

THOMAS DIBDIN.

BIOGRAPHY

Richard Henry Dana, Jr., a distinguished member of the Boston bar, author of *Two Years Before the Mast, a Personal Narrative of Life at Sea,* and son of Richard Henry Dana, poet, diplomatist, and jurist, was born in Cambridge, Mass., August 1, 1815. From early boyhood he had a strong desire for a seafaring life, and was exceedingly anxious to enter the United States navy; but his father persuaded him to seek a college education and become a lawyer. He was prepared for college at home, entered Harvard, was soon afterward rusticated as his father had been before him, and after returning to college was compelled to suspend his studies by an affection of his eyes resulting from an attack of measles.

His heart now again turned to the sea, and he determined to rough it as a common sailor on a Pacific voyage, though he had every facility for more comfortable travel and adventure. Accordingly, he set sail from Boston on the brig *Pilgrim,* for a voyage around Cape Horn to the Westward coast of North America, on August 14, 1834; performed his duty throughout with cheerfulness and an obedient spirit, and returned with the ship to Boston in September, 1836. In 1839, the manuscript of his most famous work was offered to various New York publishers, and was finally purchased by the Harpers for $250, and published in 1840.

On his return he re-entered Harvard, finished the course, was graduated in 1837, and then took the course at the Harvard Law School under Judge Story and Professor Greenleaf, and was admitted to practice in 1840. He soon attained eminence as an advocate, and also became widely noted in the practice of maritime law and as an expert on international law. In 1868, he was an unsuccessful candidate for Congress; in 1876 he failed to be confirmed as minister to England; in 1878 he went abroad with the intention of writing a great work on international law; and on January 7, 1882, he died at Rome, Italy.

CHAPTER I

"My Native Land, Good-night!"

The fourteenth of August was the day fixed upon for the sailing of the brig *Pilgrim*, on her voyage from Boston, round Cape Horn, to the western coast of North America. As she was to get under way early in the afternoon, I made my appearance on board at twelve o'clock, in full sea-rig, and with my chest, containing an outfit for a two or three years' voyage, which I had undertaken from a determination to cure, if possible, by an entire change of life, and by a long absence from books and study, a weakness of the eyes which had obliged me to give up my pursuits, and which no medical aid seemed likely to cure.

I joined the crew, and we hauled out into the stream, and came to anchor for the night. The next day we were employed in preparations for sea, reeving studding-sail gear, crossing royal-yards, putting on chafing gear, and taking on board our powder. On the following night I stood my first watch. I remained awake nearly all the first part of the night; and when I went on deck, so great were my ideas of the importance of my trust, that I walked regularly fore and aft the whole length of the vessel, looking out over the bows and taffrail at each turn, and was not a little surprised at the coolness of the old salt whom I called to take my place, in stowing himself snugly away under the longboat for a nap.

The next morning was Saturday, and, a breeze having sprung up from the southward, we took a pilot on board, and began beating down the bay. As we drew down into the lower harbor, we found the wind ahead in the bay, and were obliged to come to anchor in the roads. We remained there through the day and a part of the night. My watch began at eleven o'clock at night. About midnight the wind became fair, and, having called the captain, I was ordered to call all hands. How I accomplished this I do not know, but I am quite sure that I did not give the true hoarse boatswain call of "A-a-ll ha-a-a-nds! up anchor, a-ho-oy!" In a short time every one was in motion, the sails loosed, the yards braced, and we began to heave up the anchor. I could take but little part in these preparations. My little knowledge of a vessel was all at fault. Unintelligible orders were so rapidly given, and so immediately executed; there was such a hurrying about, and such an intermingling of strange cries and stranger actions, that I was completely bewildered. At length those peculiar, long-drawn sounds which denote that the crew are heaving at the windlass began, and in a few minutes we were under way. The noise of the water thrown from the bows began to be heard, the vessel leaned over from the damp night-breeze, and rolled with the heavy ground-swell, and we had actually begun our long, long journey.

CHAPTER II

The First Day at Sea

The first day we passed at sea was the Sabbath. As we were just from port, and there was a great deal to be done on board, we were kept at work all day, and at night the watches were set, and everything put into sea order.

I, being in the starboard or second mate's watch, had the opportunity of keeping the first watch at sea. S—, a young man making, like myself, his first voyage, was in the same watch, and as he was the son of a professional man we found that we had many friends and topics in common. We talked matters over — Boston, what our friends were probably doing, our voyage, etc., — until he went to take his turn at the look-out, and left me to myself. I had now a fine time for reflection.

But all my dreams were soon put to flight by an order from the officer to trim the yards, as the wind was getting ahead; and I could plainly see, by the looks the sailors occasionally cast to windward, and by the dark clouds that were fast coming up, that we had bad weather to prepare for, and had heard the captain say that he expected to be in the Gulf Stream by twelve o'clock. In a few minutes eight bells were struck, the watch called, and we went below. I now began to feel the first discomforts of a sailor's life. The steerage, in which I lived, was filled with coils of rigging, spare sails, old junk, and ship stores, which had not been stowed away. Moreover, there had been no berths built for us to sleep in. The sea, too, had risen, the vessel was rolling heavily, and everything was pitched about in grand confusion. There was a complete "hurrah's nest" as the sailors say, "everything on top and nothing at hand." A large hawser had been coiled away upon my chest; my hats, boots, mattress, and blankets had all *fetched away* and gone over to leeward,[*] and were jammed and broken under the boxes and coils of rigging. To crown all, I was just beginning to feel strong symptoms of sea-sickness, and that listlessness and inactivity which accompany it. Giving up all attempts to collect my things together, I lay down upon the sails, expecting every moment to hear the cry of "All hands, ahoy!" which the approaching storm would soon make necessary. I shortly heard the raindrops falling on deck thick and fast, and the watch evidently had their hands full of work, for I could hear the loud and repeated orders of the mate, the trampling of feet, the creaking of blocks, and all the accompaniments of a coming storm. In a few minutes the slide of the hatch was

[*] *Lee,* the side opposite to that from which the wind blows. *Leeward,* the lee side.

thrown back, which let down the noise and tumult of the deck still louder, the loud cry of "All hands, ahoy! Tumble up here and take in sail!" saluted our ears, and the hatch was quickly shut again. When I got upon deck, a new scene and a new experience was before me.

The little brig was close-hauled upon the wind, and lying over, as it then seemed to me, nearly upon her beam-ends. The heavy head-sea was beating against her bows with the noise and force almost of a sledge-hammer, and flying over the deck, drenching us completely through. The topsail-halyards had been let go, and the great sails were filling out and backing against the masts with a noise like thunder; the wind was whistling through the rigging; loose ropes flying about; loud, and, to me, unintelligible orders constantly given, and rapidly executed; and the sailors "singing out" at the ropes in their hoarse and peculiar strains.

In addition to all this, I had not got my "sea legs on," was dreadfully sick, with hardly strength enough to hold on to anything, and it was "pitch dark." This was my state when I was ordered aloft, for the first time, to reef topsails.

How I got along I cannot now remember. I "laid out" on the yards and held on with all my strength. I could not have been of much service, for I remember having been sick several times before I left the topsail yard. Soon all was snug aloft, and we were again allowed to go below.

This state of things continued for two days.

Wednesday, August 20th. When we came on deck at four o'clock, we found things much changed for the better. The sea and wind had gone down, and the stars were out bright.

Nothing will compare *with the early breaking of day* upon the wide, sad ocean. There is something in the first gray streaks stretching along the eastern horizon, and throwing an indistinct light upon the face of the deep, which creates a feeling of loneliness, of dread, and of melancholy foreboding, which nothing else in nature can give.

From such reflections as these, I was aroused by the order from the officer, "Forward there! rig the head-pump!" I found that no time was allowed for day-dreaming, but that we must "turn to" at the first light. Having called up the "idlers," namely carpenter, cook, steward, etc., and rigged the pump, we commenced washing down the decks. This operation, which is performed every morning at sea, takes nearly two hours; and I had hardly strength enough to get through it. After we had finished, swabbed down, and coiled up the rigging, I sat on the spars, waiting for seven bells, which was the sign for breakfast. The officer, seeing my lazy posture, ordered me to slush the mainmast, from the royal-masthead down. The vessel was then rolling a little, and I had taken no sustenance for three days, so that I felt tempted to tell him that I had rather wait till after breakfast; but I knew that if I showed any sign of want of spirit or of backwardness, I should be ruined at once. So I took my bucket of grease and climbed up to the royal-masthead. Here the rocking of the vessel, which increases the higher you go from the foot of the mast, which is the fulcrum of the lever, and the smell of the grease, upset my stomach again, and I was not a little rejoiced when I got upon the comparative *terra firma* of the deck. In a few minutes seven bells were struck, the log hove, the watch called, and we went to breakfast.

I cannot describe the change which half a pound of cold salt beef and a biscuit or two produced in me. I was a new being. We had a watch below until noon, so that I had some time to myself, and getting a huge piece of strong, cold salt beef from the cook, I kept gnawing upon it until twelve o'clock. When we went on deck I felt somewhat like a man, and could begin to learn my sea duty with considerable spirit. At about two o'clock we heard the loud cry of "Sail ho!" from aloft, and soon saw two sails to windward, going directly athwart our hawse.[*] This was the first time that I had seen a sail at sea. I thought then, and have always since, that it exceeds every other sight in interest and beauty. They passed to leeward of us, and out of hailing distance.

Thursday, August 21st. This day the sun rose clear; we had a fine wind, and everything was bright and cheerful. About six bells, that is, 3 P.M., we saw a sail on our larboard bow. I was very

[*] *Hawse,* the hole in the bows through which the cable runs.

anxious, like every new sailor, to speak her. She came down to us, backed her main-topsail, and the two vessels stood "head on," bowing and curveting at each other like a couple of war-horses reined in by their riders. It was the first vessel that I had seen near, and I was surprised to find how much she rolled and plunged in so quiet a sea. She plunged her head into the sea, and then, her stern settling gradually down, her huge bows rose up, showing the bright copper, and her stern and breast-hooks dripping with the brine. Her decks were filled with passengers, who had come up at the cry of "Sail ho!" and who by their dress and features appeared to be Swiss and French emigrants. She was the ship *La Carolina*, from Havre, for New York.

CHAPTER III

A Seaman's Daily Work

As we had now a long "spell" of fine weather, without any incident to break the monotony of our lives, there can be no better place to describe the duties, regulations, and customs of an American merchantman, of which ours was a fair specimen.

The captain, in the first place, is lord paramount. He stands no watch, comes and goes when he pleases, and is accountable to no one, and must be obeyed in everything. He has the power to turn his officers off duty, and even to make them do duty as sailors in the forecastle.

The prime minister, the official organ, and the active and superintending officer is the chief mate. The captain tells him what he wishes to have done, and leaves to him the care of overseeing, of allotting the work, and also the responsibility of its being well done. The mate also keeps the log-book, for which he is responsible to the owners and insurers, and has the charge of the stowage, safe-keeping, and delivery of the cargo.

The second mate's is proverbially a dog's berth. The men do not respect him as an officer, and he is obliged to go aloft to reef and furl the topsails, and to put his hands into the tar and slush with the rest. The crew call him the "sailor's waiter," as he has to furnish them with spun-yarn, marlins, and all other stuffs that they need in their work, and has charge of the boatswain's locker, which includes serving-boards, marline-spikes, etc., etc. His wages are usually double those of a common sailor, and he eats and sleeps in the cabin; but he is obliged to be on deck nearly all his time, and eats at the second table, that is, makes a meal out of what the captain and chief mate leave.

The steward is the captain's servant, and has charge of the pantry, from which everyone, even the mate himself, is excluded.

The cook is the patron of the crew, and those who are in his favor can get their wet mittens and stockings dried, or light their pipes at the galley in the night watch. These two worthies, together with the carpenter and sailmaker, if there be one, stand no watch, but, being employed all day, are allowed to "sleep on" at night, unless all hands are called.

The crew are divided into two watches. Of these, the chief mate commands the larboard, and the second mate the starboard. They divide the time between them, being on and off duty, or on deck and below, every other four hours. If, for instance, the chief mate with the larboard watch have the first night watch from eight to twelve; at the end of the four hours the starboard watch is called, and the second mate takes the deck, while the larboard watch and the first mate go below until four in the morning, when they come on deck again and remain until eight, having what is called the morning watch. As they will have been on deck eight hours out of the twelve, while those who had the middle watch — from twelve to four — will only have been up four hours, they have what is called "forenoon watch below," that is, from 8 A.M. till 12 M.

An explanation of the "dog-watches" may, perhaps, be of use to one who has never been at sea. They are to shift the watches each night, so that the same watch need not be on deck at the same hours. In order to effect this, the watch from 4 to 8 P.M. is divided into two half, or dog-watches, one from four to six, and the other from six to eight. By this means they divide the twenty-four hours into seven watches instead of six, and thus shift the hours every night. As the dog-watches come during twilight, after the day's work is done, and before the night-watch is set, they are the watches in which everybody is on deck. At eight o'clock eight bells are struck, the log is hove, the watch set, the wheel relieved, the galley shut up, and the other watch goes below.

The morning commences with the watch on deck's "turning to" at daybreak, and washing down, scrubbing, and swabbing the decks. This, with filling the "scuttled butt" with fresh water, and coiling up the rigging, usually occupies the time until seven bells (half after seven), when all hands get breakfast. At eight the day's work begins, and lasts until sundown, with the exception of an hour for dinner.

The discipline of the ship requires every man to be at work upon something when he is upon deck, except at night and on Sundays. It is the officers' duty to keep everyone at work, even if there is nothing to be done but to scrape the rust from the chain cables. No conversation is allowed among the crew at their duty, and though they frequently do talk when aloft, or when near one another, yet they always stop when an officer is nigh.

When I first left port, and found that we were kept regularly employed for a week or two, I supposed that we were getting the vessel into sea trim, and that it would soon be over, and we should have nothing to do but to sail the ship; but I found that it continued so for two years, and at the end of two years there was as much to be done as ever. When first leaving port, studding-sail* gear is to be rove, all the running rigging to be examined, that which is unfit for use to be got down, and new rigging rove in its place; then the standing rigging is to be overhauled, replaced, and repaired in a thousand different ways; and wherever any of the numberless ropes or the yards are chafing or wearing upon it, their "chafing gear," as it is called, must be put on. Taking off, putting on, and mending the chafing

* *Studding-sails,* light sails set outside the square sails on booms, only carried in a fair wind.

gear alone, upon a vessel, would find constant employment for two or three men during working hours for a whole voyage.

All the "small stuffs" which are used on board a ship — such as spun-yarn, marline, seizing-stuff, etc., etc. — are made on board. The owners of a vessel buy up incredible quantities of "old junk," which the sailors unlay, after drawing out the yarns, knot them together, and roll them up in balls. These "rope yarns" are used for various purposes, but the greater part is manufactured into spun-yarn. For this purpose every vessel is furnished with a "spun-yarn winch," which is very simple, consisting of a wheel and spindle.

Another method of employing the crew is "setting up" rigging. Whenever any of the standing rigging becomes slack (which is continually happening) the seizings and coverings must be taken off, tackles got up, and after the rigging is bowsed well taut, the seizings and coverings replaced, which is a very nice piece of work. If we add to this all the tarring, greasing, oiling, varnishing, painting, scraping, and scrubbing which is required in the course of a long voyage, and also remember this is all to be done in addition to watching at night, steering, reefing, furling, bracing, making and setting sail, and pulling, hauling, and climbing in every direction, one will hardly ask, "What can a sailor find to do at sea?"

If, after all this labor, the merchants and captains think that they have not earned their twelve dollars a month and their salt beef and hard bread, they keep them picking oakum — *ad infinitum.* I have seen oakum stuff placed about in different parts of the ship, so that the sailors might not be idle in the snatches between the frequent squalls upon crossing the equator. Some officers have been so driven to find work for the crew of a ship ready for sea that they have set them to pounding the anchors and scraping the chain cables. The "Philadelphia catechism" is, —

"Six days shalt thou labor and do all thou art
   able,
And on the seventh, — holystone the decks
   and scrape the cable."

CHAPTER IV

Alarm of a Pirate

After speaking the *Carolina* on the 21st of August, nothing occurred to break the monotony of our life until — *Friday, September 5th,* when we saw a sail on the weather beam. She proved to be a brig under English colors, and, passing under our stern, reported herself as forty-nine days from Buenos Ayres, bound to Liverpool. Before she had passed us, "Sail ho!" was cried again, and we made another sail, far on our weather bow, and steering athwart our hawse. She passed out of hail, but we made her out to be an hermaphrodite brig, with Brazilian colors in her main rigging.

Sunday, September 7th. Fell in with the northeast tradewinds. This morning we caught our first dolphin. I was disappointed in the colors of this fish when dying. They were certainly very beautiful, but not equal to what has been said of them.

This day was spent like all pleasant Sabbaths at sea. The decks are washed down, the rigging coiled up, and everything put in order; and throughout the day only one watch is kept on deck at a time. The men are all dressed in their best white duck trousers, and red or checked shirts, and have nothing to do but to make the necessary changes in the sails. They employ themselves in reading, talking, smoking, and mending their clothes. If the weather is pleasant, they bring their work and their books upon deck and sit down upon the forecastle and windlass.

To enhance the value of the Sabbath to the crew, they are allowed on that day a pudding, or as it is called, a "duff." This is nothing more than flour boiled with water, and eaten with molasses. It is very heavy, dark, and clammy, yet it is looked upon as a luxury, and really forms an agreeable variety with salt beef and pork.

We continued running large before the northeast tradewinds for several days, until Monday —

September 22nd, when, upon coming on deck at seven bells in the morning, we found the other watch aloft throwing water upon the sails; and, looking astern, we saw a small clipper-built brig with a black hull heading directly after us. We went to work immediately, and put all the canvas upon the brig which we could get upon her, rigging out oars for studding-sail yards, and continued wetting down the sails by buckets of water whipped up to the mast-head, until about nine o'clock, when there came on a drizzling rain. The vessel continued in pursuit, changing her course as we changed ours, to keep before the wind. The captain, who watched her with his glass, said that she was armed, and full of men, and showed no colors. We continued running dead before the wind, knowing that we sailed better so, and that clippers are fastest *on* the wind. We had also another advantage. The wind was light, and we spread more canvas than she did, having royals and sky-sails fore and aft, and ten studding-sails; while she, being an hermaphrodite brig, had only a gaff topsail* aft. Early in the morning she was overhauling us a little, but after the rain came on and the wind grew lighter, we began to leave her astern. All hands remained on deck throughout the day, and we got our arms in order; but we were too few to have done anything with her if she had proved to be what we feared. Fortunately there was no moon, and the night which followed was exceedingly dark, so that, by putting out all the lights on board and altering our course four points, we hoped to get out of her reach. At daybreak there was no sign of anything in the horizon, and we kept the vessel off to her course.

Wednesday, October 1st. Crossed the equator in long. 24° 24′ W. I now, for the first time, felt at liberty, according to the old usage, to call myself a son of Neptune, and was very glad to be able to claim the title without the disagreeable initiation which so many have to go through. After once crossing the line you can never be subjected to the process, but are considered as a son of Neptune, with full powers to play tricks upon others.

It had been obvious to all hands for some time that the second mate, whose name was Foster,

---

* *Gaff topsail,* a light sail set over a gaff, or spar, to which the head of a fore-and-aft sail is bent.

26

was an idle, careless fellow, and not much of a sailor, and that the captain was exceedingly dissatisfied with him. The power of the captain in these cases was well known, and we all anticipated a difficulty.

The second night after crossing the equator we had the watch from eight till twelve, and it was "my helm" for the last two hours. There had been light squalls through the night, and the captain told Mr. Foster, who commanded our watch, to keep a bright look-out. Soon after I came to the helm I found that he was quite drowsy, and at last he stretched himself on the companion and went fast asleep. Soon afterwards the captain came very quietly on deck, and stood by me for some time looking at the compass. The officer at length became aware of the captain's presence, but, pretending not to know it, began humming and whistling to himself, to show that he was not asleep, and went forward without looking behind him, and ordered the main royal to be loosed. On turning round to come aft he pretended surprise at seeing the master on deck. This would not do. The captain was too "wide awake" for him, and, beginning upon him at once, gave him a grand blow-up in true nautical style. "You're a lazy, good-for-nothing rascal. You're neither man, boy, *soger,* nor sailor! You're no more than a *thing* aboard a vessel! You don't earn your salt!" and other still more choice extracts from the sailor's vocabulary. After the poor fellow had taken this harangue he was sent into his stateroom, and the captain stood the rest of the watch himself.

At seven bells in the morning all hands were called aft and told that Foster was no longer an officer on board, and that we might choose one of our own number for second mate. The crew refused to take the responsibility of choosing a man of whom we would never be able to complain, and left it to the captain. He picked out an active and intelligent young sailor, born near the Kennebec, who had been several Canton voyages, and proclaimed him in the following manner: "I choose Jim Hall. He's your second mate. All you've got to do is to obey him as you would me; and remember that he is *Mr.* Hall." Foster went forward into the forecastle as a common sailor, while young foremast Jim became Mr. Hall, and took up his quarters in the land of knives and forks and tea-cups.

Sunday, October 5th. It was our morning watch, when soon after the day began to break a man on the forecastle called out, "Land ho!" I had never heard the cry before and did not know what it meant; but I soon found, by the direction of all eyes, that there was land stretching along on our weather beam.* We immediately took in studding-sails and hauled our wind, running in for the land. This was done to determine our longitude; for by the captain's chronometer we were in 25° W., but by his observations we were much

---

* *Weather,* the direction from which the wind blows.

28

farther, and he had been for some time in doubt whether it was his chronometer or his sextant which was out of order. This land-fall settled the matter, and the former instrument was condemned.

As we ran in toward the coast we found that we were directly off the port of Pernambuco, and could see with the telescope the roofs of the houses, and one large church, and the town of Olinda. It was here that I first saw one of those singular things called catamarans. They are composed of logs lashed together upon the water, have one large sail, are quite fast, and, strange as it may seem, are trusted as good sea boats. After taking a new departure from Olinda, we kept off on our way to Cape Horn.

We met with nothing remarkable until we were in the latitude of the river La Plata. Here there are violent gales from the southwest, called Pomperos, which are very destructive to the shipping in the river, and are felt for many leagues at sea. They are usually preceded by lightning. The captain told the mates to keep a bright look-out, and if they saw lightning at the southwest to take in sail at once. We got the first touch of one during my watch on deck. I was walking in the lee* gangway, and thought I saw lightning on the lee-bow. I told the second mate, who came over and looked out for some time. It was very black in the south-

*Lee, the side opposite to that from which the wind blows.

west, and in about ten minutes we saw a distinct flash. The wind, which had been southeast, had now left us, and it was dead calm. We sprang aloft immediately and furled the royals and top-gallant-sails, and took in the flying-jib, hauled up the mainsail and trysail,[*] squared the after-yards, and awaited the attack. A huge mist, capped with black clouds, came driving toward us, extending over that quarter of the horizon, and covering the stars, which shone brightly in the other part of the heavens. It came upon us at once with a blast, and a shower of hail and rain, which almost took our breath from us. We let the halyards run, and fortunately were not taken aback. The little vessel "paid off" from the wind, and ran on for some time directly before it, tearing through the water with everything flying. Having called all hands, we close-reefed the topsails and trysail, furled the courses and jib, set the foretopmast-staysail, and brought her up nearly to her course, with the weather-braces hauled in a little to ease her.

This was the first blow that I had seen which could really be called a gale. We had reefed our topsails in the Gulf Stream, and I thought it something serious, but an older sailor would have thought nothing of it. As I had now become used to the vessel and to my duty, I was of some service on a yard, and could knot my reef-point as well as anybody. I obeyed the order to lay aloft with

[*] *Trysail,* a fore-and-aft sail set with a boom and gaff, and hoisted on a small mast abaft the lower mast.

the rest, and found the reefing a very exciting scene; for one watch reefed the foretopsail, and the other the main, and every one did his utmost to get his topsail hoisted first. We had a great advantage over the larboard watch, because the chief mate never goes aloft, while our new second mate used to jump into the rigging as soon as we began to haul out the reef-tackle, and have the weather earing passed before there was a man upon the yard. In this way we were almost always able to raise the cry of "Haul out to leeward" before them, and, having knotted our points, would slide down the shrouds and backstays, and sing out at the topsail-halyards, to let it be known that we were ahead of them. Reefing is the most exciting part of a sailor's duty. All hands are engaged upon it, and after the halyards are let go, there is no time to be lost — no "sogering" or hanging back — then. If one is not quick enough, another runs over him. The first on the yard goes to the weather earing, the second to the lee and the next two to the "dog's ears"; while the others lay along into the bunt, just giving each other elbow-room. In reefing, the yard-arms (the extremes of the yards) are the posts of honor; but in furling, the strongest and most experienced stand in the slings (or middle of the yard) to make up the bunt.[*] If the second mate is a smart fellow he will never let anyone take either of these posts from him.

[*] *Bunt,* the middle of a sail.

We remained for the rest of the night, and throughout the next day, under the same close sail, for it continued to blow very fresh; and though we had no more hail, yet there was a soaking rain, and it was quite cold and uncomfortable. Toward sundown the gale moderated a little, and it began to clear off in the southwest. We shook our reefs out one by one, and before midnight had topgallant-sails upon her.

We had now made up our minds for Cape Horn and cold weather, and entered upon every necessary preparation.

Tuesday, November 4th. At daybreak saw land upon our larboard quarter. There were two islands; in a few hours we sank them in the northeast. These were the Falkland Islands. We had run between them and the mainland of Patagonia. At sunset the second mate, who was at the masthead, said that he saw land on the starboard bow. This must have been the island of Staten Land; and we were now in the region of Cape Horn, with a fine breeze from the northward, topmast and topgallant studding-sails set, and every prospect of a speedy and pleasant passage round.

CHAPTER V

Round Cape Horn

Wednesday, November 5th. The weather was fine during the previous night, and we had a clear view of the Magellan Clouds and of the Southern Cross. The Magellan Clouds consist of three small nebulæ in the southern part of the heavens — two bright, like the Milky Way, and one dark. When off Cape Horn they are nearly overhead. The Cross is composed of four stars in that form, and is said to be the brightest constellation in the heavens.

During the first part of this day the wind was light, but after noon it came on fresh, and we furled the royals.[*] We still kept the studding-sails out, and the captain said he should go round with them if he could. Just before eight o'clock (then about sundown, in that latitude) the cry of "All hands ahoy!" was sounded down the fore-scuttle and the after-hatchway, and, hurrying upon deck, we found a large black cloud rolling on toward us from the southwest, blackening the whole heavens. "Here comes Cape Horn!" said the chief mate; and we had hardly time to haul down and

---

[*] *Royal,* a light sail, next above the top-gallant sail.

clew up before it was upon us. In a few moments a heavier sea was raised than I had ever seen, and as it was directly ahead, the little brig, which was no better than a bathing-machine, plunged into it, and all the forward part of her was under water, the sea pouring in through the bow-ports and hawse-hole and over the knight-heads, threatening to wash everything overboard. We sprang aloft and double-reefed the topsails, and furled all the other sails, and made all snug. But this would not do; the brig was laboring and straining against the head-sea, and the gale was growing worse and worse. At the same time sleet and hail were driving with all fury against us. We clewed down, and hauled out the reef-tackles again, and close-reefed the fore-topsail, and furled the main, and hove her to on the starboard tack.

Throughout the night the storm was very violent — rain, hail, snow, and sleet beating upon the vessel — the wind continuing ahead, and the sea running high. At daybreak (about 3 A.M.) the deck was covered with snow. The captain sent up the steward with a glass of grog to each of the watch; and all the time that we were off the Cape grog was given to the morning watch and to all hands whenever we reefed topsails. The clouds cleared away at sunrise, and the wind becoming more fair, we again made sail and stood nearly up to our course.

Thursday, November 6th. It continued more pleasant through the first part of the day, but at night we had the same scene over again. This time we did not heave to, as on the night before, but endeavored to beat to windward under close-reefed topsails, balance-reefed trysail, and fore top-mast staysail. This night it was my turn to steer, or, as the sailors say, my trick at the helm, for two hours. Inexperienced as I was, I made out to steer to the satisfaction of the officer, and neither S— nor I gave up our tricks all the time that we were off the Cape. This was something to boast of, for it requires a good deal of skill and watchfulness to steer a vessel close-hauled in a gale of wind against a heavy head-sea. "Ease her when she pitches" is the word, and a little carelessness in letting her ship a heavy sea might sweep the decks or knock the masts out of her.

Friday, November 7th. Toward morning the wind went down, and during the whole forenoon we lay tossing about in a dead calm and in the midst of a thick fog. The calms here are unlike those in most parts of the world, for there is always such a high sea running, and the periods of calm are so short that it has no time to go down; and vessels, being under no command of sails or rudder, lie like logs upon the water. We were obliged to steady the booms and yards by guys and braces and to lash everything well below.

Toward the evening the fog cleared off, and we had every appearance of a cold blow; and soon after sundown it came on. Again it was clew up and haul down, reef and furl, until we had got her down to close-reefed topsails, double-reefed trysail, and reefed fore spenser. Snow, hail, and sleet were driving upon us most of the night, and the sea breaking over the bows and covering the forward part of the little vessel; but as she would lay her course, the captain refused to heave her to.

Sunday, November 9th. To-day the sun rose clear and continued so until twelve o'clock, when the captain got an observation. This was very well for Cape Horn, and we thought it a little remarkable that, as we had not had one unpleasant Sunday during the whole voyage, the only tolerable day here should be a Sunday. But this did not last very long. Between five and six the cry of "All starbowlines* ahoy!" summoned our watch on deck, and immediately all hands were called. A great cloud of a dark slate-color was driving on us from the southwest; and we did our best to take in sail before we were in the midst of it. We had got the light sails furled, the courses hauled up, and the topsail reef-tackles hauled out, and were just mounting the fore-rigging when the storm struck us. In an instant the sea, which had been comparatively quiet, was running higher and higher; and it became almost as dark as night. The hail and sleet were harder than I had yet felt them, seeming almost to pin us down to the rigging. We were longer taking in sail than ever

---

* *Starbowlines,* the starboard watch.

36

before, for the sails were stiff and wet, the ropes and rigging covered with snow and sleet, and we ourselves cold and nearly blinded with the violence of the storm. By the time we had got down upon deck again the little brig was plunging madly into a tremendous head-sea, which at every drive rushed in through the bow-ports and over the bows and buried all the forward part of the vessel. At this instant the chief mate, who was standing on the top of the windlass, at the foot of the spenser-mast, called out, "Lay out there and furl the jib!" This was no agreeable or safe duty, yet it must be done. An old Swede (the best sailor on board), who belonged on the forecastle, sprang out upon the bowsprit. Another must go. I was near the mate, and sprang forward, threw the down-haul over the windlass, and jumped between the knight-heads out upon the bowsprit. The crew stood abaft the windlass and hauled the jib down, while we got out upon the weather side of the jib-boom, our feet on the foot-ropes, holding on by the spar, the great jib flying off to leeward and *slatting* so as almost to throw us off the boom. For some time we could do nothing but hold on, and the vessel, diving into two huge seas, one after the other, plunged us twice into the water up to our chins. John (that was the sailor's name) thought the boom would go every moment, and called out to the mate to keep the vessel off and haul down the staysail; but the fury of the wind and the breaking of the seas against the bows defied every attempt to make ourselves heard, and we were obliged to do the best we could in our situation. Fortunately no other seas so heavy struck her, and we succeeded in furling the jib "after a fashion"; and, coming in over the staysail nettings, were not a little pleased to find that all was snug and the watch gone below, for we were soaked through, and it was very cold.

Monday, November 10th. During a part of this day we were hove to, but the rest of the time were driving on under close-reefed sails.

Tuesday, November 11th, Wednesday and Thursday. The same.

We had now got hardened to Cape weather, the vessel was under reduced sail, and everything secured on deck and below, so that we had little to do but to steer and to stand our watch. Our clothes were all wet through, and the only change was from wet to more wet. We had only to come below when the watch was out, wring out our wet clothes, hang them up, and turn in and sleep as soundly as we could until our watch was called again. The only time when we could be said to take any pleasure was at night and mornings when we were allowed a tin pot full of hot tea, sweetened with molasses. This, bad as it was, was still warm and comforting, and, together with our sea biscuit and cold salt beef, made quite a meal. Yet even this meal was attended with some uncertainty. We had to go ourselves to the galley and take our kid of beef and tin pots of tea and run the risk of losing them before we could get below. Many a kid of beef have I seen rolling in the scuppers* and the bearer lying at his length on the decks. I remember an English lad who was always the life of the crew standing for nearly ten minutes at the galley, with his pot of tea in his hand, waiting for a chance to get down into the forecastle, and, seeing what he thought was a "smooth spell," started to go forward. He had just got to the end of the windlass when a great sea broke over the bows, and for a moment I saw nothing of him but his head and shoulders; and at the next instant, being taken off his legs, he was carried aft with the sea, until her stern lifting up, and sending the water forward, he was left high and dry at the side of the long-boat, still holding on to his tin pot, which had now nothing in it but salt water. But nothing could ever daunt him, or overcome, for a moment, his habitual good-humor. Regaining his legs, he rolled below, saying, as he passed, "A man's no sailor if he can't take a joke." The ducking was not the worst of such an affair, for, as there was an allowance of tea, you could get no more from the galley; and though the sailors would never suffer a man to go without, but would always turn in a little from their own pots to fill up his, yet this was at best but dividing the loss among all hands.

Something of the same kind befell me a few days after. The cook had just made for us a mess of hot "scouse" — that is, biscuit pounded fine,

* *Scuppers,* holes cut in the water-ways for the water to run from the decks.

salt beef cut into small pieces and a few potatoes, boiled up together and seasoned with pepper. This was a rare treat, and I being the last at the galley, had it put in my charge to carry down for the mess. I got along very well as far as the hatch-way, and was just getting down the steps, when a heavy sea, lifting the stern out of water, and, passing forward, dropping it down again, threw the steps from their place, and I came down into the steerage a little faster than I meant to, with the kid on top of me, and the whole precious mess scattered over the floor.

Friday, November 14th. We were now well to the westward of the Cape, and were changing our course to the northward as much as we dared, since the strong southwest winds, which prevailed then, carried us in toward Patagonia. At 2 P.M. we saw a sail on our larboard beam, and at four we made it out to be a large ship, steering our course, under single-reefed topsails. We at that time had shaken the reefs out of our topsails, as the wind was lighter, and set the main top-gallant sail. As soon as our captain saw what sail she was under, he set the fore top-gallant sail and flying jib; and the old whaler — for such his boats and short sail showed him to be — felt a little ashamed, and shook the reefs out of his topsails, but could do no more, for he had sent down his top-gallant masts off the Cape. He ran down for us, and answered our hail as the whale-ship *New England*, of Poughkeepsie, one hundred and twenty days from New York. The ship fell astern, and continued in sight during the night. Toward morning, the wind having become light, we crossed our royal and skysail yards, and at daylight we were seen under a cloud of sail, having royals and skysails* fore and aft. The "spouter," as the sailors call a whaleman, had sent up his main top-gallant mast and set the sail, and made signal for us to heave to. About half-past seven their whale-boat came alongside, and Captain Job Terry sprang on board, a man known in every port and by every vessel in the Pacific ocean.

Captain Terry convinced our captain that our reckoning was a little out, and, having spent the day on board, put off in his boat at sunset for his ship, which was now six or eight miles astern. He began a "yarn" when he came aboard, which lasted, with but little intermission, for four hours. It would probably never have come to an end had not a good breeze sprung up which sent him off to his own vessel.

At eight o'clock we altered our course to the northward, bound for Juan Fernandez.

This day we saw the last of the albatrosses, which had been our companions a great part of the time off the Cape. I had been interested in the bird from descriptions which I had read of it, and was not at all disappointed. We caught one or two with a baited hook which we floated astern upon a shingle. Their long, flapping wings, long legs, and large, staring eyes, give them a very

* *Skysail,* a light sail, next above the royal.

peculiar appearance. They look well on the wing; but one of the finest sights that I have ever seen was an albatross asleep upon the water, during a calm, off Cape Horn, when a heavy sea was running. There being no breeze, the surface of the water was unbroken, but a long, heavy swell was rolling, and we saw the fellow, all white, directly ahead of us, asleep upon the waves, with his head under his wing; now rising on the top of a huge billow, and then falling slowly until he was lost in the hollow between. He was undisturbed for some time, until the noise of our bows, gradually approaching, roused him, when, lifting his head, he stared upon us for a moment, and then spread his wide wings and took his flight.

CHAPTER VI

A Man Overboard

Monday, November 17th. This was a black day in our calendar. At seven o'clock in the morning we were aroused from a sound sleep by the cry of "All hands ahoy! a man overboard!" This unwonted cry sent a thrill through the heart of everyone, and hurrying on deck, we found the vessel hove flat aback, with all her studding-sails set; for the boy who was at the helm left it to throw something overboard, and the carpenter, who was an old sailor, knowing that the wind was light, put the helm down and hove her aback. The watch on deck were lowering away the quarter-boat, and I got on deck just in time to heave myself into her as she was leaving the side; but it was not until out upon the wide Pacific in our little boat that I knew we had lost George Ballmer, a young English sailor, who was prized by the officers as an active and willing seaman, and by the crew as a lively, hearty fellow, and a good shipmate. He was going aloft to fit a strap round the main topmast-head for ringtail halyards, and had the strap and block, a coil of halyards, and a marline-spike about his neck. He fell from the starboard futtock shrouds, and not knowing how

43

to swim, and being heavily dressed, with all those things round his neck, he probably sank immediately. We pulled astern in the direction in which he fell, and though we knew that there was no hope of saving him, yet no one wished to speak of returning, and we rowed about for nearly an hour without the hope of doing anything, but unwilling to acknowledge to ourselves that we must give him up. At length we turned the boat's head and made toward the vessel.

Death is at all times solemn, but never so much so as at sea. When a man falls overboard at sea and is lost, there is a suddenness in the event, and a difficulty in realizing it, which give to it an air of awful mystery. Then, too, at sea — to use a homely but expressive phrase — you *miss* a man so much. A dozen men are shut up together in a little bark upon the wide sea, and for months and months see no forms and hear no voices but their own, and one is taken suddenly from among them, and they miss him at every turn.

All these things make such a death peculiarly solemn, and the effect of it remains upon the crew for some time. There is more kindness shown by the officers to the crew, and by the crew to one another. There is more quietness and seriousness. The officers are more watchful, and the crew go more carefully aloft. The lost man is seldom mentioned, or is dismissed with a sailor's rude eulogy — "Well, poor George is gone! His cruise is up soon! He knew his work, and did his duty, and was a good shipmate."

44

We had hardly returned on board with our sad report, before an auction was held of the poor man's clothes. The captain had first, however, called all hands aft and asked them if they were satisfied that everything had been done to save the man, and if they thought there was any use in remaining there longer. The crew all said that it was in vain, for the man did not know how to swim, and was very heavily dressed. So we then filed away, and kept her off to her course.

The laws regulating navigation make the captain answerable for the effects of a sailor who dies during the voyage, and it is either a law or a universal custom, established for convenience, that the captain should immediately hold an auction of his things, in which they are bid off by the sailors, and the sums which they give are deducted from their wages at the end of the voyage. Accordingly, we had no sooner got the ship before the wind than his chest was brought up upon the forecastle, and the sale began. The jackets and trousers in which we had seen him dressed but a few days before were exposed and bid off while the life was hardly out of his body, and his chest was taken aft and used as a store-chest, so that there was nothing left which could be called *his*.

The night after this event, when I went to the galley to get a light, I found the cook inclined to be talkative, so I sat down on the spars and gave him an opportunity to hold a yarn. He talked about George's having spoken of his friends, and said he believed few men died without having a warning of it, which he supported by a great many stories of dreams, and the unusual behavior of men before death. From this he went on to other superstitions — the Flying Dutchman, etc. — and talked rather mysteriously, having something evidently on his mind. At length he put his head out of the galley and looked carefully about to see if anyone was within hearing, and, being satisfied on that point, asked me, in a low tone:

"I say, you know what countryman 'e carpenter be?"

"Yes," said I; "he's a German."

"What kind of a German?" said the cook.

"He belongs to Bremen," said I.

"Are you sure o' dat?" said he.

I satisfied him on that point by saying that he could speak no language but the German and English.

"I'm plaguy glad o' dat," said the cook. "I was mighty afraid he was a Finn."

I asked him the reason of this, and found that he was fully possessed with the notion that Finns are wizards, and especially have power over winds and storms. I tried to reason with him about it, but he had the best of all arguments, that from experience, at hand, and was not to be moved. He had been in a vessel at the Sandwich Islands in which the sailmaker was a Finn, and could do anything he felt inclined to do. This sailmaker kept a junk bottle in his berth, which was always just half full of rum, though he got drunk upon it nearly every day.

He had heard of ships, too, beating up the Gulf of Finland against a head wind, and having a ship heave in sight astern, overhaul, and pass them, with as fair a wind as could blow and all studding-sails out, and find she was from Finland.

"Oh, oh," said he; "I've seen too much of them men to want to see 'em 'board a ship."

As I still doubted, he said he would leave it to John, who was the oldest seaman aboard, and would know if anybody did. John, to be sure, was the oldest, and at the same time the most ignorant man in the ship; but I consented to have him called. The cook stated the matter to him, and John, as I anticipated, sided with the cook, and said that he himself had been in a ship where they had a head wind for a fortnight, and the captain found out at last that one of the men, whom he had had some hard words with a short time before, was a Finn, and immediately told him if he didn't stop the head wind he would shut him down in the fore-peak. The Finn would not give in, and the captain shut him down in the fore-peak, and would not give him anything to eat. The Finn held out for a day and a half, when he could not stand it any longer, and did something or other which brought the wind round again, and they let him up.

"There," said the cook, "what do you think o' dat?"

I told him I had no doubt it was true, and that it would have been odd if the wind had not changed in fifteen days, Finn or no Finn.

CHAPTER VII

Juan Fernandez

We continued sailing along with a fair wind and fine weather until —

Tuesday, November 25th, when at daylight we saw the Island of Juan Fernandez directly ahead, rising like a deep blue cloud out of the sea. We were then probably nearly seventy miles from it; and so high and so blue did it appear that I mistook it for a cloud resting over the island, and looked for the island under it until it gradually turned to a deader and greener color, and I could mark the inequalities upon its surface. At length we could distinguish trees and rocks; and by the afternoon this beautiful island lay fairly before us, and we directed our course to the only harbor. Arriving at the entrance, soon after sundown, we found a Chilian man-of-war brig, the only vessel, coming out. She hailed us, and an officer on board advised us to run in before night, and said that they were bound to Valparaiso. We ran immediately for the anchorage, but owing to the winds which drew about the mountains and came to us in flaws from every point of the compass, we did not come to an anchor until nearly midnight.

I was called on deck to stand my watch at about three in the morning, and I shall never forget the peculiar sensation which I experienced on finding myself once more surrounded by land, feeling the night-breeze coming from off shore and hearing the frogs and crickets.

When all hands were called it was nearly sunrise, and between that time and breakfast I had a good view of the objects about me. The harbor was nearly land-locked, and at the head of it was a landing-place, protected by a small breakwater of stones, upon which two large boats were hauled up, with a sentry standing over them. Near this was a variety of huts or cottages, nearly a hundred in number, the best of them built of mud and white-washed, but the greater part only — Robinson Crusoe like — of posts and branches of trees. The governor's house was the most conspicuous, being large, with grated windows, plastered walls, and roof of red tiles; yet, like all the rest, only of one story. Near it was a small chapel, distinguished by a cross, and a long, low, brown-looking building surrounded by something like a palisade, from which an old and dingy-looking Chilian flag was flying. This was the *Presidio*. A sentinel was stationed at the chapel, another at the governor's house, and a few soldiers, armed with bayonets, looking rather ragged, with shoes out at the toes, were strolling about among the houses, or waiting at the landing-place for our boat to come ashore.

The mountains were high, but not so overhanging as they appeared to be by starlight. They seemed to bear off toward the center of the island, and were green and well wooded, with some large, and, I am told, exceedingly fertile valleys, with mule-tracks leading to different parts of the island.

After breakfast, the second mate was ordered ashore with five hands to fill the water-casks, and, to my joy, I was among the number. We pulled ashore with the empty casks; and here again fortune favored me, for the water was too thick and muddy to be put into the casks, and the governor had sent men up to the head of the stream to clear it out for us, which gave us nearly two hours of leisure. This leisure we employed in wandering about among the houses and eating a little fruit which was offered to us. Ground apples, melons, grapes, strawberries of an enormous size, and cherries abound here. The island belongs to Chili, and had been used by the government as a sort of Botany Bay for nearly two years; and the governor — an Englishman who had entered the Chilian navy — with a priest, half-a-dozen task-masters, and a body of soldiers, were stationed there to keep the convicts in order. The worst part of them, I found, were locked up under sentry, in caves dug into the side of the mountain, nearly half-way up, with mule-tracks leading to them, whence they were taken by day and set to work under task-masters upon building an aqueduct, a wharf, and other public works; while the rest lived in the houses which they put up for themselves, had their families with them, and seemed to me to be the laziest people on the face of the earth.

Having filled our casks we returned on board, and soon after, the governor, dressed in a uniform like that of an American militia officer, the *Padre,* in the dress of the Grey Friars, with hood and all complete, and the *Capitan,* with big whiskers and dirty regimentals, came on board to dine.

A small boat which came from the shore to take away the governor and suite — as they styled themselves — brought, as a present to the crew, a large pail of milk, a few shells, and a block of sandal-wood. The milk, which was the first we had tasted since leaving Boston, we soon despatched; a piece of the sandal-wood I obtained, and learned that it grew on the hills in the center of the island.

About an hour before sundown, having stowed our water-casks, we commenced getting under way, and were not a little while about it, for we were in thirty fathoms water, and in one of the gusts which came from off shore had let go our other bow anchor; and as the southerly wind draws round the mountains and comes off in uncertain flaws, we were continually swinging round, and had thus got a very foul hawse. We hove in upon our chain, and after stoppering and unshackling it again and again, and hoisting and hauling down sail, we at length tipped our anchor and stood out to sea. It was bright starlight when we were clear of the bay, and the lofty island lay behind us in its still beauty, and I gave a parting look and bid farewell to the most romantic spot of earth that my eyes had ever seen. I did then and have ever since felt an attachment for that island, altogether peculiar. It was partly, no doubt, from its having been the first land that I had seen since leaving home, and still more from the associations which everyone has connected with it in their childhood from reading *Robinson Crusoe*.

It is situated in about 33° 30′ S., and is distant a little more than three hundred miles from Valparaiso, on the coast of Chili, which is in the same latitude. It is about fifteen miles in length and five in breadth. The harbor in which we anchored (called by Lord Anson Cumberland Bay) is the only one in the island. The best anchorage is at the western side, where we lay at about three cables' length from the shore, in a little more than thirty fathoms water.

There is an abundance of the best water upon the island, small streams running through every valley, and leaping down from the sides of the hills. One stream of considerable size flows through the center of the lawn upon which the houses are built, and furnishes an easy and abundant supply to the inhabitants. This, by means of a short wooden aqueduct, was brought quite down to our boats.

The island in the month of November, when we were there, being in all the freshness and beauty of spring, appeared covered with trees.

These were chiefly aromatic, and the largest was the myrtle. The soil is very loose and rich, and wherever it is broken up, there spring up immediately radishes, turnips, ground apples, and other garden fruits. Goats, we were told, were not abundant, and we saw none, though it was said we might if we had gone into the interior.

It is perhaps needless to say that we saw nothing of the interior; but all who have seen it give very glowing accounts of it.

A steady, though light southwesterly wind carried us well off from the island, and when I came on deck for the middle watch I could just distinguish it from its hiding a few low stars in the southern horizon, though my unpracticed eyes would hardly have known it for land. At the close of the watch a few trade wind clouds which had arisen, though we were hardly yet in their latitude, shut it out from our view, and the next day,

Thursday, November 27th, upon coming on deck in the morning, we were again upon the wide Pacific, and saw no more land until we arrived upon the western coast of the great continent of America.

CHAPTER VIII

Effects of Long Sea Voyage

As we saw neither land nor sail from the time of leaving Juan Fernandez until our arrival in California, nothing of interest occurred except our own doings on board. We caught the southeast trades, and ran before them for nearly three weeks, without so much as altering a sail or bracing a yard. The captain took advantage of this fine weather to get the vessel in order for coming upon the coast. Everything was set up taut, the lower rigging rattled down, or rather rattled up, an abundance of spun-yarn and seizing-stuff made, and finally the whole standing-rigging, fore and aft, was tarred down. This was my first essay at this latter business, and I had enough of it; for nearly all of it came upon my friend S— and myself. We put on short duck frocks, and, taking a small bucket of tar and a bunch of oakum in our hands, went aloft, one at the main royal-mast-head, and the other at the fore, and began tarring down. This is an important operation, and is usually done about once in six months in vessels upon a long voyage. It was done in our vessel several times afterwards, but by the whole crew at once, and finished off in a day; but at this time,

54

as most of it came upon two of us, and we were new at the business, it took us several days. In this operation they always begin at the mast-head, and work down, tarring the shrouds, back-stays, standing parts of the lifts, the ties, runners, etc., and go on to the yard-arms, and come in, tarring as they come, the lifts and foot-ropes. Tarring the stays is more difficult, and is done by an operation which the sailors call "riding down." A long piece of rope — top-gallant-studding-sail halyards, or something of the kind — is taken up to the mast-head from which the stay leads, and rove through a block for a girt-line, or as the sailors call it, a *gant*-line; with the end of this a bowline is taken round the stay, into which the man gets with his bucket of tar and a bunch of oakum; and the other end being fast on deck, with some one to tend it, he is lowered down gradually, and tars the stay carefully as he goes. In this manner I tarred down all the head-stays, but found the rigging about the jib-boom, martingale, and sprit-sail-yard, upon which I was afterwards put, the hardest.

This dirty work could not last forever; and on Saturday night we finished it, scraped all the spots from the deck and rails, and what was of more importance to us, cleaned ourselves thoroughly, rolled up our tarry frocks and trousers, and laid them away for the next occasion, and put on our clean duck clothes, and had a good comfortable sailor's Saturday night. The next day was pleasant, and indeed we had but one unpleasant Sunday during the whole voyage, and that was off Cape Horn, where we could expect nothing better. On Monday we commenced painting and getting the vessel ready for port. We painted her, both inside and out, from the truck to the water's edge. In the midst of our painting, on —

Friday, December 19th, we crossed the equator for the second time.

Thursday, December 25th. This day was Christmas, but it brought us no holiday. The only change was that we had a "plum duff" for dinner, and the crew quarreled with the steward because he did not give us our usual allowance of molasses to eat with it. He thought the plums would be a substitute for the molasses, but we were not to be cheated out of our rights in this way.

Such are the trifles which produce quarrels on shipboard. In fact, we had been too long from port. We were getting tired of one another, and were in an irritable state, both forward and aft. Our fresh provisions were, of course, gone, and the captain had stopped our rice, so that we had nothing but salt beef and salt pork throughout the week, with the exception of a very small "duff" on Sunday. This added to the discontent, and a thousand little things, daily and almost hourly occurring, which no one who has not himself been on a long and tedious voyage can conceive of or properly appreciate, brought us into a state in which everything seemed to go wrong.

In the midst of this state of things, my messmate S— and myself petitioned the captain for leave to shift our berths from the steerage, where we had previously lived, into the forecastle. This, to our delight, was granted, and we turned in to bunk and mess with the crew forward. We now began to feel like sailors, which we never did when we were in the steerage. While there, however useful and active you may be, you are but a mongrel. You are immediately under the eye of the officers, cannot dance, sing, play, smoke, make a noise, or growl, or take any other sailor's pleasure; and you live with a steward, who is usually a go-between; and the crew never feel as though you were one of them. But if you live in the forecastle you hear sailors' talk, learn their ways, their peculiarities of feeling as well as speaking and acting; and, moreover, pick up a great deal of curious and useful information in seamanship, ships' customs, foreign countries, etc., from their long yarns and equally long disputes. After I had been a week there, nothing would have tempted me to go back to my old berth, and never afterwards, even in the worst of weather, when in a close and leaking forecastle off Cape Horn, did I for a moment wish myself in the steerage. Another thing which you learn better in the forecastle than you can anywhere else is to make and mend clothes, and this is indispensable to sailors. A large part of their watches below they spend at this work, and here I learned that art which stood me in so good stead afterwards.

But to return to the state of the crew. Upon our coming into the forecastle there was some difficulty about the uniting of the allowances of bread, by which we thought we were to lose a few pounds. This set us into a ferment. The captain would not condescend to explain, and we went aft in a body, with a Swede, the oldest and best sailor of the crew, for spokesman. The recollection of the scene that followed always brings up a smile, especially the quarter-deck dignity and eloquence of the captain. He was walking the weather side of the quarter-deck, and, seeing us coming aft, stopped short in his walk, and with a voice and look intended to annihilate us, called out, "Well, what do you want now?" Whereupon we stated our grievances as respectfully as we could, but he broke in upon us, saying that we were getting fat and lazy, didn't have enough to do, and that made us find fault. This provoked us, and we began to give word for word. This would never answer. He clenched his fist, stamped and swore, and sent us all forward, saying, with oaths enough interspersed to send the words home, "Away with you! Go forward, every one of you! I'll haze you! I'll work you up! You don't have enough to do! . . . You've mistaken your man! I'm F— T—, all the way from 'down east.' I've been through the mill, ground and bolted, and come out a regular-built down-east johnny-cake — good when it's hot; but when it's cold, sour and indigestible; and you'll find me so!"

So much for our petition for the redress of grievances. The matter was, however, set right, for the mate, after allowing the captain time to cool off, explained it to him; and at night we were all called aft to hear another harangue, in which, of course, the whole blame of the misunderstanding was thrown upon us. Thus the affair blew over, but the irritation caused by it remained, and we never had peace or good understanding again so long as the captain and crew remained together.

We continued sailing along in the beautiful temperate climate of the Pacific. We sailed well to the westward to have the full advantage of the northeast trades, and when we had reached the latitude of Point Conception, where it is usual to make the land, we were several hundred miles to the westward of it. We immediately changed our course due east, and sailed in that direction for a number of days. At length we began to heave-to after dark, for fear of making the land at night, on a coast where there are no lighthouses, and but indifferent charts, and at daybreak on the morning of —

Tuesday, January 13th, 1835, we made the land at Point Conception, lat. 34° 32′ N., lon. 120° 06′ W. The port of Santa Barbara, to which we were bound, lying about sixty miles to the southward of this point, we continued sailing down the coast during the day and following night, and on the next morning,

January 14th, 1835, we came to anchor in the spacious bay of Santa Barbara, after a voyage of one hundred and fifty days from Boston.

CHAPTER IX

First Landing in California

California extends along nearly the whole of the
western coast of Mexico, between the Gulf of
California in the south and the Bay of Sir Francis
Drake[*] on the north, or between the twenty-sec-
ond and thirty-eighth degrees of north latitude.
The bay, or, as it was commonly called, the canal
of Santa Barbara, is very large, being formed by
the mainland on one side, which here bends in
like a crescent, and three large islands opposite
to it and at the distance of twenty miles. This is
just sufficient to give it the name of a bay, while
at the same time it is so large and so much exposed to the southeast and northwest winds, that
it is little better than an open roadstead; and the
whole swell of the Pacific ocean rolls in here
before a southeaster and breaks with so heavy a
surf in the shallow waters, that it is highly dangerous to lie near in to the shore during the southeaster season, that is, between the months of
November and April.

This wind is the bane of the coast of California.
Between the months of November and April,

* Now called the Bay of San Francisco.

60

which is the rainy season, you are never safe from it; and accordingly, in the ports which are open to it, vessels are obliged, during these months, to lie at anchor at a distance of three miles from the shore, with slip-ropes on their cables, ready to slip and go to sea at a moment's warning. The only ports which are safe from this wind are San Francisco and Monterey in the north, and San Diego in the south.

As it was January when we arrived, and the middle of the southeaster season, we accordingly came to anchor at the distance of three miles from the shore, in eleven fathoms water, and bent a slip-rope and buoys to our cables, cast off the yard-arm gaskets from the sails, and stopped them all with rope-yarns. After we had done this, the boat went ashore with the captain, and returned with orders to the mate to send a boat ashore for him at sundown. I did not go in the first boat, and was glad to find that there was another going before night; for after so long a voyage as ours had been, a few hours is long to pass in sight and out of reach of land.

It was a beautiful day, and so warm that we had on straw hats, duck trousers, and all the summer gear, and as this was midwinter, it spoke well for the climate; and we afterwards found that the thermometer never fell to the freezing-point throughout the winter, and that there was very little difference between the seasons, except that during a long period of rainy and southeasterly weather thick clothes were not uncomfortable.

The large bay lay about us, nearly smooth, as there was hardly a breath of wind stirring, though the boat's crew who went ashore told us that the long ground-swell broke into a heavy surf on the beach. There was only one vessel in the port — a long sharp brig of about three hundred tons, with raking masts, and very square yards, and English colors at her peak. We afterwards learned that she was built at Guayaquil, and named the *Ayacucho*, after the place where the battle was fought that gave Peru her independence, and was now owned by a Scotchman named Wilson, who commanded her, and was engaged in the trade between Callao, the Sandwich islands, and California. She was a fast sailor, as we frequently afterwards perceived, and had a crew of Sandwich Islanders on board. Two points ran out as the horns of the crescent, one of which — the one to the westward — was low and sandy, and is that to which vessels are obliged to give a wide berth when running out for a southeaster; the other is high, bold, and well wooded, and, we were told, has a mission upon it, called St. Buenaventura, from which the point is named. In the middle of this crescent, directly opposite the anchoring ground, lie the mission and town of Santa Barbara, on a low, flat plain, but little above the level of sea, covered with grass, though entirely without trees, and surrounded on three sides by an amphitheater of mountains, which slant off to the distance of fifteen or twenty miles.

Just before sundown the mate ordered a boat's

crew ashore, and I went as one of the number. We passed under the stern of the English brig, and had a long pull ashore. I shall never forget the impression which our first landing on the beach of California made upon me. The sun had just gone down; it was getting dusky; the damp night-wind was beginning to blow, and the heavy swell of the Pacific was setting in, and breaking in loud and high "combers" upon the beach. We lay on our oars in the swell, just outside of the surf, waiting for a good chance to run in, when a boat, which had put off from the *Ayacucho* just after us, came alongside of us, with a crew of dusky Sandwich Islanders, talking and hallooing in their outlandish tongue. They knew that we were novices in this kind of boating and waited to see us go in. The second mate, however, who steered our boat, determined to have the advantage of their experience, and would not go in first. Finding at length how matters stood, they gave a shout, and taking advantage of a great comber which came swelling in, rearing its head, and lifting up the stern of our boat nearly perpendicular, and again dropping it in the trough, they gave three or four long and strong pulls, and went in on top of the great wave, throwing their oars overboard and as far from the boat as they could throw them, and jumping out the instant that the boat touched the beach, and then seizing hold of her, and running her up high and dry upon the sand. We saw at once how it was to be done, and also the necessity of keeping the boat stern on to the sea; for the instant the sea should strike upon her broadside or quarter she would be driven up broadside on and capsized. We pulled strongly in, and as soon as we felt that the sea had got hold of us, and was carrying us in with the speed of a racehorse, we threw the oars as far from the boat as we could, and took hold of the gunwale, ready to spring out and seize her when she struck, the officer using his utmost strength to keep her stern on. We were shot up upon the beach like an arrow from a bow, and seizing the boat, ran her up high and dry, and soon picked up our oars, and stood by her, ready for the captain to come down.

Finding that the captain did not come immediately, we walked about the beach to see what we could of the place. It was growing dark, so that we could just distinguish the thin outlines of the two vessels in the offing. The Sandwich Islanders had turned their boat round and ran her down into the water, and were loading her with hides and tallow. As this was the work in which we were soon to be engaged we looked on with some curiosity. They ran the boat into the water so far that every large sea might float her, and two of them, with their trousers rolled up, stood by the bows, one on each side, keeping her in her right position. This was hard work; for beside the force they had to use upon the boat, the large seas nearly took them off their legs. The others were running from the boat to the bank, upon which, out of the reach of the water, was a pile of dry bullock's hides, doubled lengthwise in the middle, and nearly as stiff as boards. These they took upon their heads, one or two at a time, and carried down to the boat, where one of their number stowed them away. "Well, Dana," said the second mate to me, "this does not look much like college, does it? This is what I call head work."

After they had got through with the hides they laid hold of the bags of tallow, and lifting each upon the shoulders of two men, one at each end, walked off with them to the boat, and prepared to go aboard. Here, too, was something for us to learn. The man who steered shipped his oar and stood up in the stern, and those that pulled the after oars sat upon their benches, with their oars shipped, ready to strike out as soon as she was afloat. The two men standing at the bows kept their places, and when at length a large sea came in and floated her, seized hold of the gunwale and ran out with her till they were up to their armpits, and then tumbled over the gunwale into the bows, dripping with water. The men at the oars struck out, but it wouldn't do; the sea swept back and left them nearly high and dry. The two fellows jumped out again, and the next time they succeeded better, and with the help of a deal of outlandish hallooing and bawling got her well off.

The sand of the beach began to be cold to our bare feet, the frogs set up their croaking in the marshes, and one solitary owl, from the end of the distant point, gave out his melancholy note, mellowed by the distance, and we began to think that it was high time for the "old man" to come down. Presently the captain appeared; and we winded the boat round, shoved her down, and prepared to go off. The captain, who had been on the coast before and "knew the ropes," took the steering oar, and we went off in the same way as the other boat. We went off well, though the seas were high. Some of them lifted us up, and, sliding from under us, seemed to let us drop through the air like a flat plank upon the body of the water. In a few minutes we were in the low, regular swell, and pulled for a light, which, as we came up, we found had been run up to our trysail gaff.

Coming aboard, we hoisted up all the boats, and, diving down into the forecastle, changed our wet clothes, and got our supper. After supper the sailors lighted their pipes, and we had to tell all we had seen ashore. At eight bells all hands were called aft, and the "anchor watch" set. We were to stand two in a watch, and, as the nights were pretty long, two hours were to make a watch. The second mate was to keep the deck until eight o'clock, all hands were to be called at daybreak, and the word was passed to keep a bright look-out, and to call the mate if it should come on to blow from the southeast. We had, also, orders to strike the bells every half hour through the night, as at sea. At daylight all hands were called, and we went through the usual process of washing down, swabbing, etc., and got breakfast at eight o'clock. In the course of the forenoon a boat went aboard of the *Ayacucho* and brought off a quarter of beef, which made us a fresh bite for dinner. This we were glad enough to have, and the mate told us that we should live upon fresh beef while we were on the coast, as it was cheaper here than the salt. While at dinner the cook called "Sail ho!" and, coming on deck, we saw two sails coming round the point. One was a large ship under top-gallant sails, and the other a small hermaphrodite brig. They both backed their topsails and sent boats aboard of us. The ship's colors had puzzled us, and we found that she was from Genoa, with an assorted cargo, and was trading on the coast. She filled away again, and stood out, being bound up the coast to San Francisco. The crew of the brig's boat were Sandwich Islanders, but one of them, who spoke a little English, told us that she was the *Loriotte*, Captain Nye, from Oahu, and was engaged in this trade.

The three captains went ashore after dinner, and came off again at night. When in port everything is attended to by the chief mate; the captain, unless he is also supercargo, has little to do, and is usually ashore much of his time. This we thought would be pleasanter for us, as the mate was a good-natured man, and not very strict. So it was for a time, but we were worse off in the end; for wherever the captain is a severe, energetic man, and the mate is wanting in both these qualities, there will always be trouble. And trouble we had already begun to anticipate. The captain had several times found fault with the mate in presence of the crew, and hints had been dropped that all was not right between them.

CHAPTER X

A Southeaster

This night, after sundown, it looked black at the southward and eastward, and we were told to keep a bright look-out. Expecting to be called up, we turned in early. Waking up about midnight, I found a man who had just come down from his watch striking a light. He said that it was beginning to puff up from the southeast, and that the sea was rolling in, and he had called the captain; and as he threw himself down on his chest with all his clothes on I knew that he expected to be called. I felt the vessel pitching at her anchor and the chain surging and snapping, and lay awake, expecting an instant summons. In a few minutes it came — three knocks on the scuttle, and "All hands ahoy! bear a hand up and make sail." We sprang up for our clothes and were about half-way dressed when the mate called out, down the scuttle, "Tumble up here, men! tumble up! before she drags her anchor." We were on deck in an instant. "Lay aloft and loose the topsails!" shouted the captain, as soon as the first man showed himself. Springing into the rigging, I saw that the *Ayacucho*'s topsails were loosed, and heard her crew singing out at the sheets as they were hauling them home. This had probably started our captain, as "Old Wilson" had been many years on the coast, and knew the signs of the weather. We soon had the topsails loosed; and one hand remaining, as usual, in each top, to overhaul the rigging and light the sail out, the rest of us laid down to man the sheets. While sheeting home we saw the *Ayacucho* standing athwart our bows, sharp upon the wind, cutting through the head-sea like a knife, with her raking masts, and sharp bows running up like the head of a greyhound. It was a beautiful sight. She was like a bird which had been frightened and had spread her wings in flight. After the topsails had been sheeted home, the head yards braced aback, the fore-topmast staysail hoisted, and the buoys streamed, and all ready forward for slipping, we went aft and manned the slip-rope which came through the stern port with a turn round the timber-heads. "All ready forward?" asked the captain. "Aye, aye, sir; all ready," answered the mate. "Let go!" "All gone, sir"; and the iron cable grated over the windlass and through the hawse-hole, and the little vessel's head swinging off from the wind under the force of her backed head sails brought the strain upon the slip-rope. "Let go aft!" Instantly all was gone and we were under way. As soon as she was well off from the wind we filled away the head yards, braced all up sharp, set the foresail and trysail, and left our anchorage well astern, giving the point a good berth.

It now began to blow fresh, the rain fell fast,

and it grew very black, but the captain would not take in sail until we were well clear of the point. As soon as we left this on our quarter and were standing out to sea the order was given, and we sprang aloft, double-reefed each topsail, furled the foresail, and double-reefed the trysail, and were soon under easy sail. In these cases of slipping for southeasters there is nothing to be done, after you have got clear of the coast, but to lie to under easy sail and wait for the gale to be over, which seldom lasts more than two days, and is often over in twelve hours, but the wind never comes back to the southward until there has a good deal of rain fallen. "Go below, the watch," said the mate; but here was a dispute which watch it should be, which the mate soon, however, settled by sending his watch below, saying that we should have our turn the next time we got under way. We remained on deck till the expiration of the watch, the wind blowing very fresh, and the rain coming down in torrents. When the watch came up we wore ship and stood on the other tack, in toward land. When we came up again, which was at four in the morning, it was very dark, and there was not much wind, but it was raining as I thought I had never seen it rain before. We had on oilcloth suits and southwester caps, and had nothing to do but to stand bolt upright and let it pour down upon us.

Toward morning the captain put his head out of the companion-way and told the second mate, who commanded our watch, to look out for a change of wind, which usually followed a calm and heavy rain; and it was well that he did, for in a few minutes it fell dead calm, the vessel lost her steerage-way, and the rain ceased. We hauled up the trysail and courses, squared the after-yards, and waited for the change, which came in a few minutes, with a vengeance, from the north-west, the opposite point of the compass. Owing to our precautions we were not taken aback, but ran before the wind with square yards. The captain coming on deck, we braced up a little and stood back for our anchorage. With the change of wind came a change of weather, and in two hours the wind moderated into the light, steady breeze which blows down the coast the greater part of the year, and, from its regularity, might be called a trade-wind. The sun came up bright, and we set royals, sky-sails, and studding-sails, and were under fair way for Santa Barbara.

The *Ayacucho* got to the anchoring-ground about half-an-hour before us, and was furling her sails when we came up to it. This picking up your cables is a very nice piece of work. It requires some seamanship to come to at your former moorings, without letting go another anchor. Captain Wilson was remarkable among the sailors on the coast for his skill in doing this; and our captain never let go a second anchor during all the time that I was with him. Coming a little to windward of our buoy, we clewed up the light sails, backed our main topsail, and lowered a boat which pulled off, and made fast a spare hawser to the buoy on the end of the slip-rope. We brought the other end to the capstan, and hove in upon it until we came to the slip-rope, which we took to the windlass, and walked her up to her chain, the captain helping her by backing and filling the sails. The chain is then passed through the hawse-hole and round the windlass, and bitted, the slip-rope taken round outside and brought into the stern port, and she is safe in her old berth.

After we had furled the sails and got dinner we saw the *Loriotte* nearing, and she had her anchor before night. At sundown we went ashore again, and found the *Loriotte*'s boat waiting on the beach. The Sandwich Islander who could speak English told us that he had been up to the town, that our agent, Mr. R—, and some other passengers, were going to Monterey with us, and that we were to sail the same night. In a few minutes, Captain T—, with two gentlemen and one female, came down, and we got ready to go off. I pulled the after-oar, so that I heard the conversation, and learned that one of the men, who, as well as I could see in the darkness, was a young-looking man, in the European dress, and covered up in a large cloak, was the agent of the firm to which our vessel belonged; and the other, who was dressed in the Spanish dress of the country, was a brother of our captain, who had been many years a trader on the coast, and had married the lady who was in the boat. As soon as we got on board, the boats were hoisted up, the sails loosed,

73

the windlass manned, the slip-ropes and gear cast off; and after about twenty minutes of heaving at the windlass, making sail, and bracing yards, we were well under way, and going with a fair wind up the coast to Monterey. We had a fair wind, which is something unusual when going up, as the prevailing wind is the north, which blows directly down the coast; whence the northern are called the windward, and the southern the lee-ward ports.

CHAPTER XI

A Fresh Breeze

We got clear of the islands before sunrise the next morning, and by twelve o'clock we were out of the canal, and off Point Conception. This is the largest point on the coast, and is an uninhabited headland, stretching out into the Pacific, and has the reputation of being very windy. Any vessel does well which gets by it without a gale, especially in the winter season. We were going along with studding-sails set on both sides, when, as we came round the point, we had to haul our wind, and took in the lee studding-sails. As the brig came more upon the wind, she felt it more, and we doused the sky-sails, but kept the weather studding-sails on her, bracing the yards forward so that the swinging-boom nearly touched the sprit-sail yard. She now lay over to it, the wind was freshening, and the captain was evidently "dragging on to her." He stood up to windward, holding on by the back stays, and looking up at the sticks, to see how much they would bear; when a puff came which settled the matter. Then it was "haul down," and "clew up," royals, flying-jib, and studding-sails, all at once. The mate and some men forward were trying to haul in the lower studding-sail, which had blown over the sprit-sail yard-arm, and round the guys, while the topmast-studding-sail boom, after buckling up and springing out again like a piece of whalebone, broke off at the boom-iron. I sprang aloft to take in the main top-gallant studding-sail, but before I got into the top, the tack parted, and away went the sail, swinging forward of the top-gallant sail, and tearing and slatting itself to pieces. The halyards were at this moment let go by the run; and such a piece of work I never had before in taking in a sail. After great exertions I got it, or the remains of it, into the top, and was making it fast, when the captain, looking up, called out to me, "Lay aloft there, Dana, and furl that main royal." Leaving the studding-sail, I went up to the cross-trees; and here it looked rather squally. The foot of the top-gallant-mast was working between the cross and trussel trees, and the royal-mast lay over at a fearful angle with the mast below, while everything was working, and cracking, strained to the utmost.

There's nothing for Jack to do but to obey orders, and I went up upon the yard; and there was a worse mess, if possible, than I had left below. The braces had been let go, and the yard was swinging about like a turnpike gate, and the whole sail, having blown over to leeward, the lee leach was over the yard-arm, and the sky-sail was all adrift and flying over my head. I looked down, but it was in vain to attempt to make myself heard, for everyone was busy below, and the wind roared, and sails were flapping in every direction. Fortunately, it was noon and broad daylight, and the man at the wheel, who had his eyes aloft, soon saw my difficulty, and after numberless signs and gestures got some one to haul the necessary ropes taut. At the other royal-mast-head was S—, working away at the sail, which was blowing from him as fast as he could gather it in. The top-gallant sail below me was soon clewed up, which relieved the mast, and in a short time I got my sail furled and went below. In an hour from the time the squall struck us, from having all our flying kites abroad, we came down to double-reefed top-sails and the storm-sails.

The wind had hauled ahead during the squall, and we were standing directly in for the point. So, as soon as we had got all snug, we wore round and stood off again, and had the pleasant prospect of beating up to Monterey, a distance of a hundred miles, against a violent head wind. Before night it began to rain; and we had five days of rainy, stormy weather, under close sail all the time, and were blown several hundred miles off the coast. In the midst of this we discovered that our fore topmast was sprung, and were obliged to send down the fore top-gallant-mast and carry as little sail as possible forward. On the sixth day it cleared off, and the sun came out bright, but the wind and sea were still very high. It was quite like being at sea again; no land for hundreds of miles, and the captain taking the sun every day at noon.

After a few days we made the land at Point Pinos, which is the headland at the entrance of the bay of Monterey. As we drew in, and ran down the shore, we could distinguish well the face of the country, and found it better wooded than that to the southward of Point Conception.

The bay of Monterey is very wide at the entrance, being about twenty-four miles between the two points, Año Nuevo at the north, and Pinos at the south, but narrows gradually as you approach the town, which is situated in a bend or large cove at the southeastern extremity, and about eighteen miles from the points, which makes the whole depth of the bay. We came to anchor within two cable-lengths of the shore, and the town lay directly before us, making a very pretty appearance; its houses being plastered, which gives a much better effect than those of Santa Barbara, which are of a mud color. The red tiles, too, on the roofs contrasted well with the white plastered sides, and with the extreme greenness of the lawn upon which the houses — about a hundred in number — were dotted about here and there irregularly.

It was a fine Saturday afternoon when we came to anchor, the sun about an hour high, and everything looking pleasant. The Mexican flag was flying from the little square Presidio, and the drums and trumpets of the soldiers, who were out on parade, sounded over the water, and gave great life to the scene. Everyone was delighted with the appearance of things. We felt as though we had got into a Christian country.

We landed the agent and passengers, and found several persons waiting for them on the beach, among whom were some who, though dressed in the costume of the country, spoke English; and who, we afterwards learned, were English and Americans who had married and settled in the country.

CHAPTER XII

Trading in California

On Monday, the cargo having been entered in due form, we began trading. The trade-room was fitted up in the steerage, and furnished out with the lighter goods and with specimens of the rest of the cargo; and M—, a young man who came out from Boston with us before the mast, was taken out of the forecastle and made supercargo's clerk. He was well qualified for the business, having been clerk in a counting-house in Boston. The people came off to look and to buy — men, women, and children; and we were continually going in the boats, carrying goods and passengers — for they have no boats of their own. Everything must dress itself and come aboard and see the new vessel, if it were only to buy a paper of pins. The agent and his clerk managed the sales, while we were busy in the hold or in the boats. Our cargo was an assorted one; that is, it consisted of everything under the sun. We had spirits of all kinds, teas, coffee, sugars, spices, raisins, molasses, hardware, crockery-ware, tin-ware, cutlery, clothing of all kinds, boots and shoes from Lynn, calicoes and cottons from Lowell, crapes, silks; also shawls, scarfs, necklaces, jewelry, and combs for the ladies; furniture, and, in fact, everything that can be imagined, from Chinese fireworks to English cart-wheels — of which we had a dozen pairs with their iron rims on.

By being thus continually engaged in transporting passengers with their goods to and fro we gained considerable knowledge of the character, dress, and language of the people. The women wore gowns of various texture — silks, crape, calicoes, etc. — made after the European style, except that the sleeves were short, leaving the arm bare, and that they were loose about the waist, having no corsets. They wore shoes of kid or satin, sashes or belts of bright colors, and almost always a necklace and ear-rings. Bonnets they had none. They wear their hair (which is almost invariably black or a very dark brown) long in their necks, sometimes loose, and sometimes in long braids; though the married women often do it up on a high comb. Their only protection against the sun and weather is a large mantle which they put over their heads, drawing it close round their faces when they go out of doors, which is generally only in pleasant weather. When in the house, or sitting out in front of it, which they often do in fine weather, they usually wear a small scarf or neckerchief of a rich pattern. A band also about the top of the head, with a cross, star, or other ornament in front, is common. Their complexions are various, depending — as well as their dress and manner — upon their rank; or, in other words, upon the amount of

Spanish blood they can lay claim to.

Next to the love of dress, I was most struck with the fineness of the voices and beauty of the intonations of both sexes. Every common ruffian-looking fellow, with a slouched hat, blanket cloak, dirty under-dress, and soiled leather leggings appeared to me to be speaking elegant Spanish. It was a pleasure simply to listen to the sound of the language before I could attach any meaning to it. A common bullock-driver on horseback delivering a message seemed to speak like an ambassador at an audience. In fact, they sometimes appeared to me to be a people on whom a curse had fallen, and stripped them of everything but their pride, their manners, and their voices.

I had never studied Spanish while at college, and could not speak a word when at Juan Fernandez; but during the latter part of the passage out, I borrowed a grammar and dictionary from the cabin, and by a continual use of these, and a careful attention to every word that I heard spoken, I soon got a vocabulary together, and began talking for myself. As I soon knew more Spanish than any of the crew, and had been at college, and knew Latin, I got the name of a great linguist, and was always sent by the captain and officers to get provisions or to carry letters and messages to different parts of the town. This was a good exercise for me, and no doubt taught me more than I should have learned by months of study and reading; it also gave me opportunities of seeing the customs, characters, and domestic arrangements of the people; beside being a great relief from the monotony of a day spent on board ship.

But to return to Monterey. The houses here, as everywhere else in California, are of one story, built of clay made into large bricks, about a foot and a half square, and three or four inches thick, and hardened in the sun. The floors are generally of earth, the windows grated and without glass, and the doors, which are seldom shut, open directly into the common room, there being no entries. Some of the more wealthy inhabitants have glass to their windows and board floors; and in Monterey nearly all the houses are plastered on the outside. The better houses, too, have red tiles upon the roofs. The common ones have two or three rooms, which open into each other, and are furnished with a bed or two, a few chairs and tables, a looking-glass, a crucifix of some material or other, and small daubs of paintings inclosed in glass, and representing some miracle or martyrdom. They have no chimneys or fireplaces in the houses, the climate being such as to make a fire unnecessary; and all their cooking is done in a small cookhouse separated from the house.

In Monterey there are a number of English and Americans, who have married Californians, become united to the Catholic Church, and acquired considerable property. Having more industry, frugality, and enterprise than the natives, they soon get nearly all the trade into their hands.

The men in Monterey appeared to me to be always on horseback. Horses are as abundant here as dogs and chickens were in Juan Fernandez. There are no stables to keep them in, but they are allowed to run wild, and graze wherever they please, being branded, and having long leather ropes, called "lassos," attached to their necks, and dragging along behind them, by which they can easily be taken. The men usually catch one in the morning, throw a saddle and bridle upon him, and use him for the day, and let him go at night, catching another the next day. When they go on long journeys, they ride one horse down, and catch another, throw the saddle and bridle upon him, and after riding him down, take a third, and so on to the end of the journey. There are probably no better riders in the world. The stirrups are covered or boxed up in front, to prevent their catching when riding through the woods; and the saddles are large and heavy, strapped very tight upon the horse, and have pommels in front, round which the "lasso" is coiled when not in use. They can hardly go from one house to another without getting on a horse, there being generally several standing tied to the door-posts of the little cottages. When they wish to show their activity they make no use of their stirrups in mounting, but striking the horse, spring into the saddle as he starts, and sticking their long spurs into him, go off on the full run. They frequently give exhibitions of their horsemanship in races, bull-baitings, etc.; but as we were not ashore during any holiday we saw nothing of it.

Nothing but the character of the people prevents Monterey from becoming a great town. The soil is as rich as man could wish — climate as good as any in the world — water abundant, and situation extremely beautiful. The harbor, too, is a good one, being subject only to one bad wind — the north; and though the holding-ground is not the best, yet I have heard of but one vessel being driven ashore here.

The only vessel in port with us was the little *Loriotte.* I frequently went on board her, and became very well acquainted with her Sandwich Island crew. They were well formed and active, with black eyes, intelligent countenances, dark-olive or copper complexions, and coarse black hair, but not woolly like the negro's. The language is extremely guttural, and not pleasant at first, but improves as you hear it more, and is said to have great capacity. They use a good deal of gesticulation, and are exceedingly animated, saying with their might what their tongues find to say. They are complete water-dogs, and therefore very good in boating. They are also quick and active in the rigging, and good hands in warm weather; but those who have been with them round Cape Horn, and in high latitudes, say that they are useless in cold weather. In their dress they are precisely like our sailors. In addition to these Islanders, the vessel had two English sailors, who acted as boatswains over the Islanders, and took care of the rigging. One of them I shall always remember as the best specimen of the thoroughbred English sailor that I ever saw. He had been to sea from a boy, having served a regular apprenticeship of seven years, as all English sailors are obliged to do, and was then about four or five and twenty.

He called himself Bill Jackson; and I know no one of all my accidental acquaintances to whom I would more gladly give a shake of the hand than to him.

Sunday came again while we were at Monterey, but, as before, it brought us no holiday. The people on shore came off in greater numbers than ever, and we were employed all day in boating and breaking out cargo, so that we had hardly time to eat. Our *ci-devant* second mate, who was determined to get liberty if it was to be had, dressed himself in a long coat and black hat, and polished his shoes, and went aft and asked to go ashore. He could not have done a more imprudent thing, for he knew that no liberty would be given; and besides, sailors, however sure they may be of having liberty granted them, always go aft in their working clothes, to appear as though they had no reason to expect anything, and then wash, dress, and shave, after they have got their liberty. We looked to see him go aft, knowing pretty well what his reception would be. The captain was walking the quarter-deck, smoking his morning cigar, and Foster went as far as the break of the deck, and there waited for him to notice him. The captain took two or three turns, and then walking directly up to him, surveyed him from head to foot, and lifting up his fore-finger, said a word or two, in a tone too low for us to hear, but which had a magical effect upon poor Foster. He walked forward, sprang into the forecastle, and in a moment more made his appearance in his common clothes, and went quietly to work again. What the captain said to him we never could get him to tell, but it certainly changed him outwardly and inwardly in a most surprising manner.

CHAPTER XIII

The Seamen Discontented

After a few days, finding the trade beginning to slacken, we hove our anchor up, set our topsails, ran the stars and stripes up to the peak, and left the little town astern, running out of the bay, and bearing down the coast again for Santa Barbara. As we were now going to leeward, we had a fair wind, and plenty of it. After doubling Point Pinos, we bore up, set studding-sails alow and aloft, and were walking off at the rate of eight or nine knots, promising to traverse in twenty-four hours the distance which we were nearly three weeks in traversing on the passage up. We passed Point Conception at a flying rate, the wind blowing so that it would have seemed half a gale to us if we had been going the other way and close hauled. As we drew near the islands of Santa Barbara it died away a little, but we came to at our old anchoring-ground in less than thirty hours from the time of leaving Monterey.

Here everything was pretty much as we left it — the large bay without a vessel in it; the surf roaring and rolling in upon the beach; the white mission, the dark town, and the high treeless mountains. Here, too, we had our southeaster tacks aboard again. We lay here about a fortnight, employed in landing goods and taking off hides occasionally when the surf was not high; but there did not appear to be one-half the business doing here that there was in Monterey.

The hides are always brought down dry, or they would not be received. When they are taken from the animal they have holes cut in the ends, and are staked out, and thus dried in the sun without shrinking. They are then doubled once lengthwise with the hair side usually in, and sent down upon mules or in carts, and piled above high-water mark; and then we take them upon our heads and wade out with them, and throw them into the boat. We all provided ourselves with thick Scotch caps, which would be soft to the head, and at the same time protect it; for we soon found that however it might look or feel at first, the "head-work" was the only system for California.

After we had got our heads used to the weight and had learned the true Californian style of tossing a hide, we could carry off two or three hundred in a short time without much trouble; but it was always wet work, and if the beach was stony, hard for our feet; for we, of course, always went barefooted on this duty, as no shoes could stand such constant wetting with salt water. Then, too, we had a long pull of three miles with a loaded boat, which often took a couple of hours.

We had now got well settled down into our harbor duties, which, as they are a good deal different from those at sea, it may be well enough to describe. In the first place, all hands are called at daylight, or rather — especially if the days are short — before daylight, as soon as the first gray of the morning. The cook makes his fire in the galley; the steward goes about his work in the cabin; and the crew rig the head pump, and wash down the decks. The washing, swabbing, squilgeeing, etc., lasts, or is made to last, until eight o'clock, when breakfast is ordered fore and aft. After breakfast, for which half an hour is allowed, the boats are lowered down and made fast astern, or out to the swinging-booms by geswarps, and the crew are turned-to upon their day's work. This is various, and its character depends upon circumstances. There is always more or less of boating in small boats; and if heavy goods are to be taken ashore, or hides are brought down to the beach for us, then all hands are sent ashore with an officer in the long-boat. Then there is always a good deal to be done in the hold; goods to be broken out; and cargo to be shifted, to make room for hides, or to keep the trim of the vessel. In addition to this, the usual work upon the rigging must be going on. The great difference between sea and harbor duty is in the division of time. Instead of having a watch on deck and a watch below, as at sea, all hands are at work together except at meal times, from daylight till dark; and at night an "anchor-watch" is kept. An hour is allowed for dinner; and at dark the decks are cleared up, the boats hoisted, supper ordered; and at eight the lights put out, except in the binnacle, where the glass stands and the anchor-watch is set. Thus when at anchor the crew have more time at night, but have no time to themselves in the day; so that reading, mending clothes, etc., has to be put off until Sunday, which is usually given. Some religious captains give their crews Saturday afternoons to do their washing and mendings in, so that they may have their Sundays free. We were well satisfied if we got Sunday to ourselves, for if any hides came down on that day, as was often the case when they were brought from a distance, we were obliged to bring them off, which usually took half a day.

But all these little vexations and labors would have been nothing were it not for the uncertainty, or worse than uncertainty, which hung over the nature and length of our voyage. Here we were in a little vessel with a small crew on a half-civilized coast at the ends of the earth, and with the prospect of remaining an indefinite period, two or three years at the least. When we left Boston we supposed that it was to be a voyage of eighteen months, or two years at most; but upon arriving on the coast we learned something more of the trade, and found that in the scarcity of hides, which was yearly greater and greater, it would take us a year at least to collect our own cargo, beside the passage out and home, and that we were also to collect a cargo for a large ship belonging to the same firm, which was soon to come on the coast, and to which we were to act as tender.

The ship *California*, belonging to the same firm, had been nearly two years on the coast, had collected a full cargo, and was now at San Diego, from which port she was expected to sail in a few weeks for Boston; and we were to collect all the hides we could and deposit them at San Diego, when the new ship, which would carry forty thousand, was to be filled and sent home; and then we were to begin anew and collect our own cargo. Here was a gloomy prospect before us indeed. The *California* had been twenty months on the coast, and the *Lagoda*, a smaller ship, carrying only thirty-one or thirty-two thousand, had been two years getting her cargo, and we were to collect a cargo of forty thousand beside our own, which would be twelve or fifteen thousand. Besides, we were not provided for so long a voyage, and clothes and all sailors' necessaries were excessively dear — three or four hundred per cent advance upon the Boston prices. This was bad enough for them; but still worse was it for me, who did not mean to be a sailor for life, having intended only to be gone eighteen months or two years. Three or four years would make me a sailor in every respect, mind and habits as well as body, and would put all my companions so far ahead of me that college and a profession would be in vain to think of.

Beside the length of the voyage and the hard and exposed life, we were at the ends of the earth, in a country where there is neither law nor gospel, and where sailors are at their captain's mercy, there being no American consul, or anyone to whom a complaint could be made. We lost all interest in the voyage, cared nothing about the cargo, which we were only collecting for others, began to patch our clothes, and felt as though we were fixed beyond all hope of change.

In addition to, and perhaps partly as a consequence of, this state of things, there was trouble brewing on board the vessel. Our mate was a worthy man — a more honest, upright, and kind-hearted man I never saw; but he was too good for the mate of a merchantman. He wanted the energy and spirit for such a voyage as ours and for such a captain. Captain T— was a vigorous, energetic fellow. During all the time that I was with him I never saw him sit down on deck. He was always active and driving; severe in his discipline, and expected the same of his officers. The mate not being enough of a driver for him, and being perhaps too easy with the crew, he was dissatisfied with him, became suspicious that discipline was getting relaxed, and began to interfere in everything. He drew the reins tauter, and in his attempt to remedy the difficulty by severity he made everything worse. Severity created discontent, and signs of discontent provoked severity. Then, too, ill-treatment and dissatisfaction are no *"linimenta laborum";* and many a time have I heard the sailors say that they should not mind the length of the voyage and the hardships if they were only kindly treated, and if they could feel that something was done to make things lighter and easier. But the contrary policy was pursued. We were kept at work all day when in port, which, together with a watch at night, made us glad to turn in as soon as we got below. Thus we got no time for reading or for washing and mending our clothes. And then, when we were at sea, sailing from port to port, instead of giving us "watch and watch," as was the custom on board every other vessel on the coast, we were all kept on deck and at work, rain or shine, making spun-yarn and rope, and at other work in good weather, and picking oakum when it was too wet for anything else.

While lying at Santa Barbara we encountered another southeaster, and, like the first, it came on in the night — the great black clouds coming round from the southward, covering the mountain, and hanging down over the town, appearing almost to rest upon the roofs of the houses. We made sail, slipped our cable, cleared the point, and beat about for four days in the offing under close sail, with continual rain and high seas and winds. On the fifth day it cleared up, and we found ourselves drifted nearly ten leagues from the anchorage, and, having light head winds, we did not return until the sixth day. Having recovered our anchor we made preparations for getting under way to go down to leeward. Just before sailing the captain took on board a short, red-haired, round-shouldered, vulgar-looking fellow, who had lost one eye and squinted with the other, and, introducing him as Mr. Russell, told us that

94

he was an officer on board. This was too bad. We had lost overboard on the passage one of the best of our number, another had been taken from us and appointed clerk; and thus weakened and reduced, instead of shipping some hands to make our work easier, he had put another officer over us to watch and drive us. We had now four officers, and only six in the forecastle.

Leaving Santa Barbara we coasted along down, the country appearing level or moderately uneven, and for the most part sandy and treeless, until, doubling a high sandy point, we let go our anchor at a distance of three or three and a half miles from shore. As soon as everything was snug on board the boat was lowered, and we pulled ashore, our new officer, who had been several times in the port before, taking the place of steersman. As we drew in we found the tide low and the rocks and stones covered with kelp and seaweed, lying bare for the distance of nearly an eighth of a mile. Just in front of the landing, and immediately over it, was a small hill which we had not perceived from our anchorage. Over this hill we saw three men come down, dressed partly like sailors and partly like Californians. When they came down to us we found that they were Englishmen, and they told us that they had belonged to a small Mexican brig which had been driven ashore here in a southeaster, and now lived in a small house just over the hill. Going up this hill with them we saw just behind it a small, low building, with one room, containing a fireplace, cooking apparatus, etc., and the rest of it unfinished, and used as a place to store hides and goods. This, they told us, was built by some traders in the Pueblo (a town about thirty miles in the interior, to which this was the port), and used by them as a storehouse, and also as a lodging-place when they came down to trade with the vessels. These three men were employed by them to keep the house in order and to look out for the things stored in it. They said that they had been there nearly a year, and had nothing to do most of the time. The nearest house, they told us, was a rancho or cattle-farm about three miles off; and one of them went up, at the request of our officer, to order a horse to be sent down, with which the agent, who was on board, might go up to the Pueblo. From one of them I learned a good deal in a few minutes' conversation about the place, its trade, and the news from the southern ports. San Diego, he said, was about eighty miles to the leeward of San Pedro; that they had heard from there, by a Spaniard who came up on horseback, that the *California* had sailed for Boston, and that the *Lagoda*, which had been in San Pedro only a few weeks before, was taking in her cargo for Boston.

I also learned, to my surprise, that the desolate-looking place we were in was the best place on the whole coast for hides. It was the only port for a distance of eighty miles, and about thirty miles in the interior was a fine plane country, filled with herds of cattle, in the center of which was the

Pueblo de los Angelos — the largest town in California — and several of the wealthiest missions, to all of which San Pedro was the seaport.

The next day we pulled the agent ashore, and he went up to visit the Pueblo and the neighboring missions; and in a few days, as the result of his labors, large ox-carts and droves of mules, loaded with hides, were seen coming over the flat country. We loaded our long boat with goods of all kinds, light and heavy, and pulled ashore. After landing and rolling them over the stones upon the beach, we stopped, waiting for the carts to come down the hill and take them; but the captain soon settled the matter by ordering us to carry them all up to the top, saying that that was "California fashion." So what the oxen would not do we were obliged to do. The hill was low, but steep, and the earth, being clayey and wet with the recent rains, was but bad holding ground for our feet. The heavy barrels and casts we rolled up with some difficulty, getting behind and putting our shoulders to them; now and then our feet slipping added to the danger of the casks rolling back upon us. But the greatest trouble was with the large boxes of sugar. These we had to place upon oars, and, lifting them up, rest the oars upon our shoulders and creep slowly up the hill with the gait of a funeral procession. After an hour or two of hard work we got them all up, and found the carts standing full of hides, which we had to unload and also to load again with our own goods.

Now the hides were to be got down; and for this purpose we brought the boat round to a place where the hill was steeper, and threw them down, letting them slide over the slope. Many of them lodged, and we had to let ourselves down and set them agoing again, and in this way got covered with dust, and our clothes torn. After we had got them all down we were obliged to take them on our heads and walk over the stones, and through the water, to the boat. For several days we were employed in this manner, until we had landed forty or fifty tons of goods, and brought on board about two thousand hides, when the trade began to slacken, and we were kept at work on board during the latter part of the week either in the hold or upon the rigging.

CHAPTER XIV

A Tyrannical Captain

For several days the captain seemed very much out of humor. He quarreled with the cook, and threatened to flog him for throwing wood on deck; and had a dispute with the mate about reeving a Spanish burton, the mate saying that he was right, and had been taught how to do it by a man *who was a sailor!* This the captain took in dudgeon, and they were at swords' points at once. But his displeasure was chiefly turned against a large, heavy-molded fellow, from the Middle States, who was called Sam. This man hesitated in his speech, and was rather slow in his motions, but was a pretty good sailor, and always seemed to do his best; but the captain took a dislike to him, found fault with everything he did, and hazed him for dropping a marline-spike from the main-yard, where he was at work. We worked late on Friday night, and were turned-to early on Saturday morning. About ten o'clock the captain ordered our new officer, Russell, to get the gig ready to take him ashore. John, the Swede, was sitting in the boat alongside, and Russell and myself were standing by the main hatchway, waiting for the captain, who was down in the hold,

99

where the men were at work, when we heard his voice raised in violent dispute with somebody. Then came blows and scuffling. I ran to the side and beckoned to John, who came up, and we leaned down the hatchway; and though we could see no one, yet we knew that the captain had the advantage, for his voice was loud and clear: —

"You see your condition! Will you ever give me any more of your *jaw?*" No answer; and then came wrestling and heaving, as though the man was trying to turn him. "You may as well keep still, for I have got you," said the captain. Then came the question, "Will you ever give me any more of your jaw?"

"I never gave you any, sir," said Sam; for it was his voice that we heard.

"That's not what I ask you. Will you ever be impudent to me again?"

"I never have been, sir," said Sam.

"Answer my question, or I'll make a spread-eagle of you!"

"I'm no negro slave," said Sam.

"Then I'll make you one," said the captain; and he came to the hatchway and sprang on deck, threw off his coat, and rolling up his sleeves, called out to the mate, "Seize that man up, Mr. A— I seize him up! Make a spread-eagle of him! I'll teach you all who is master aboard!"

The crew and officers followed the captain up the hatchway, and after repeated orders the mate laid hold of Sam, who made no resistance, and carried him to the gangway.

"What are you going to flog that man for, sir?" said John, the Swede, to the captain.

Upon hearing this the captain turned upon him, but, knowing him to be quick and resolute, he ordered the steward to bring the irons, and calling upon Russell to help him, went up to John.

"Let me alone," said John. "You need not use any force"; and putting out his hands, the captain slipped the irons on, and set him aft to the quarter-deck. Sam by this time was seized up — that is, placed against the shrouds, with his wrists made fast to the shrouds, his jacket off, and his back exposed. The captain stood on the break of the deck, a few feet from him, and a little raised, so as to have a good swing at him, and held in his hand the bight of a thick, strong rope. The officers stood round, and the crew grouped together in the waist. All these preparations made me feel sick and almost faint, angry and excited as I was. A man — a human being, made in God's likeness — fastened up and flogged like a beast! The first and almost uncontrollable impulse was resistance. But what was to be done? The time for it had gone by. The two best men were fast, and there were only two beside myself, and a small boy of ten or twelve years of age. And then there were, beside the captain, three officers, steward, agent, and clerk. But beside the numbers, what is there for sailors to do? If they resist, it is mutiny; and if they succeed, and take the vessel, it is piracy. Bad as it was it must be borne.

It is what a sailor ships for. Swinging the rope over his head, and bending his body so as to give it full force, the captain brought it down upon the poor fellow's back. Once, twice — six times. "Will you ever give me any more of your jaw?" The man writhed with pain, but said not a word. Three times more. This was too much, and he muttered something which I could not hear. This brought as many more as the man could stand, when the captain ordered the man to be cut down and to go forward.

"Now for you," said the captain, making up to John, and taking his irons off. As soon as he was loose, he ran forward to the forecastle. "Bring that man aft!" shouted the captain. The second mate, who had been a shipmate of John's, stood still in the waist, and the mate walked slowly forward; but our third officer, anxious to show his zeal, sprang over the windlass and laid hold of John; but he soon threw him from him. At this moment I would have given worlds for the power to help the poor fellow; but it was all in vain. The captain stood on the quarter-deck, bareheaded, his eyes flashing with rage, and his face as red as blood, swinging the rope, and calling out to his officers, "Drag him aft! lay hold of him! I'll sweeten him!" etc., etc.

The mate now went forward and told John quietly to go aft; and he, seeing resistance was in vain, threw the blackguard third mate from him, said he would go aft of himself, that they should not drag him, and went up to the gangway and held out his hands; but as soon as the captain began to make him fast, the indignity was too much, and he began to resist; but the mate and Russell holding him, he was soon seized up. When he was made fast he turned to the captain, who stood turning up his sleeves and getting ready for the blow, and asked him what he was to be flogged for. "Have I ever refused my duty, sir? Have you ever known me to hang back, or to be insolent, or not to know my work?"

"No," said the captain; "it is not that that I flog you for; I flog you for your interference — for asking questions."

"Can't a man ask a question here without being flogged?"

"No," shouted the captain; "nobody shall open his mouth aboard this vessel but myself"; and began laying the blows upon his back, swinging half round between each blow to give it full effect. As he went on his passion increased, and he danced about the deck, calling out as he swung the rope, "If you want to know what I flog you for, I'll tell you. It's because I like to do it! — because I like to do it! — It suits me! That's what I do it for!"

The man writhed under the pain. My blood ran cold. I could look on no longer. Disgusted, sick, and horror-struck, I turned away and leaned over the rail and looked down into the water. A few rapid thoughts of my own situation, and of the prospect of future revenge crossed my mind; but the falling of the blows and the cries of the man called me back at once. At length they ceased, and, turning round, I found that the mate, at a signal from the captain, had cut him down.

Almost doubled up with pain the man walked slowly forward, and went down into the forecastle. Everyone else stood still at his post, while the captain, swelling with rage and with the importance of his achievement, walked the quarter-deck, and at each turn, as he came forward, calling out to us. "You see your condition! You see where I've got you all, and you know what to expect! You've been mistaken in me — you didn't know what I was! Now you know what I am! — I'll make you toe the mark, every soul of you, or I'll flog you all, fore and aft, from the boy, up! — You've got a driver over you! Yes, a slave-driver — a negro-driver!"

With this and the like matter, equally calculated to quiet us, and to allay any apprehensions of future trouble, he entertained us for about ten minutes, when he went below. Soon after John came aft, with his bare back covered with stripes and wales in every direction, and dreadfully swollen, and asked the steward to ask the captain to let him have some salve or balsam to put upon it.

"No," said the captain, who heard him from below; "tell him to put his shirt on; that's the best thing for him; and pull me ashore in the boat. Nobody is going to lay-up on board this vessel." He then called Mr. Russell to take those two men and two others in the boat and pull him ashore.

I went for one. The two men could hardly bend their backs, and the captain called to them to "give way, give way!" but finding they did their best he let them alone.

The agent was in the stern-sheets, but during the whole pull not a word was spoken. We landed; the captain, agent, and officer went up to the house, and left us with the boat. I, and the man with me, stayed near the boat, while John and Sam walked slowly away and sat down on the rocks. They talked some time together, but at length separated, each sitting alone.

After the day's work was done we went down into the forecastle and ate our supper, but not a word was spoken. It was Saturday night, but there was no song — no "sweethearts and wives." A gloom was over everything. The two men lay in their berths groaning with pain, and we all turned in — but, for myself, not to sleep. A sound coming now and then from the berths of the two men showed that they were awake, as awake they must have been, for they could hardly lie in one posture a moment; the dim, swinging lamp of the forecastle shed its light over the dark hole in which we lived; and many and various reflections and purposes coursed through my mind. I thought of our situation, living under a tyranny; of the character of the country we were in; of the length of the voyage, and of the uncertainty attending our return to America; and then, if we should return, of the prospect of obtaining justice and satisfaction for these poor men; and vowed that, if ever

I should have the means, I would do something to redress the grievances and relieve the sufferings of that poor class of beings of whom I then was one.

The next day was Sunday. We worked as usual, washing decks, etc., until breakfast-time. After breakfast we pulled the captain ashore, and finding some hides there which had been brought down the night before, he ordered me to stay ashore and watch them, saying that the boat would come again before night. They left me; and I spent a quiet day on the hill eating dinner with the three men at the little house. Unfortunately, they had no books; and after talking with them and walking about I began to grow tired of doing nothing.

I looked anxiously for a boat during the latter part of the afternoon, but none came until toward sundown, when I saw a speck on the water, and as it drew near I found it was the gig with the captain. The hides, then, were not to go off. The captain came up the hill, with a man bringing my monkey jacket and a blanket. He looked pretty black, but inquired whether I had enough to eat, told me to make a house out of the hides and keep myself warm, as I should have to sleep there among them, and to keep good watch over them. I got a moment to speak to the man who brought my jacket.

"How do things go aboard?" said I.

"Bad enough," said he; "hard work, and not a kind word spoken."

"What," said I, "have you been at work all day?"

"Yes! no more Sunday for us. Everything has been moved in the hold from stem to stern and from the water-ways to the keelson."

I went up to the house to supper. After our meal the three men sat down by the light of a tallow candle, with a pack of greasy Spanish cards, to the favorite game of "treinta uno," a sort of Spanish "everlasting." I left them and went out to take up my bivouac among the hides. It was now dark, the vessel was hidden from sight, and except the three men in the house there was not a living soul within a league. The coati (a wild animal of a nature and appearance between that of the fox and the wolf) set up their sharp, quick bark, and two owls, at the end of two distant points running out into the bay, on different sides of the hill where I lay, kept up their alternate dismal notes. Mellowed by the distance, and heard alone at night, I thought it was the most melancholy, boding sound I had ever heard. Through nearly all the night they kept it up, answering one another slowly at regular intervals. The next morning, before sunrise, the long-boat came ashore, and the hides were taken off.

We lay at San Pedro about a week, engaged in taking off hides and in other labors, which had now become our regular duties. I spent one more day on the hill, watching a quantity of hides and goods, and this time succeeded in finding a part of a volume of Scott's *Pirate* in a corner of the house, but it failed me at a most interesting moment, and I betook myself to my acquaintances on shore, and from them learned a good deal about the customs of the country, the harbors, etc.

On board the *Pilgrim* everything went on regularly, each one trying to get along as smoothly as possible; but the comfort of the voyage was evidently at an end. The flogging was seldom if ever alluded to by us in the forecastle. If anyone was inclined to talk about it, the others, with a delicacy which I hardly expected to find among them, always stopped him or turned the subject. But the behavior of the two men who were flogged toward one another showed a delicacy and a sense of honor which would have been worthy of admiration in the highest walks of life. Sam knew that the other had suffered solely on his account, and in all his complaints he said that if he alone had been flogged it would have been nothing, but that he never could see that man without thinking that he had been the means of bringing that disgrace upon him; and John never, by word or deed, let anything escape him to remind the other that it was by interfering to save his shipmate that he had suffered.

Having got all our spare room filled with hides, we hove up our anchor and made sail for San Diego. In no operation can the disposition of a crew be discovered better than in getting under way. Where things are done "with a will" everyone is like a cat aloft, sails are loosed in an instant, each one lays out his strength on his handspike, and the windlass goes briskly round with the loud cry of "Yo, heave ho! Heave and pawl! Heave hearty, ho!" But with us at this time it was all dragging work. The mate, between the knight-heads, exhausted all his offcial rhetoric in calls of "Heave with a will!" "Heave hearty, men! — heave hearty!" "Heave and raise the dead!" "Heave and away!" etc., etc.; but it would not do. Nobody broke his back or his handspike by his efforts. And when the cat-tackle-fall was strung along, and all hands — cook, steward, and all — laid hold to cat the anchor, instead of the lively song of "Cheerily, men!" in which all hands join in the chorus, we pulled a long, heavy, silent pull, and the anchor came to the cat-head pretty slowly. "Give us 'Cheerily!' " said the mate; but there was no "cheerily" for us, and we did without it. The captain walked the quarter-deck and said not a word.

We sailed leisurely down the coast before a light fair wind, keeping the land well aboard, and saw two other missions, looking like blocks of white plaster, shining in the distance. At sunset on the second day, we had a large and well wooded headland directly before us, behind which lay the little harbor of San Diego. We were becalmed off this point all night; but the next morning, which was Saturday, the 14th of March, having a good breeze, we stood round the point, and hauling our wind, brought the little harbor which is rather the outlet of a small river, right before us. A chain of high hills, beginning at the point (which was on our larboard hand, coming in), protected the harbor on the north and west, and ran off into the interior as far as the eye could reach. On the other sides the land was low and green, but without trees. The entrance is so narrow as to admit but one vessel at a time, the current swift, and the channel runs so near to a low stony point that the ship's sides appeared almost to touch it. There was no town in sight; but on the smooth sand-beach, abreast, and within a cable's-length of which three vessels lay moored, were four large houses, built of rough boards, with piles of hides standing round them, and men in red shirts and large straw hats walking in and out of the doors. These were the hide-houses. Of the vessels, one we recognized as our old acquaintance the *Loriotte*; another, newly painted and tarred, and glittering in the morning sun, with the blood-red banner and cross of St. George at her peak, was the handsome *Ayacucho*. The third was a large ship, with topgallant-masts housed, and sails unbent, and looking as rusty and worn as two years' "hide droghing" could make her. This was the *Lagoda*. As we drew near we overhauled our anchor and clewed up the topsails. "Let go the anchor!" said the captain; but either there was not chain enough forward of the windlass, or the anchor went down foul, or we had too much headway on, for it did not bring us up. "Pay out chain!" shouted the captain; and we gave it to her; but it would not do. Before the other anchor could be let go, we drifted down, broadside on, and went smash into the *Lagoda*.

Fortunately no great harm was done. Her jib-boom ran between our fore and main-masts, carrying away some of our rigging, and breaking down the rail. She lost her martingale.* This brought us up; and as they paid out chain we swung clear of them, and let go the other anchor; but this had as bad luck as the first, for before anyone perceived it, we were drifting on to the *Loriotte*. The captain now gave out his orders rapidly and fiercely, sheeting home the topsails, and backing and filling the sails, in hope of starting or clearing the anchors; but it was all in vain; and he sat down on the rail, taking it very leisurely, and calling out to Captain Nye that he was coming to pay him a visit. We drifted fairly into the *Loriotte*, her larboard bow into our starboard quarter, carrying away a part of our starboard quarter railing, and breaking off her larboard bumpkin, and one or two stanchions above the deck. After paying out chain we swung clear, but our anchors were no doubt afoul of hers. We manned the windlass, and hove, and hove away, but to no purpose. Sometimes we got a little upon the cable, but a good surge would take it all back again. We now began to drift down toward the *Ayacucho*, when her boat put off, and brought her commander, Captain Wilson, on board. He was

* *Martingale,* a short perpendicular spar under the bow-sprit end, used for guying down the head-stays.

a short, active, well-built man, between fifty and sixty years of age; and being nearly thirty years older than our captain, he did not hesitate to give his advice, and from giving advice, he gradually came to taking the command, ordering us when to heave and when to pawl, and backing and filling the topsails, setting and taking in jib and trysails, whenever he thought best. We had no objections to this state of things; for Wilson was a kind old man, and had an encouraging and pleasant way of speaking to us, which made everything go easily. After two or three hours of constant labor at the windlass, heaving and "Yo ho!"-ing with all our might, we brought up an anchor, with the *Loriotte*'s small bower fast to it. Having cleared this and let it go, and cleared our hawse, we got out our other anchor, which had dragged half over the harbor. "Now," said Wilson, "I'll find you a good berth"; and setting both the topsails, he carried us down, and brought us to anchor, in handsome style, directly abreast of the hide-house which we were to use. Having done this, he took his leave, while we furled the sails, and got our breakfast. After breakfast and until night we were employed in getting out the boats and mooring ship.

After supper two of us took the captain on board the *Lagoda*. As he came alongside, he gave his name, and the mate, in the gangway, called out to the captain down the companion-way — "Captain T— has come aboard, sir!" "Has he brought his brig with him?" said the rough old fellow, in a tone which made itself heard fore and aft. The captain went down into the cabin, and we walked forward and put our heads down the forecastle, where we found the men at supper. "Come down, shipmates! come down!" said they as soon as they saw us; and we went down, and found a large high forecastle, well lighted, and a crew of twelve or fourteen men, eating out of their kids and pans, and drinking their tea, and talking and laughing, all as independent and easy as so many "wood-sawyer's clerks."

We spent an hour or two with them, talking over California matters, until the word was passed — "Pilgrims away!" — and we went back with our captain to the brig.

CHAPTER XV

On Shore

The next day being Sunday, after washing and clearing decks, and getting breakfast, the mate came forward with leave for one watch to go ashore on liberty. We drew lots, and it fell to the larboard, which I was in. Instantly all was preparation. Buckets of fresh water (which we were allowed in port), and soap, were put in use; go-ashore jackets and trousers got out and brushed; pumps, neckerchiefs, and hats overhauled; one lending to another; so that among the whole each one got a good fit-out. A boat was called to pull the "liberty-men" ashore, and we sat down in the stern-sheets, "as big as pay-passangers," and jumping ahore, set out on our walk for the town, which was nearly three miles off.

It is a pity that some other arrangement is not made in merchant vessels with regard to the liberty-day. I have heard of a religious captain who gave his crew liberty on Saturdays after twelve o'clock. This would be a good plan, if shipmasters would bring themselves to give their crews so much time. As it is, it can hardly be expected that a crew on a long and hard voyage will refuse a few hours of freedom from toil and the restraints of a vessel, and an opportunity to tread the ground and see the sights of society and humanity because it is on a Sunday.

I shall never forget the delightful sensation of being in the open air, with the birds singing around me, and escape from the confinement, labor, and strict rule of a vessel — of being once more in my life, though only for a day, my own master. A sailor's liberty is but for a day, yet while it lasts it is perfect. He is under no one's eye, and can do whatever, and go wherever he pleases. This day, for the first time, I may truly say, in my whole life, I felt the meaning of a term which I had often heard — the sweets of liberty. It was wonderful how the prospect brightened, and how short and tolerable the voyage appeared, when viewed in this new light. Things looked differently from what they did when we talked them over in the little dark forecastle the night after the flogging at San Pedro.

S— and myself determined to keep as much together as possible, though we knew that it would not do to cut our shipmates; for, knowing our birth and education, they were a little suspicious that we would try to put on the gentleman when we got ashore, and would be ashamed of their company; and this won't do with Jack. Our crew fell in with some men who belonged to the other vessels, and, sailor-like, steered for the first grog-shop. This was a small mud-building, of only one room, in which were liquors, dry and West India goods, shoes, bread, fruits, and everything which is vendible in California. S— and I followed in our shipmates' wake, knowing that to refuse to drink with them would be the highest affront, but determining to slip away at the first opportunity. When we first came in there was some dispute between our crew and the others, whether the new-comers or the old California rangers should treat first; but it being settled in favor of the latter, each of the crews of the other vessels treated all round in their turn, and as there were a good many present, and the liquor was a *real* (12½ cents) a glass, it made somewhat of a hole in their lockers. It was now our ship's turn, and S — and I, anxious to get away, stepped up to call for glasses; but we soon found that we must go in order — the oldest first, for the old sailors did not choose to be preceded by a couple of youngsters, and we had to wait our turn, with the twofold apprehension of being too late for our horses and of taking too much; for drink you must every time; and if you drink with one and not with another it is always taken as an insult.

Having at length gone through our turns, and acquitted ourselves of all obligations, we slipped out, and went about among the houses, endeavoring to get horses for the day, so that we might ride round and see the country. At first we had but little success, but after several efforts we fell in with a little Sandwich Island boy, who belonged to Captain Wilson of the *Ayacucho*, and was well acquainted with the place; he, knowing where to go, soon procured us two horses, ready saddled and bridled, each with a lasso coiled over the pommel. Mounted on our horses, which were spirited beasts, we started off on a fine run over the country. The first place we went to was the old ruinous Presidio which stands on a rising ground near the village, which it overlooks. From the Presidio we rode off in the direction of the mission, which we were told was three miles distant. The country was rather sandy, and there was nothing for miles which could be called a tree; but the grass grew green and rank, and there were many bushes and thickets; and the soil is said to be good. After a pleasant ride of a couple of miles we saw the white walls of the mission, and fording a small river we came directly before it. There was something decidedly striking in its appearance: a number of irregular buildings, connected with one another, and disposed in the form of a hollow square, with a church at one end, rising above the rest, with a tower containing five belfries, in each of which hung a large bell, and with an immense rusty iron cross at the top. Just outside of the buildings, and under the walls, stood twenty or thirty small huts, built of straw and of the branches of trees, in which a few Indians lived, under the protection and in the service of the mission.

Entering a gateway, we rode into the open square, in which the stillness of death reigned. Not a living creature could we see. We rode twice round the square in the hope of waking up some one; and in one circuit saw a tall monk with shaven head, sandals, and the dress of the Grey Friars pass rapidly through a gallery, but he disappeared without noticing us. After two circuits we stopped our horses, and saw at last a man show himself in front of one of the small buildings. We rode up to him and found him dressed in the common dress of the country, with a silver chain round his neck supporting a large bunch of keys. From this we took him to be the steward of the mission, and addressing him as "Mayordomo" received a low bow and an invitation to walk into his room. It was a plain room, containing a table, three or four chairs, a small picture or two, and a few dishes and glasses. "Hay algunas cosas á comer?" said I. "Si, Señor!" said he. "Que gusta Usted?" Mentioning frijoles, which I knew they must have if they had nothing else, and beef and bread, and a hint for wine, if they had any, he went off to another building, across the court, and returned in a few moments with a couple of Indian boys, bearing dishes and a decanter of wine. The dishes contained baked meats, frijoles stewed with peppers and onions, boiled eggs, and a kind of macaroni. These, together with the wine, made the most sumptuous meal we had eaten since we left Boston. After despatching our meal, we took out some money and asked him how much we were to pay. He shook his head, and crossed himself, saying that it was charity — the Lord gave it to us. We gave him ten or twelve *reals,* which he pocketed with admirable nonchalance, saying, "Dios se lo pague." Taking leave of him, we rode out to the Indians' huts.

Leaving the mission, we returned to the village, going nearly all the way on a full run. The California horses have no medium gait which is pleasant between walking and running; for as there are no streets and parades, they have no need of the genteel trot, and their riders usually keep them at the top of their speed until they are tired, and then let them rest themselves by walking. The fine air of the afternoon, the rapid rate of the animals, who seemed almost to fly over the ground, and the excitement and novelty of the motion to us who had been so long confined on shipboard, were exhilarating beyond expression, and we felt willing to ride all day long. Coming into the village we found things looking very lively. The Indians, who always have a holiday on Sunday, were engaged at playing a kind of running game of ball on a level piece of ground near the houses. Several blue-jackets were reeling about among the houses, which showed that the pulperias had been well patronized. One or two of the sailors had got on horseback, but being rather indifferent horsemen, and the Spaniards having given them vicious horses, they were soon thrown, much to the amusement of the people. A half-dozen Sandwich Islanders, from the hide-houses and the two brigs, who are bold riders, were dashing about on the full gallop, hallooing and laughing like so many wild men.

It was now nearly sundown, and S— and myself

went into a house and sat quietly down to rest ourselves before going down to the beach. Thus ended our first liberty-day on shore. We were well tired, but had had a pleasant holiday, and were more willing to go back to our old duties.

CHAPTER XVI

San Diego

The next sound that we heard was "All hands ahoy!" and looking up the scuttle, saw that it was just daylight. Our liberty had now truly taken flight, and putting on old duck trousers, red shirts, and Scotch caps, we began taking out and landing our hides. For three days we were hard at work in this duty, from the gray of the morning until starlight, with the exception of a short time allowed for meals. We took possession of one of the hide-houses, which belonged to our firm, and had been used by the *California*. It was built to hold forty thousand hides, and we had the pleasing prospect of filling it before we could leave the coast; and toward this, our thirty-five hundred, which we brought down with us, would do but little.

The hides, as they come rough and uncured from the vessels, are piled up outside of the houses, whence they are taken and carried through a regular process of pickling, drying, cleaning, etc., and stowed away in the house, ready to be put on board. This process is necessary in order that they may keep during a long voyage and in warm latitudes. For the purpose of curing and taking care of these hides, an officer and a part of the crew of each vessel are usually left ashore; and it was for this business, we found, that our new officer had joined us. As soon as the hides were landed he took charge of the house, and the captain intended to leave two or three of us with him, hiring Sandwich Islanders to take our places on board; but he could not get any Sandwich Islanders to go, though he offered them fifteen dollars a month; for the report of the flogging had got among them, and he was called "aole maikai" (no good), and that was an end of the business. They were, however, willing to work on shore, and four of them were hired and put with Mr. Russell to cure the hides.

After landing our hides we next sent ashore all our spare spars and rigging — all the stores which we did not want to use in the course of one trip to windward — and, in fact, everything which we could spare, so as to make room for hides; among other things the pig-sty, and with it "Old Bess." This was an old sow that we had brought from Boston, and which lived to get round Cape Horn, where all the other pigs died from cold and wet. She had been the pet of the cook during the whole passage, and he had fed her with the best of everything, and taught her to do a number of strange tricks for his amusement. It almost broke our poor darky's heart when he heard that Bess was to be taken ashore. He had depended upon her as a solace during the long trips up and down the coast. We got a whip up on the main-yard, and hooking it to a strap round her body, swayed away; and giving a wink to one another, ran her chock up to the yard-arm. " 'Vast there! vast!' " said the mate; "none of your skylarking! Lower away!" But he evidently enjoyed the joke. The pig squealed like the "crack of doom," and tears stood in the poor darky's eyes, and he muttered something about having no pity on a dumb beast. "Dumb beast!" said Jack; "if she's what you call a dumb beast, then my eyes a'n't mates." This produced a laugh from all but the cook. He was too intent upon seeing her safe in the boat. He watched her all the way ashore, where, upon her landing, she was received by a whole troop of her kind, who had been set ashore from the other vessels. From the door of his galley the cook used to watch them in their maneuver setting up a shout and clapping his hands whenever Bess came off victorious in the struggle for pieces of raw hide and half picked bones which were lying about the beach. We told him that he thought more about the pig than he did about his wife; and, indeed, he could hardly have been more attentive, for he actually, on several nights after dark, when he thought he would not be seen, sculled himself ashore in a boat with a bucket of nice swill.

The next Sunday the other half of our crew went ashore on liberty, and left us on board, to enjoy the first quiet Sunday which we had had upon the coast. Here were no hides to come off, and no southeasters to fear. We washed and mended our clothes in the morning, and spent the rest of the day in reading and writing. Several of us wrote letters to send home by the *Lagoda*.

At the close of the week we were ready to sail, but were delayed a day or two by the running away of Foster, the man who had been our second mate. From the time that he was "broken" he had had a dog's berth on board the vessel, and determined to run away at the first opportunity. Having shipped for an officer when he was not half a seaman, he found little pity with the crew, and was not man enough to hold his ground among them. He had had several difficulties with the captain, and asked leave to go home in the *Lagoda*; but this was refused him. One night he was insolent to an officer on the beach, and refused to come aboard in the boat. He was reported to the captain; and as he came on board — it being past the proper hour — he was called aft and told that he was to have a flogging. Immediately he fell down on the deck, calling out, "Don't flog me, Captain T—; don't flog me!" and the captain, angry with him and disgusted with his cowardice, gave him a few blows over the back with a rope's-end and sent him forward. He was not much hurt, but a good deal frightened, and made up his mind to run away that very night.

This was managed better than anything he ever did in his life, and seemed really to show some spirit and forethought. He gave his bedding and mattress to one of the *Lagoda*'s crew, who took it aboard his vessel as something which he had bought, and promised to keep it for him. He then unpacked his chest, putting all his valuable clothes into a large canvas bag, and told one of us, who had the watch, to call him at midnight. Finding no officer on deck, and all still aft, he lowered his bag into a boat, got softly down into it, cast off the painter, and let it drop down silently with the tide until he was out of hearing, when he sculled ashore.

The next morning when all hands were mustered there was a great stir to find Foster. Of course, we would tell nothing; and all they could discover was that he had left an empty chest behind him, and that he went off in a boat. After breakfast the captain went up to the town and offered a reward of twenty dollars for him; and for a couple of days the soldiers, Indians, and all others who had nothing to do were scouring the country for him on horseback, but without effect; for he was safely concealed all the time within fifty rods of the hide-houses. As soon as he had landed, he went directly to the *Lagoda*'s hide-house; and a part of her crew who were living there on shore promised to conceal him and his traps until the *Pilgrim* should sail, and then to intercede with Captain Bradshaw to take him on board his ship. Just behind the hide-houses, among the thickets and underwood, was a small cave, the entrance to which was known only to the two men on the beach. To this cave he was carried before daybreak in the morning, and supplied with bread and water, and there remained until he saw us under way and well round the point.

Friday, March 27th. The captain, having given up all hope of finding Foster, gave orders for unmooring ship, and we made sail, dropping slowly down with the tide. The wind, which was very light, died away soon after we doubled the point, and we lay becalmed for two days. On the third day about noon a cool sea-breeze came rippling and darkening the surface of the water, and by sundown we were off St. Juan's. Our crew was now considerably weakened. Yet there was not one who was not glad that Foster had escaped; for shiftless and good-for-nothing as he was, no one could wish to see him dragging on a miserable life, cowed down and disheartened; and we were all rejoiced to hear, upon our return to San Diego about two months afterwards, that he had been immediately taken aboard the *Lagoda*.

After a slow passage of five days, we arrived on Wednesday, the first of April, at our old anchoring-ground at San Pedro. In a few days the hides began to come slowly down, and we got into the old business of rolling goods up the hill, pitching hides down, and pulling our long league off and on.

On board things went on in the common monotonous way. The excitement which immediately followed the flogging scene had passed off, but the effect of it upon the crew, and especially upon the two men themselves, remained.

After a stay of about a fortnight, during which

we slipped for one southeaster, and were at sea two days, we got under way for Santa Barbara. There we found lying at anchor the large Genoese ship which we saw in the same place on the first day of our coming upon the coast. She had been up to San Francisco, had stopped at Monterey on the way down, and was shortly to proceed to San Pedro and San Diego, and thence, taking in her cargo, to sail for Valparaiso and Cadiz. It was now the close of Lent, and on Good Friday she had all her yards a'-cock-bill, which is customary among Catholic vessels. Some also have an effigy of Judas, which the crew amuse themselves with keel-hauling and hanging by the neck from the yard-arms.

CHAPTER XVII

Easter in California

The next Sunday was Easter day, and as there had been no liberty at San Pedro, it was our turn to go ashore and misspend another Sabbath. Soon after breakfast a large boat, filled with men in blue jackets, scarlet caps, and various colored under-clothes, bound ashore on liberty, left the Italian ship and passed under our stern, the men singing beautiful Italian boat-songs all the way in fine full chorus. Supposing that the whole day would be too long a time to spend ashore, as there was no place to which we could take a ride, we remained quietly on board until after dinner. We were then pulled ashore in the stern of the boat, and with orders to be on the beach at sundown, we took our way for the town. There everything wore the appearance of a holiday. Under the piazza of a "pulperia" two men were seated, decked out with knots of ribands and bouquets, and playing the violin and the Spanish guitar. As it was now too near the middle of the day to see any dancing, and hearing that a bull was expected down from the country to be baited in the Presidio square in the course of an hour or two, we took a stroll among the houses. Inquiring for an American who, we had been told, had married in the place, and kept a shop, we were directed to a long, low building, at the end of which was a door with a sign over it in Spanish. Entering the shop we found no one in it, and the whole had a deserted appearance. In a few minutes the man made his appearance, and apologized for having nothing to entertain us with, saying that he had had a *fandango* at his house the night before, and the people had eaten and drunk up everything.

"Oh, yes," said I; "Easter holidays."

"No," said he, with a singular expression on his face; "I had a little daughter die the other day, and that's the custom of the country."

At this I felt a little strangely, not knowing what to say, or whether to offer consolation or no, and was beginning to retire when he opened a side-door and told us to walk in. Here I was no less astonished; for I found a large room filled with young girls from three or four years of age up to fifteen and sixteen, dressed all in white, with wreaths of flowers on their heads and bouquets in their hands. Following our conductor among all these girls, who were playing about in high spirits, we came to a table at the end of the room, covered with a white cloth, on which lay a coffin about three feet long with the body of his child. Through an open door we saw in another room a few elderly people in common dresses; while the benches and tables thrown up in a corner and the stained walls gave evident signs of the last night's "high go."

To pass away the time we hired horses and rode down to the beach. There we found three or four Italian sailors mounted and riding up and down on the hard sand at a furious rate. We joined them, and found it fine sport. From the beach we returned to the town, and finding that the funeral procession had moved, rode on and over-took it about half way to the mission. Here was as peculiar a sight as we had seen before in the house — the one looking as little like a funeral procession as the other did like a house of mourn-ing. The coffin was borne by eight girls, who were continually relieved by others, running forward from the procession and taking their places. Be-hind it came a straggling company of girls, dressed as before, in white and flowers, and in-cluding, I should suppose by their numbers, nearly all the girls between five and fifteen in the place. They played along on the way, frequently stopping and running altogether to talk to some one, or to pick up a flower, and then running on again to overtake the coffin. There were a few elderly women in common colors; and a herd of young men and boys, some on foot and others mounted, followed them, or walked or rode by their side, frequently interrupting them by jokes and questions. But the most singular thing of all was that two men walked, one on each side of the coffin, carrying muskets in their hands, which they continually loaded and fired into the air.

As we drew near the mission we saw the great

gate thrown open and the padre standing on the steps with a crucifix in his hand. Just at this moment the bells set up their harsh, discordant clang, and the procession moved into the court. I was anxious to follow and see the ceremony, but the horse of one of my companions had become frightened and was tearing off toward the town, and having thrown his rider and got one of his feet caught in the saddle, which had slipped, was fast dragging and ripping it to pieces. Knowing that my shipmate could not speak a word of Spanish, and fearing that he would get into difficulty, I was obliged to leave the ceremony and ride after him.

Having returned to the town, we saw a great crowd collected in the square before the principal pulperia, and found that all these people — men, women, and children — had been drawn together by a couple of bantam cocks.

We heard some talk about *"cabellas"* and *"carréra,"* and seeing the people all streaming off in one direction, we followed, and came upon a level piece of ground just out of the town which was used as a racecourse. Here the crowd soon became thick again; the ground was marked off, the judges stationed, and the horses led up to one end. Two fine-looking old gentlemen — Don Carlos and Don Domingo, so called — held the stakes, and all was now ready. We waited some time, during which we could just see the horses twisting round and turning, until at length there was a shout along the lines, and on they came, heads stretched out and eyes starting, working all over, both man and beast. The steeds came by us like a couple of chain-shot — neck and neck, and now we could see nothing but their backs, and their hind-hoofs flying in the air. As fast as the horses passed the crowd broke up behind them and ran to the goal. When we got there we found the horses returning on a slow walk, having run far beyond the mark, and heard that the long, bony one had come in head and shoulders before the other. The horses were noble-looking beasts — not so sleek and combed as our Boston stable-horses, but with fine limbs and spirited eyes.

Returning to the large pulperia, we found the violin and guitar screaming and twanging away under the piazza, where they had been all day. As it was now sundown there began to be some dancing. The Italian sailors danced, and one of our crew exhibited himself in a sort of West Indian shuffle, to the amusement of the bystanders, who cried out "Bravo!" "Otra vez!" and "Vivan los marineros!" but the dancing did not become general, as the women and the "genta de razón" had not yet made their appearance. We wished very much to stay and see the style of dancing, but, although we had had our own way during the day, yet we were after all but 'foremast Jacks, and having been ordered to be on the beach by sundown, did not venture to be more than an hour behind the time; so we took our way down.

On Monday morning, as an off-set to our day's sport, we were all set to work "tarring down" the rigging. After breakfast we had the satisfaction of seeing the Italian ship's boat go ashore filled with men gaily dressed, as on the day before, and singing their barcarollas. The Easter holidays are kept up on shore during three days, and being a Catholic vessel, the crew had the advantage of them. For two successive days, while perched up in the rigging covered with tar and engaged in our disagreeable work, we saw these fellows going ashore in the morning and coming off again at night in high spirits.

About noon a man aloft called out "Sail ho!" and looking round we saw the head sails of a vessel coming round the point. As she drew round she showed the broadside of a full-rigged brig, with the Yankee ensign at her peak. We ran up our stars and stripes, and, knowing that there was no American brig on the coast but ourselves, expected to have news from home. She rounded-to and let her anchor go; but the dark faces on her yards, when they furled the sails, and the Babel on deck, soon made known that she was from the Islands. Immediately afterwards a boat's crew came aboard, bringing her skipper, and from them we learned that she was from Oahu, and was engaged in the same trade with the *Ayacucho*, *Loriotte*, etc., between the coast, the Sandwich Islands, and the leeward coast of Peru and Chili. Her captain and officers were Americans, and also a part of her crew; the rest were Islanders. She was called the *Catalina*, and, like all the other vessels in that trade, except the *Ayacucho*, her papers and colors were from Uncle Sam.

After lying here about a fortnight, and collecting all the hides the place afforded, we set sail again for San Pedro.

We lay about a week in San Pedro, and got under way for San Diego, intending to stop at San Juan as the southeaster season was nearly over, and there was little or no danger.

This being the spring season, San Pedro, as well as all the other open ports upon the coast, was filled with whales that had come in to make their annual visit upon soundings. For the first few days that we were here and at Santa Barbara we watched them with great interest, calling out "There she blows!" every time we saw the spout of one breaking the surface of the water; but they soon became so common that we took little notice of them. We once very nearly ran one down in the gig, and should probably have been knocked to pieces or blown sky-high. We had been on board the little Spanish brig, and were returning, stretching out well at our oars, the little boat going like a swallow; our backs were forward, and the captain, who was steering, was not looking out, when all at once we heard the spout of a whale directly ahead. "Back water! back water, for your lives!" shouted the captain, and we backed our blades in the water, and brought the boat to in a smother of foam. Turning our heads, we saw a great, rough, hump-backed whale slowly crossing our forefoot, within three or four yards of the boat's stem. Had we not backed water just as we did we should inevitably have gone smash upon him. He took no notice of us, but passed slowly on, and dived a few yards beyond us, throwing his tail high in the air. This kind differs much from the sperm in color and skin, and is said to be fiercer. We saw a few sperm whales; but most of the whales that come upon the coast are fin-backs, hump-backs, and right-whales, which are more difficult to take, and are said not to give oil enough to pay for the trouble.

Coasting along on the quiet shore of the Pacific, we came to anchor in twenty fathoms' water, almost out at sea, as it were, and directly abreast of a steep hill which overhung the water, and was twice as high as our royal-masthead. We had heard much of this place from the *Lagoda*'s crew, who said it was the worst place in California. The shore is rocky, and directly exposed to the south-east, so that vessels are obliged to slip and run for their lives on the first sign of a gale; and, late as it was in the season, we got up our slip-rope and gear, though we meant to stay only twenty-four hours. We pulled the agent ashore, and were ordered to wait for him, while he took a circuitous way round the hill to the mission, which was hidden behind it.

San Juan is the only romantic spot we saw in California. The country here for several miles is high table-land, running boldly to the shore, and breaking off in a steep hill, at the foot of which the waters of the Pacific are constantly dashing. For several miles the water washes the very base of the hill, or breaks upon ledges and fragments of rocks which run out into the sea. Just where we landed was a small cove, or "bight," which gave us, at high tide, a few square feet of sand-beach between the sea and the bottom of the hill. This was the only landing-place. Directly before us rose the perpendicular height of four or five hundred feet. How we were to get hides down, or goods up, upon the table-land on which the mission was situated was more than we could tell. The agent had taken a long circuit, and yet had frequently to jump over breaks and climb up steep places in the ascent. No animal but a man or a monkey could get up it. However, that was not our look-out, and knowing that the agent would be gone an hour or more, we strolled about, picking up shells, and following the sea where it tumbled in, roaring and spouting, among the crevices of the great rocks. What a sight, thought I, must this be in a southeaster! Besides, there was a grandeur in everything around, which gave almost a solemnity to the scene; a silence and solitariness which affected everything! Not a human being but ourselves for miles; and no sound heard but the pulsations of the great Pacific! the steep hill rising like a wall, and cutting us off from all the world but the "world of waters!" I separated myself from the rest, and sat down on a rock, just where the sea ran in and formed a fine spouting-horn. Compared with the plain, dull sand-beach of the rest of the coast this grandeur was as refreshing as a great rock in a weary land.

It was almost the first time that I had been positively alone — free from the sense that human beings were at my elbow, if not talking with me — since I had left home. My better nature returned strong upon me. Everything was in accordance with my state of feeling, and I experienced a glow of pleasure at finding that what of poetry and romance I ever had in me had not been entirely deadened by the laborious life I had been lately leading. Nearly an hour did I sit, almost lost in the luxury of this entire new scene of the play in which I had been so long acting, when I was aroused by the distant shouts of my companions, and saw that they were collecting together, as the agent had made his appearance on his way back to our boat.

We pulled aboard, and found the long-boat hoisted out, and nearly laden with goods; and after dinner we all went on shore in the quarter-boat, with the long-boat in tow. As we drew in, we found an ox-cart and a couple of men standing directly on the brow of the hill; and having landed, the captain took his way round the hill, ordering me and one other to follow him. We followed, picking our way out, and jumping and scrambling up, walking over briars and prickly pears, until we came to the top. Here the country stretched out for miles, as far as the eye could reach, on a level table surface; and the only habitation in sight was the small white mission of San Juan Campestrano with a few Indian huts about it, standing in a small hollow about a mile from where we were. Reaching the brow of the hill where the cart stood, we found several piles of hides, and the Indians sitting round them. One or two other carts were coming slowly on from the mission, and the captain told us to begin and throw the hides down. This, then, was the way they were to be got down; thrown down, one at a time, a distance of four hundred feet!

Down this height we pitched the hides, throwing them as far out into the air as we could; and as they were all large, stiff, and doubled, like the cover of a book, the wind took them, and they swayed and eddied about, plunging and rising in the air like a kite when it has broken its string. As it was now low tide there was no danger of their falling into the water, and as fast as they came to ground the men below picked them up and, taking them on their heads, walked off with them to the boat. It was really a picturesque sight.

Some of the hides lodged in cavities which were under the bank and out of our sight, being directly under us, but by sending others down in the same direction we succeeded in dislodging them.

Having thrown them all down, we took our way back again, and found the boat loaded and ready to start. We pulled off, took the hides all aboard, hoisted in the boats, hove up our anchor, made sail, and before sundown were on our way to San Diego.

Friday, May 8th, 1835. Arrived at San Diego. Here we found the little harbor deserted. The

Lagoda, Ayacucho, Loriotte, and all, had left the coast, and we were nearly alone. All the hide-houses on the beach but ours were shut up; and the Sandwich Islanders, a dozen or twenty in number, who had worked for the other vessels and had been paid off when they sailed, were living on the beach, keeping up a grand carnival. A Russian discovery-ship, which had been in this port a few years before, had built a large oven for baking bread, and went away leaving it standing. This the Sandwich Islanders took possession of, and had kept ever since undisturbed. It was big enough to hold six or eight men, had a door at the side, and a vent-hole at top. They covered it with Oahu mats for a carpet, stopped up the vent-hole in bad weather, and made it their head-quarters. It was now inhabited by as many as a dozen or twenty men, who lived there in complete idleness — drinking, playing cards, and carousing in every way. They bought a bullock once a week, which kept them in meat, and one of them went up to town every day to get fruit, liquor, and provisions. Captain T— was anxious to get three or four of them to come on board of the *Pilgrim,* as we were so much diminished in numbers, and went up to the oven and spent an hour or two trying to negotiate with them. One of them, a finely-built, active, strong, and intelligent fellow, who was a sort of king among them, acted as spokesman. He was called Mannini, and was known all over California. Through him the captain offered them fifteen dollars a month, and one month's pay in advance; but so long as they had money they would not work for fifty dollars a month, and when their money was gone they would work for ten.

We discharged our hides and tallow, and in about a week were ready to set sail again for the windward. We unmoored, and got everything ready, when the captain made another attempt upon the oven. This time he had more regard to the *"mollia tempora fandi,"* and succeeded very well. He got Mr. Mannini in his interest, and, as the shot was getting low in the locker, prevailed upon him and three others to come on board with their chests and baggage, and sent a hasty summons to me and the boy to come ashore with our things, and join the gang at the hide-house. This was unexpected to me, but anything in the way of variety I liked; so we got ready, and were pulled ashore. I stood on the beach while the brig got under way, and watched her until she rounded the point, and then went up to the hide-house to take up my quarters for a few months.

CHAPTER XVIII

Sandwich Islanders and Hide Curing

Here was a change in my life as complete as it had been sudden. In the twinkling of an eye I was transformed into a "beach-comber" and hide-curer; yet the novelty and the comparative independence of the life were not unpleasant. Our hide-house was a large building made of rough board and intended to hold forty thousand hides. In one corner of it a small room was parted off, in which four berths were made, where we were to live, with mother earth for our floor. It contained a table, a small locker for pots, spoons plates, etc., and a small hole cut to let in the light. Over our head was another small room, in which Mr. Russell lived, who had charge of the hide-house. There he lived in solitary grandeur; eating and sleeping alone, and communing with his own dignity. The boy was to act as cook; while myself, a giant of a Frenchman named Nicholas, and four Sandwich Islanders were to cure hides. Sam, the boy, the Frenchman, and myself lived together in the room, and the four Sandwich Islanders worked and ate with us, but generally slept at the oven. My new messmate, Nicholas, was the most immense man that I had ever seen in my life. He was considerably over six feet, and of a frame so large that he might have been shown for a curiosity. His strength was in proportion to his size, and his ignorance to his strength — "strong as an ox, and ignorant as strong." He neither knew how to read nor to write. He had been to sea from a boy, and had seen all kinds of service, and been in every kind of vessels: merchantmen, men-of-war, privateers, and slavers; and from what I could gather from the accounts of himself, and from what he once told me in confidence after we had been better acquainted, he had even been in worse business than slave-trading. He was once tried for his life in Charleston, South Carolina, and though acquitted, yet he was so frightened that he never would show himself in the United States again.

Though I knew what his life had been, yet I never had the slightest fear of him. We always got along very well together; and though so much stronger and larger than I, he showed a respect for my education, and from what he had heard of my situation before coming to sea. "I'll be good friends with you," he used to say, "for by-and-by you'll come out here captain, and then you'll *haze* me well!" By holding well together we kept the officer in good order, for he was evidently afraid of Nicholas, and never ordered us, except when employed upon the hides.

A considerable trade has been carried on for several years between California and the Sandwich Islands; and most of the vessels are manned with Islanders, who, as they for the most part sign no articles, leave whenever they choose, and let themselves out to cure hides at San Diego, and to supply the places of the men of the American vessels while on the coast. In this way, quite a colony of them had become settled at San Diego as their headquarters. Some of these had recently gone off in the *Ayacucho*, the *Loriotte*, and the *Pilgrim*, so that there were not more than twenty left. Of these four were on pay at the *Ayacucho*'s house, four more working with us, and the rest were living at the oven.

I had been but a few hours on the beach, and the *Pilgrim* was hardly out of sight, when the cry of "Sail ho!" was raised, and a small hermaphrodite brig rounded the point, bore up into the harbor, and came to anchor. It was the Mexican brig *Fazio*, which we had left at San Pedro, and which had come down to land her tallow, try it all over, and make new bags, and then take it in, and leave the coast. They moored ship, erected their try-works on shore, put up a small tent, in which they all lived, and commenced operations. They made an addition to our society, and we spent many evenings in their tent, where, amid the babel of English, Spanish, French, Indian, and Kanaka, we found some words that we could understand in common.

The morning after my landing I began the duties of hide-curing. The great weight of the wet hides, which we were obliged to roll about in wheelbarrows, the continual stooping upon those which were pegged out to be cleaned, and the smell of the vats, into which we were often obliged to get, knee-deep, to press down the hides — all made the work disagreeable and fatiguing. But we soon got hardened to it, and the comparative independence of our life reconciled us to it, for when we had finished our work we had only to wash and change our clothes, and our time was our own. There was, however, one exception to the time being our own, which was, that on two afternoons of every week we were obliged to go off and get wood for the cook to use in the galley. Wood is very scarce in the vicinity of San Diego, and two afternoons in the week, generally Monday and Thursday, as soon as we had finished our dinner, we started off for the bush, each of us furnished with a hatchet and a long piece of rope, and dragging the hand-cart behind us, and followed by the whole colony of dogs, who were always ready for the bush, and were half mad whenever they saw our preparations. We went with the hand-cart as far as we could conveniently drag it, and, leaving it in an open, conspicuous place, separated ourselves, each taking his own course, and looking about for some good place to begin upon. Having lighted upon a good thicket, the next thing was to clear away the under-brush, and have fair play at the trees. These trees are seldom more than five or six feet high; so that, with lopping off the branches and clearing away the underwood, we had a good deal of cutting to do for a very little wood. Having cut enough for a "back-load," the next thing was to make it well and fast with the rope, and heaving the bundle upon our backs, and taking the hatchet in hand, to walk off, up hill and down dale, to the hand-cart. Two good back-loads apiece filled the hand-cart, and that was each one's proportion. When each had brought down his second load, we filled the hand-cart, and took our way again slowly back to the beach.

These wooding excursions had always a mixture of something rather pleasant in them. Roaming about the woods, with hatchet in hand, like a backwoodsman, followed by a troop of dogs; starting up of birds, snakes, hares, and foxes, and examining the various kinds of trees, flowers, and birds' nests, was at least a change from the monotonous drag and pull on shipboard. Frequently, too, we had some amusement and adventure. The coati,[*] of which I have before spoken, fierce little animals, with bushy tails and large heads, and a quick, sharp bark, abound here, as in all other parts of California. These the dogs were very watchful for, and whenever they saw them started off in full run after them. We had many fine chases, yet, although our dogs ran finely, the rascals generally escaped. They are a match for the dog, one to one; but as the dogs generally went in squads there was seldom a fair fight. A smaller dog belonging to us once attacked a coati, single, and got a good deal worsted, and might, perhaps,

[*] Coyote.

145

have been killed, had we not come to his assistance. We had, however, one dog which gave them a good deal of trouble and many hard runs. He was a fine tall fellow, and united strength and agility better than any dog that I have ever seen. He was born at the Islands, his father being an English mastiff and his mother a greyhound. He had the high head, long legs, narrow body, and springing gait of the latter, and the heavy jaw, thick jowls, and strong fore-quarters of the mastiff. He always led the dogs by several yards in the chase, and had killed two coati at different times in single combats. We often had fine sport with these fellows. A quick, sharp bark from a coati, and in an instant every dog was at the height of his speed. Pursuit by us was in vain, and in about half an hour a few of them would come panting and straggling back.

Beside the coati, the dogs sometimes made prizes of rabbits and hares, which are very plentiful here, and great numbers of which we often shot for our dinners. There was another animal that I was not much disposed to find amusement from, and that was the rattlesnake. These are very abundant. The latter part of the time that I was on shore I did not meet with so many; but for the first two months we seldom went into "the bush" without one of our number starting some of them. The first that I ever saw I remember perfectly well. I had left my companions, and was beginning to clear away a fine clump of trees, when, just in the midst of the thicket, not more than eight yards from me, one of these fellows set up his hiss. Once or twice the noise stopped for a short time, which gave me a little uneasiness, and, retreating a few steps, I threw something into the bush, at which he would set his rattle going; and finding that he had not moved from his first place, I was easy again. In this way I continued at my work till I had cut a full load, never suffering him to be quiet for a moment. Having cut my load, I strapped it together and got everything ready for starting. I felt that I could now call the others without the imputation of being afraid, and went in search of them. In a few minutes we were all collected and began an attack upon the bush. The big Frenchman I found as little inclined to approach the snake as I had been. The dogs, too, seemed afraid of the rattle, and kept up a barking at a safe distance; but the Kanakas showed no fear, and getting long sticks went into the bush, and keeping a bright look-out stood within a few feet of him. One or two blows struck near him, and a few stones thrown started him, and we lost his track, and had the pleasant consciousness that he might be directly under our feet. By throwing stones and chips in different directions we made him spring his rattle again, and began another attack. This time we drove him into the clear ground, and saw him gliding off, with head and tail erect, when a stone, well aimed, knocked him over the bank, down a declivity of fifteen or twenty feet, and stretched him at his length. Having made sure of him by a few more stones we went down, and one of the Kanakas cut off his rattle. These rattles vary in number, it is said, according to the age of the snake; though the Indians think they indicate the number of creatures they have killed.

Hares and rabbits, as I said before, were abundant, and during the winter months the waters are covered with wild ducks and geese. Crows, too, were very numerous, and frequently alighted in great numbers upon our hides, picking at the pieces of dried meat and fat. Bears and wolves are numerous in the upper parts and in the interior, but there were none in our immediate neighborhood. The only other animals were horses. Over a dozen of these were owned by different people on the beach, and were allowed to run loose among the hills, with a long lasso attached to them, and pick up feed wherever they could find it. These horses were bought at from two to six dollars apiece, and were held very much as common property. We generally kept one fast to one of the houses every day, so that we could mount him and catch any of the others. Some of them were really fine animals, and gave us many good runs up to the Presidio and over the country.

CHAPTER XIX

Burning the Water

After we had been a few weeks on shore, and had begun to feel broken into the regularity of our life, its monotony was interrupted by the arrival of two vessels from the windward. As they drew near we soon discovered the high poop and top-gallant forecastle and other marks of the Italian ship *Rosa*, and the brig proved to be the *Catalina*, which we saw at Santa Barbara, just arrived from Valparaiso. They came to anchor, moored ship, and commenced discharging hides and tallow. The *Rosa* had purchased the house occupied by the *Lagoda*, and the *Catalina* took the other spare one between ours and the *Ayacucho*'s, so that now each one was occupied, and the beach for several days was all alive. The *Catalina* had several Kanakas on board, who were immediately besieged by the others, and carried up to the oven, where they had a long pow-wow and a smoke. Two Frenchmen, who belonged to the *Rosa*'s crew, came in every evening to see Nicholas; and from them we learned that the *Pilgrim* was at San Pedro, and was the only other vessel now on the coast. Several of the Italians slept on shore at their hide-house; and there, and at the tent in which the *Fazio*'s crew lived, we had some very good singing almost every evening. The Italians sang a variety of songs — barcarollas, provincial airs, etc. — in several of which I recognized parts of our favorite operas and sentimental songs.

The greater part of the crews of the vessels came ashore every evening, and we passed the time in going about from one house to another, and listening to all manner of languages. The Spanish was the common ground upon which we all met, for everyone knew more or less of that. We had now, out of forty or fifty representatives from almost every nation under the sun, two Englishmen, three Yankees, two Scotchmen, two Welshmen, one Irishman, three Frenchmen, one Dutchman, one Austrian, two or three Spaniards, half a dozen of Spanish-Americans and half-breeds, two native Indians from Chili and the Island of Chiloe, one negro, one mulatto, about twenty Italians from all parts of Italy, as many more Sandwich Islanders, one Otaheitan, and one Kanaka from the Marquesas Islands.

The night before the vessels were ready to sail, all the Europeans united and had an entertainment at the *Rosa*'s hide-house, and we had songs of every nation and tongue. A German gave us "Och! mein lieber Augustin!"; the three Frenchmen roared through the Marseillaise Hymn; the English and Scotchmen gave us "Rule Britannia" and "Wha'll be King but Charlie?"; the Italians and Spaniards screamed through some national affairs, for which I was none the wiser; and we three Yankees made an attempt at the "Star Spangled Banner." After these national tributes had been paid the Austrian gave us a very pretty little love-song, and the Frenchman sang a spirited thing called "Sentinelle! O prenez garde à vous!"

The next day the two vessels got under way for the windward, and left us in quiet possession of the beach. Our numbers were somewhat enlarged by the opening of the new houses, and the society of the beach a little changed. In charge of the *Catalina*'s house was an old Scotchman, who, like most of his countrymen, had a pretty good education, and like many of them, was rather pragmatical, and had a ludicrously solemn conceit. Everything was as neat as a pin in the house, and he was as regular in his hours as a chronometer, but as he kept very much by himself was not a great addition to our society. He had been a petty officer on board the British frigate *Dublin*, Captain Lord James Townshend, and had great ideas of his own importance. The man in charge of the *Rosa*'s house was an Austrian by birth, but spoke, read, and wrote four languages with ease and correctness. He was between forty and fifty years of age, and was a singular mixture of the man-of-war's-man and Puritan. He talked a great deal about propriety and steadiness, and gave good advice to the youngsters and Kanakas, but seldom went up to the town without coming down "three sheets in the wind." One holiday he and the Scotchman went up to the town and got so cozy, talking over old stories and giving one another good advice, that they came down, double-backed, on a horse, and both rolled off into the sand as soon as the horse stopped. This put an end to their pretensions, and they never heard the last of it from the rest of the men.

In about six weeks from the time when the *Pilgrim* sailed we had got all the hides which she left us cured and stowed away; and having cleared up the ground, and emptied the vats, and set everything in order, had nothing more to do until she should come down again, but to supply ourselves with wood. Instead of going twice a week for this purpose we determined to give one whole week to getting wood, and then we should have enough to last us half through the summer. Accordingly, we started off every morning and cut wood until the sun was over the point — which was our only mark of time, as there was not a watch on the beach — and then came back to dinner, and after dinner started off again with our hand-cart and ropes, and carted it down until sunset. This we kept up for a week until we had collected enough to last us for six or eight weeks, when we "knocked off" altogether, much to my joy; for though I liked straying in the woods and cutting very well, yet the backing the wood for so great a distance over an uneven country, was without exception, the hardest work I had ever done.

We were now through all our work, and had nothing more to do until the *Pilgrim* should come down again. We had nearly got through our provisions too, as well as our work; for our officer had been very wasteful of them, and the tea, flour, sugar, and molasses were all gone. Finding wheat, coffee and dry bread rather poor living, we clubbed together, and I went up to the town on horseback, with a great salt-bag behind the saddle, and a few reals in my pocket, and brought back the bag full of onions, pears, beans, watermelons, and other fruits. With these we lived like fighting-cocks for a week or two, and had, besides, what the sailors call "a blow-out on sleep"; not turning out in the morning until breakfast was ready. I employed several days in overhauling my chest and mending up all my old clothes, until I had got everything in order — patch upon patch, like a sand-barge's mainsail. That done, and there being no signs of the *Pilgrim*, I made a descent upon Schmidt, and borrowed and read all the books there were upon the beach. I found at the bottom of Schmidt's chest, "*Mandeville*, a romance by Godwin, in five volumes." I bore it off, and for two days I was up early and late, reading with all my might, and actually drinking in delight. It is no extravagance to say that it was like a rock in a desert land.

Wednesday, July 18th, brought us the brig *Pilgrim* from the windward. As she came in, we found that she was a good deal altered in her countenance. Then there was a new voice giving orders, and a new face on the quarter-deck — a short, dark-complexioned man, in a green jacket and a high leather cap. These changes, of course, set the whole beach on the *qui vive,* and we were all waiting for the boat to come ashore that we might have things explained. At length, after the sails were furled and the anchor carried out, the boat pulled ashore, and the news soon flew that the expected ship had arrived at Santa Barbara, and that Captain T— had taken command of her, and her captain, Faucon, had taken the *Pilgrim,* and was the green-jacketed man on the quarter-deck. The boat put directly off again, without giving us time to ask any more questions, and we were obliged to wait till night, when we took a little skiff that lay on the beach and paddled off. When I stepped aboard, the second mate called me aft, and gave me a large bundle, directed to me, and marked "Ship *Alert.*" Diving down into the forecastle I found the same old crew, and was really glad to see them again. Numerous inquiries passed as to the new ship, the latest news from Boston, etc., etc. The *Alert* was agreed on all hands to be a fine ship, and a large one: "Larger than the *Rosa*" — "Big enough to carry off all the hides in California." Captain T— took command of her, and she went directly up to Monterey; from thence she was to go to San Francisco, and probably would not be in San Diego under two or three months. Some of the *Pilgrim*'s crew spent an hour or two in her forecastle the evening before she sailed. They said her decks were as white as snow — holystoned every morning, like a man-of-war's; everything on board "ship-shape and Bristol fashion"; a fine crew, three mates, a sail-

154

maker and carpenter, and all complete. "They've got a *man* for mate of that ship, and not a *sheep* about decks!" — "A mate that knows his duty, and makes everybody do theirs, and won't be imposed upon either by captain or crew."

Having got all the news we could, we pulled ashore; and as soon as we reached the house, I, as might be supposed, proceeded directly to open my bundle, and found a reasonable supply of duck, flannel shirts, shoes, etc., and, what was still more valuable, a packet of eleven letters. These I sat up nearly all the night to read. Then came half a dozen newspapers, the last of which gave notice of Thanksgiving, and of the clearance of "ship *Alert*, Edward H. Faucon, master, for Callao and California, by Bryant, Sturgis & Co." No one has ever been on distant voyages, and after a long absence received a newspaper from home, who cannot understand the delight that they give one.

The *Pilgrim* discharged her hides, which set us at work again, and in a few days we were in the old routine of dry hides, wet hides, cleaning, beating, etc. Captain Faucon came quietly up to me as I was at work with my knife, cutting the meat from a dirty hide, asked me how I liked California, and repeated:

"Tityre, tu patulæ recubans sub tegmine fagi."

Saturday, July 11th. The *Pilgrim* set sail for the windward, and left us to go on in our old way.

155

Having laid in such a supply of wood, and the days being now long, and invariably pleasant, we had a good deal of time to ourselves. Reading, mending, sleeping, with occasional excursions into the bush, with the dogs, in search of coati, hares and rabbits, or to encounter a rattlesnake, and now and then a visit to the Presidio, filled up our spare time after hide-curing was over for the day.

Another amusement which we sometimes indulged in was "burning the water" for craw-fish. For this purpose we procured a pair of grains, with a long staff like a harpoon, and making torches with tarred rope twisted round a long pine stick, took the only boat on the beach, a small skiff, and with a torch-bearer in the bow, a steersman in the stern, and one man on each side with the grains, went off, on dark nights, to burn the water. This is fine sport. Keeping within a few rods of the shore, where the water is not more than three or four feet deep, with a clear sandy bottom, the torches light everything up so that one could almost have seen a pin among the grains of sand. The craw-fish are an easy prey, and we used soon to get a load of them. The *Pilgrim* brought us down a supply of fish-hooks, which we had never had before on the beach, and for several days we went down to the Point, and caught a quantity of cod and mackerel.

On one of these expeditions, we saw a battle between two Sandwich Islanders and a shark. "Johnny" had been playing about our boat for

156

some time, driving away the fish, and showing his teeth at our bait, when we missed him, and in a few moments heard a great shouting between two Kanakas who were fishing on the rock opposite to us, and saw them pulling away on a stout line, and "Johnny Shark" floundering at the other end. The line soon broke; but the Kanakas would not let him off so easily, and sprang directly into the water after him. Now came the tug of war. Before he could get into deep water one of them seized him by the tail, and ran up with him upon the beach, but Johnny twisted round, turning his head under his body, and showing his teeth in the vicinity of the Kanaka's hand, made him let go and spring out of the way. The shark now turned tail and made the best of his way, by flapping and floundering, toward deep water; but here again, before he was fairly off, the other Kanaka seized him by the tail, and made a spring toward the beach, his companion at the same time paying away upon him with stones and a large stick. As soon, however, as the shark could turn he was obliged to let go his hold; but the instant he made toward deep water they were both behind him, watching their chance to seize him. In this way the battle went on for some time, the shark, in a rage, splashing and twisting about, and the Kanakas in high excitement, yelling at the top of their voices; but the shark at last got off, carrying away a hook and line, and not a few severe bruises.

CHAPTER XX

New Ship – The *"Alert"*

Saturday, July 18th. This day sailed the Mexican hermaphrodite *Fazio* for San Blas and Mazatlan. The owner of her had had a good deal of difficulty with the government about the duties, etc., and her sailing had been delayed for several weeks; but everything having been arranged she got under way with a light breeze, and was floating out of the harbor when two horsemen came dashing down to the beach at full speed, and tried to find a boat to put after her; but there being none on the beach, they offered a handful of silver to any Kanaka who would swim off and take a letter on board. One of the Kanakas, a fine, active, well-made young fellow, instantly threw off everything but his duck trousers, and putting the letter into his hat, swam off after the vessel. Fortunately, the wind was very light, and the vessel was going slowly, so that although she was nearly a mile off when he started he gained on her rapidly. He went through the water leaving a wake like a small steamboat. They saw him coming from the deck, but did not heave-to, suspecting the nature of his errand; yet, the wind continuing light, he swam alongside and got on board, and delivered his

158

letter. The captain read the letter, told the Kanaka there was no answer, and giving him a glass of brandy, left him to jump overboard and find the best of his way to the shore. The Kanaka swam in for the nearest point of land, and in about an hour made his appearance at the hide-house. He did not seem at all fatigued, had made three or four dollars, got a glass of brandy, and was in fine spirits.

It was now nearly three months since the *Alert* arrived at Santa Barbara, and we began to expect her daily. About half-a-mile behind the hide-house was a high hill, and every afternoon, as soon as we had done our work, some one of us walked up to see if there were any sail in sight. Each day after the latter part of July we went up the hill and came back disappointed. I was anxious for her arrival: for I had been told by letter that the owners in Boston, at the request of my friends, had written to Captain T— to take me on board the *Alert*, in case she returned to the United States before the *Pilgrim*; and I, of course, wished to know whether the order had been received, and what was the destination of the ship. One year more or less might be of small consequence to others, but it was everything to me. It was now just a year since we sailed from Boston, and at the shortest, no vessel could expect to get away under eight or nine months, which would make our absence two years in all. This would be pretty long, but would not be fatal. It would not necessarily be decisive of my future life.

But one year more would settle the matter. I should be a sailor for life; and although I had made up my mind to it before I had my letters from home, and was, as I thought quite satisfied; yet as soon as an opportunity was held out to me of returning, and the prospect of another kind of life was opened to me, my anxiety to return, and, at least, to have the chance of deciding upon my course for myself was beyond measure. Beside that, I wished to be "equal to either fortune," and to qualify myself for an officer's berth; and a hide-house was no place to learn seamanship in. I had become experienced in hide-curing, and everything went on smoothly, and I had many opportunities of becoming acquainted with the people, and much leisure for reading and studying navigation; yet practical seamanship could only be got on board ship; therefore I determined to ask to be taken on board the ship when she arrived. By the first of August we finished curing all our hides, stored them away, cleaned out our vats, and got in readiness for the arrival of the ship, and had another leisure interval of three or four weeks, which I spent as usual in reading, writing, studying, making and mending my clothes, and getting my wardrobe in complete readiness, in case I should go on board the ship.

Tuesday, August 25th. This morning the officer in charge of our house went off beyond the point fishing in a small canoe with two Kanakas; and we were sitting quietly in our room at the hide-house when, just before noon, we heard a complete yell of "Sail ho!" breaking out from all parts of the beach at once. In an instant everyone was out of his house; and there was a fine, tall ship, with royals and skysails set, bending over before the strong afternoon breeze, and coming rapidly round the point. The Yankee ensign was flying from her mizzen-peak; and having the tide in her favor, she came up like a race horse. It was nearly six months since a new vessel had entered San Diego, and of course everyone was on the *qui vive*. She certainly made a fine appearance. Her light sails were taken in as she passed the low, sandy tongue of land, and clewing up her head-sails, she rounded handsomely to under her miz-zentopsail, and let go the anchor at about a ca-ble's-length from the shore. In a few minutes the topsail yards were manned, and all three of the topsails furled at once. From the fore top-gallant yard the men slid down the stay to furl the jib, and from the mizzen top-gallant yard by the stay into the main-top, and thence to the yard; and the men on the topsail-yards came down the lifts to the yard-arms of the courses. The sails were furled with great care, the bunts triced up by jiggers, and the jibs stowed in cloth. The royal-yards were then struck, tackles got upon the yard-arms and the stay, the long-boat hoisted out, a large anchor carried astern, and the ship moored. Then the captain's gig was lowered away from the quarter, and a boat's crew of fine lads, be-tween the ages of fourteen and eighteen, pulled the captain ashore. We immediately attacked the boat's crew, and got very thick with them in a few minutes. We had much to ask about Boston, their passage out, etc., and they were very curious to know about the life we were leading upon the beach. One of them offered to exchange with me, which was just what I wanted; and we had only to get the permission of the captain.

After dinner the crew began discharging their hides, and as we had nothing to do at the hide-houses, we were ordered aboard to help them. She looked as well on board as she did from without. Her decks were wide and roomy, flush fore and aft, and as white as snow. There was no rust, no dirt, no rigging hanging slack, no fag-ends of ropes and "Irish pendants" aloft, and the yards were squared "to a T" by lifts and braces. The mate was a fine, hearty, noisy fellow, with a voice like a lion, and always wide awake. There was also a second and third mate, a carpenter, sailmaker, steward, mate, cook, etc., and twelve, including boys, before the mast. She had on board seven thousand hides, which she had col-lected at the windward, and also horns and tallow. All these we began discharging from both gang-ways at once into the two boats, the second mate having charge of the launch, and the third mate of the pinnace. For several days we were em-ployed in this way until all the hides were taken out, when the crew began taking in ballast, and we returned to our old work, hide-curing.

Saturday, August 29th. Arrived brig *Catalina* from the windward.

Sunday, August 30th. This was the first Sunday that the crew had been in San Diego, and of course they were all for going up to see the town. The Indians came down early with horses to let for the day, and all the crew who could obtain liberty went off to the Presidio and Mission, and did not return until night. I had seen enough of San Diego, and went on board, and spent the day with some of the crew, whom I found quietly at work in the forecastle, mending and washing their clothes, and reading and writing. The forecastle in which they lived was large, tolerably well lighted by bulls' eyes, and being kept perfectly clean had quite a comfortable appearance; at least it was far better than the little, black, dirty hole in which I had lived so many months on board the *Pilgrim.* In the after part of the ship was a handsome cabin, a dining-room, and a trade-room, fitted out with shelves, and furnished with all sorts of goods. Between these and the forecastle was the "between decks," as high as the gun-deck of a frigate, being six feet and a half under the beams. These between decks were kept in the most perfect order, the carpenter's bench and tools being in one part, the sailmaker's in another, the boatswain's locker, with the spare rigging in a third. A part of the crew slept here in hammocks swung fore and aft from the beams, and triced up every morning.

This ship lay about a week longer in port, when, having discharged her cargo and taken in ballast, she prepared to get under way. I now made my application to the captain to go on board. He said he had no objections, if I could find one of my own age to exchange with me for the time. This I easily accomplished, for they were glad to change the scene by a few months on shore, and, moreover, escape the winter and the southeasters; and I went on board the next day, and found myself once more afloat.

CHAPTER XXI

Tom Harris

Tuesday, September 8th. This was my first day's duty on board the ship, and though a sailor's life is a sailor's life wherever it may be, yet I found everything very different here from the customs of the brig *Pilgrim*. After all hands were called at daybreak the head-pump was then rigged, and the decks washed down by the second and third mates, the chief mate walking the quarter-deck and keeping a general supervision, but not deigning to touch a bucket or a brush. There were five boats belonging to the ship — launch, pinnace, jolly-boat, larboard quarter-boat, and gig — each of which had a coxswain, who had charge of it, and was answerable for the order and cleanness of it. The rest of the cleaning was divided among the crew. When the decks were dry the lord paramount made his appearance on the quarter-deck and took a few turns, when eight bells were struck, and all hands went to breakfast. Half an hour was allowed for breakfast, when all hands were called again, the kids, pots, bread-bags, etc., stowed away; and, this morning, preparations were made for getting under way.

We paid out on the chain by which we swung,

hove in on the other, catted the anchor, and hove short on the first. This work was done in shorter time than was usual on board the brig; for though everything was more than twice as large and heavy yet there was plenty of room to move about in, more discipline and system, more men, and more good-will. Everyone seemed ambitious to do his best: officers and men knew their duty, and all went well. As soon as she was hove short, the mate, on the forecastle, gave the order to loose the sails, and in an instant everyone sprung into the rigging, up the shrouds and out on the yards, scrambling by one another, cast off the yard-arm gaskets and bunt gaskets, and one man remained on each yard, holding the bunt jigger with a turn round the tye, all ready to let go, while the rest laid down to man the sheets and halyards. The mate then hailed the yards, "All ready forward?" "All ready the cross-jack yards?" etc., etc.; and "Aye, aye, sir!" being returned from each, the word was given to let go; and in the twinkling of an eye the ship, which had shown nothing but her bare yards was covered with her loose canvas from the royal-mast-heads to the decks. Everyone then laid down, except one man in each top, to overhaul the rigging, and the topsails were hoisted and sheeted home, all three yards going to the mast-head at once, the larboard watch hoisting the fore, the starboard watch the main, and five light hands (of whom I was one) picked from the two watches, the mizzen. The yards were then trimmed, the anchor weighed, the cat-block hooked on, the fall stretched out, manned by "all hands and the cook," and the anchor brought to the head with "cheerily men!" in full chorus. The ship being now under way, the light sails were set, one after another, and she was under full sail before she had passed the sandy point. The fore royal, which fell to my lot (being in the mate's watch), was more than twice as large as that of the *Pilgrim*, and though I could handle the brig's easily, I found my hands full with this.

As soon as we were beyond the point, and all sail out, the order was given, "Go below the watch!" and the crew said that ever since they had been on the coast they had had "watch and watch" while going from port to port, and, in fact, everything showed that, though strict discipline was kept, and the utmost required of every man in the way of his duty, yet on the whole there was very good usage on board.

It being the turn of our watch to go below, the men went to work, mending their clothes and doing other little things for themselves.

While on deck the regular work of the ship went on. The sailmaker and carpenter worked between decks, and the crew had their work to do upon the rigging, drawing yarns, making spun-yarn, etc., as usual in merchantmen. The night watches were much more pleasant than on board the *Pilgrim*. The sailmaker was the head man of the watch, and was generally considered the most experienced seaman on board. He was a thorough-bred old man-of-war's-man, had been to sea twenty-two years in all kinds of vessels — men-of-war, privateers, slavers, and merchant-men — everything except whalers, which a thorough sailor despises and will always steer clear of if he can. He had, of course, been in all parts of the world, and was remarkable for drawing a long-bow. His yarns frequently stretched through a watch, and kept all hands awake. They were always amusing from their improbability, and, indeed, he never expected to be believed, but spun them merely for amusement; and as he had some humor and a good supply of man-of-war slang and sailor's salt phrases he always made fun.

Next to him in age and experience, and, of course, in standing in the watch, was an Englishman named Harris. Then came two or three Americans, who had been the common run of European and South American voyages, and one who had been in a "spouter," and, of course, had all the whaling stories to himself. Last of all was a broad-backed, thick-headed boy from Cape Cod, who had been in mackerel schooners, and was making his first voyage in a square-rigged vessel. The other watch was composed of about the same number. A tall, fine-looking Frenchman, with coal-black whiskers and curly hair, a first-rate seaman, and named John, was the head man of the watch. Then came two Americans, a German, an English lad named Ben, and two Boston boys just from the public schools. The carpenter sometimes mustered in the starboard watch, and was an old sea-dog, a Swede by birth, and accounted the best helmsman in the ship. This was our ship's company, beside cook and steward, who were blacks, three mates, and the captain.

The second day out the wind drew ahead, and we had to beat up the coast, so that, in tacking ship, I could see the regulations of the vessel. Instead of going wherever was most convenient, and running from place to place, wherever work was to be done, each man had his station. A regular tacking and wearing bill was made out. The chief mate commanded on the forecastle, and had charge of the head sails and the forward part of the ship. Two of the best men in the ship — the sailmaker from our watch, and John, the Frenchman, from the other — worked the forecastle. The third mate commanded in the waist, and, with the carpenter and one man, worked the main tack and bowline; the cook, *ex officio*, the fore sheet; and the steward the main. The second mate had charge of the after yards, and let go the lee fore and main braces. I was stationed at the weather cross-jack braces, three other light hands at the lee, one boy at the spanker-sheet and guy, a man and a boy at the main topsail, top-gallant, and royal braces, and all the rest of the crew — men and boys — tallied on to the main brace.

As soon as all hands are at their stations, the captain, who stands on the weather side of the quarter-deck, makes a sign to the man at the wheel to put it down, and calls out, "Helm's a lee'!" "Helm's a lee'!" answers the mate on the forecastle, and the head sheets are let go. "Raise tacks and sheets!" says the captain. "Tacks and sheets" is passed forward, and the fore tack and main sheet are let go. The next thing is to haul taut for a swing. The weather cross-jack braces and the lee main braces are each belayed together upon two pins, and ready to be let go, and the opposite braces hauled taut. "Main topsail haul!" shouts the captain. The braces are let go; and if he has taken his time well the yards swing round like a top; but if he is too late or too soon it is like drawing teeth. The after yards are then braced up and belayed, the main sheet hauled aft, the spanker eased over to leeward, and the men from the braces stand by the head yards. "Let go and haul!" says the captain. The second mate lets go the weather fore braces, and the men haul in to leeward. The mate, on the forecastle, looks out for the head yards. "Well, the fore topsail yard!" "Top-gallant yard's well!" "Royal yard too much! Haul in to windward! So! well *that!*" "Well *all!*" Then the starboard watch board the main tack, and the larboard watch lay forward and board the fore tack and haul down the jib sheet, clapping a tackle upon it if it blows very fresh. The after yards are then trimmed, the captain generally looking out for them himself. "Well the cross-jack yard!" "Small pull the main top-gallant yard!" "Well *that!*" "Well the mizzen topsail yard!" "Cross-jack yards all *well!*" "Well all aft!" "Haul taut to windward!" Everything being now trimmed and in order, each man coils up the rigging at his own station, and the order is given, "Go below the watch!"

Friday, September 11th. This morning at four o'clock went below, San Pedro point being about two leagues ahead, and the ship going on under studding-sails. In about an hour we were waked up by the hauling of the chain about decks, and in a few minutes "All hands ahoy!" was called; and we were all at work, hauling in and making up the studding-sails, overhauling the chain forward, and getting the anchors ready. "The *Pilgrim* is there at anchor," said some one, as we were running about decks; and taking a moment's look over the rail I saw my old friend, deeply laden, lying at anchor inside of the kelp.

From the moment of letting go the anchor, when the captain ceases his care of things, the chief mate is the great man. With a voice like a young lion he was hallooing and bawling in all directions, making everything fly, and at the same time doing everything well. He was quite a contrast to the worthy, quiet, unobtrusive mate of the *Pilgrim*: not so estimable a man, perhaps, but a far better mate of a vessel; and the entire change in Captain T—'s conduct since he took command of the ship was owing, no doubt, in a great measure, to this fact. Mr. Brown (the mate of the *Alert*) wanted no help from anybody; took everything into his own hands; and was more likely to encroach upon the authority of the master than to need any spurring. Captain T— gave his directions to the mate in private, and, except in coming to anchor, getting under way, tacking, reefing topsails, and other "all-hands'-work," seldom appeared in person. This is the proper state of things; and while this lasts, and there is a good understanding aft, everything will go on well.

Having furled all the sails, the royal yards were next to be sent down. The English lad and myself sent down the main; two more light hands the fore; and one boy the mizzen. This order we always kept while on the coast, sending them up and down every time we came in and went out of port. No sooner was she all snug than tackles were got up on the yards and stays and the long-boat and pinnace hove out. The swinging booms were then guyed out, and the boats made fast by geswarps, and everything in harbor style. After breakfast the hatches were taken off, and all got ready to receive hides from the *Pilgrim*. All day boats were passing and repassing until we had taken her hides from and left her in ballast trim. These hides made but little show in our hold, though they had loaded the *Pilgrim* down to the water's edge. This changing of the hides settled the question of the destination of the two vessels, which had been one of some speculation to us. We were to remain in the leeward ports, while the *Pilgrim* was to sail the next morning for San Francisco.

About seven o'clock the mate came down into the steerage in fine trim for fun, roused the boys out of the berth, turned up the carpenter with his fiddle, sent the steward with lights to put in the between-decks, and set all hands to dancing. The between-decks were high enough to allow of jumping; and being clear and white from holy-stoning, made a fine dancing-hall. Some of the *Pilgrim*'s crew were in the forecastle, and we all turned to and had a regular sailor's shuffle till eight bells. The Cape Cod boy could dance the true fisherman's jig barefooted, knocking with his heels, and slapping the decks with his bare feet, in time with the music. This was a favorite amusement of the mate's, who always stood at the steerage door looking on.

The next morning, according to the orders of the agent, the *Pilgrim* set sail for the windward, to be gone three or four months. She got under way with very little fuss, and came so near us as to throw a letter on board, Captain Faucon standing at the tiller himself, and steering her as he would a mackerel smack. When Captain T— was in command of the *Pilgrim* there was as much preparation and ceremony as there would be in getting a seventy-four under way. Captain Faucon was a sailor, every inch of him; he knew what a ship was, and was as much at home in one as a cobbler in his stall.

After the *Pilgrim* left us we lay three weeks at San Pedro, from the 11th of September until the 2d of October, engaged in the usual port duties of landing cargo, taking off hides, etc., etc. These duties were much easier, and went on much more agreeably than on board the *Pilgrim*. "The more the merrier" is the sailor's maxim; and a boat's crew of a dozen could take off all the hides brought down in a day without much trouble by a division of labor; and on shore, as well as on board, a good will, and no discontent or grumbling, make everything go well. The officer, too, who usually went with us, the third mate, was a fine young fellow, and made no unnecessary trouble; so that we generally had quite a sociable time, and were glad to be relieved from the restraint of the ship. A light whale-boat, handsomely painted, and fitted out with stern seats, yoke, tiller-ropes, etc., hung on the starboard quarter, and was used as the gig. The youngest lad in the ship, a Boston boy about thirteen years old, was coxswain of this boat, and had the entire charge of her, to keep her clean, and have her in readiness to go and come at any hour. Four light hands, of about the same size and age, of whom I was one, formed the crew. Each had his oar and seat numbered, and we were obliged to be in our places, have our oars scraped white, our tholepins in, and the fenders over the side. Our duty was to carry the captain and agent about and passengers off and on, which last was no trifling duty, as the people on shore have no boats, and every purchaser was to be taken off and on in our boat. Some days, when people were coming and going fast, we were in the boat, pulling off and on, all day long, making, as we lay nearly three miles from shore, from forty to fifty miles rowing in a day. Still we thought it the best berth in the ship, for when the gig was employed we had nothing to do with the cargo. The rest of the crew never left the ship except for bringing heavy goods and taking off hides; and though we were always in the water, the surf hardly leaving us a dry thread from morning to night, yet we were young, and the climate was good, and we thought it much better than the quiet, hum-drum drag and pull on board ship.

The brig *Catalina* came in from San Diego, and being bound up to windward, we both got under way at the same time, for a trial of speed up to Santa Barbara, a distance of about eighty miles. We hove up and got under sail about eleven o'clock at night, with a light land-breeze, which died away toward morning, leaving us becalmed only a few miles from our anchoring-place. The *Catalina* being less than half our size, put out sweeps and got a boat ahead, and pulled out to sea during the night, so that she had the sea-breeze earlier and stronger than we did, and we had the mortification of seeing her standing up the coast with a fine breeze, the sea all ruffled about her, while we were becalmed inshore. When the sea-breeze died away she was nearly out of sight; and, toward the latter part of the afternoon, the regular northwest wind set in fresh; we braced sharp upon it, took a pull at every sheet, tack, and halyard, and stood after her in fine style, our ship being very good upon a taut bowline. We had nearly five hours of fine sailing, beating up to windward, by long stretches in and off shore, and evidently gaining upon the *Catalina* at every tack. Fortunately, the wind died away when we were on our inward tack, and she on her outward, so we were in-shore, and caught the land breeze first, which came off upon our quarter, about the middle of the first watch. All hands were turned up, and we set all sail, to the skysails and the royal studding-sails; and with these, we glided quietly through the water, leaving the *Catalina* gradually astern, and by daylight were off St. Buenaventura, and our antagonist nearly out of sight. The sea-breeze, however, favored her again, while we were becalmed under the headland, and laboring slowly along, she was abreast of us by noon. Thus we continued, ahead, astern, and abreast of one another alternately; now far out at sea, and again, close in under the shore. On the third morning we came into the great bay of Santa Barbara, two hours behind the brig, and thus lost the bet; though, if the race had been to the point, we should have beaten her by five or six hours. This, however, settled the relative sailing of the vessels, for it was admitted that although she could gain upon us in very light winds, yet whenever there was breeze enough to set us agoing, we walked away from her like hauling in a line; and in beating to windward, which is the best trial of a vessel, we had much the advantage of her.

Sunday, October 4th. This was the day of our arrival; and somehow or other, our captain always managed not only to sail, but to come into port, on a Sunday. The main reason for sailing on the Sabbath is not, as many people suppose, because Sunday is thought a lucky day, but because it is a leisure day.* During the six days the crew are employed upon the cargo and other ship's works, and, Sunday being their only day of rest, whatever additional work can be thrown into it is so much gain to the owners. Thus it was with us, nearly all the time we were on the coast, and many of our Sundays were lost entirely to us. The Catholics on shore have no trading, and make no journeys, on Sunday; but the American has no national religion, and likes to show his independence of priestcraft by doing as he chooses on the Lord's day.

Santa Barbara looked very much as it did when I left it five months before: the long sand beach, with the heavy rollers breaking upon it in a continuous roar, and the little town, imbedded on the plain, girt by its amphitheater of mountains. We had a few visitors, and collected about a hundred hides; and every night, at sundown, the gig was sent ashore to wait for the captain, who spent his evenings in the town. We always took our monkey-jackets with us, and flint and steel, and made a fire on the beach with the driftwood and the bushes we pulled from the neighboring thickets, and lay down by it on the sand. Some-

---

* English seamen like sailing on Sunday because they have the prayers of the Church "for all who travel by land or water."

times earlier and sometimes later the captain came down; when, after a good drenching in the surf, we went aboard, changed our clothes, and turned in for the night — yet not for all the night, for there was the anchor watch to stand.

This leads me to speak of my watchmate for nine months — and, taking him all in all, the most remarkable man I have ever seen — Tom Harris. An hour every night while lying in port, Harris and myself had the deck to ourselves, and walking fore and aft, night after night, for months, I learned his whole character and history, and more about foreign nations, the habits of different people, and especially the secret of sailors' lives and hardships, and also of practical seamanship, than I could ever have learned. But the most remarkable thing about him was the power of his mind. His memory was perfect; seeming to form a regular chain, reaching from his earliest childhood up to the time I knew him, without one link wanting. His power of calculation, too, was remarkable. He carried in his head not only a log-book of the whole voyage, in which everything was complete and accurate, and from which no one ever thought of appealing, but also an accurate registry of all the cargo; knowing precisely where each thing was, and how many hides we took in at every port. One night he made a rough calculation of the number of hides that could be stowed in the lower hold, between the fore and main mast, and the average area and thickness of a hide; he came surprisingly near the number, as it afterwards turned out. The mate frequently came to him to know the capacity of different parts of the vessel, and he could tell the sailmaker very nearly the amount of canvas he would want for each sail in the ship; for he knew the hoist of every mast, and spread of every sail, on the head and foot, in feet and inches. Calculation of all kinds was his delight. I doubt if he ever forgot anything that he read. The only thing in the way of poetry that he ever read was Falconer's "Ship-wreck," which he was delighted with, and whole pages of which he could repeat. He knew the name of every sailor that had ever been his ship-mate, and also of every vessel, captain, and offi-cer, and the principal dates of each voyage. His reasoning powers were remarkable. I have had harder work maintaining an argument with him in a watch, even when I knew myself to be right, and he was only doubting, than I ever had before — not from his obstinacy, but from his acute-ness. With an iron memory, he seemed to have your whole past conversation at command, and if you said a thing now which ill agreed with something said months before, he was sure to have you on the hip. In fact, I always felt, when with him, that I was with no common man. I had a positive respect for his powers of mind, and felt often that if half the pains had been spent upon his education which are thrown away yearly in our colleges, he would have been a man of great weight in society. Like most self-taught men, he over-estimated the value of an education; and this

I often told him, though I profited by it myself; for he always treated me with respect, and often unnecessarily gave way to me from an over-estimate of my knowledge.

I recollect his posing me once on the subject of the Corn Laws. He asked me my opinion about them, which I gave him; and my reasons, my small stock of which I set forth to the best advantage. When I had got through he took the liberty of differing from me, and, to my surprise, brought arguments and facts connected with the subject which were new to me, and to which I was entirely unable to reply. He knew every lunar star in both hemispheres, and was a perfect master of his quadrant and sextant. Such was the man who, at forty, was still a dog before the mast, at twelve dollars a month. The reason of this was to be found in his whole past life, as I had it, at different times, from himself.

He was a native of Ilfracombe, in North Devon. His father was skipper of a small coaster from Bristol, and dying, left him, when quite young, to the care of his mother, by whose exertions he received a common school education, passing his winters at school and his summers in the coasting trade, until his seventeenth year, when he left home to go upon foreign voyages. Of his mother he often spoke with the greatest respect, and said that she was a strong-minded woman, and had the best system of education he had ever known — a system which had made respectable men of his three brothers, and failed only in him from his own indomitable obstinacy. It was no fault of hers that he was what I saw him; and so great was his sense of gratitude for her efforts, though unsuccessful, that he determined at the close of the voyage to embark for home with all the wages he could get, to spend with and for his mother, if perchance he should find her alive.

After leaving home he had spent nearly twenty years sailing upon all sorts of voyages, generally out of the ports of New York and Boston. Twenty years of vice! Every sin that a sailor knows he had gone to the bottom of. Several times, from his known capacity, he had been promoted to the office of chief mate, and as often his conduct when in port, especially his drunkenness, which neither fear nor ambition could induce him to abandon, put him back into the forecastle. One night, when giving me an account of his life, and lamenting the years of manhood he had thrown away, he said that there, in the forecastle, at the foot of the steps — a chest of old clothes — was the result of twenty-two years' hard labor and exposure — worked like a horse, and treated like a dog. As he grew older he began to feel the necessity of some provision for his later years, and came gradually to the conviction that rum had been his worst enemy. One night, in Havana, a young shipmate of his was brought aboard drunk, with a dangerous gash in his head, and his money and new clothes stripped from him. Harris had seen and been in hundreds of such scenes as these, but in his then state of mind it fixed his

181

determination, and he resolved never to drink another drop of strong drink of any kind. He signed no pledge and made no vow, but relied on his own strength of purpose. The first thing with him was a reason, and then a resolution, and the thing was done. The date of his resolution he knew, of course, to the very hour. It was three years before I knew him, and during all that time nothing stronger than cider or coffee had passed his lips. The sailors never thought of enticing Tom to take a glass any more than they would of talking to the ship's compass.

He understood the management of a ship upon scientific principles, and could give the reason for hauling every rope; and a long experience, added to careful observation at the time, and a perfect memory, gave him a knowledge of the expedients and resorts in times of hazard which was remarkable, and for which I became much indebted to him, as he took the greatest pleasure in opening his stores of information to me in return for what I was enabled to do for him.

In fact, taking together all that I learned from him of seamanship, of the history of sailors' lives, of practical wisdom, and of human nature under new circumstances, I would not part with the hours I spent in the watch with that man for any given hours of my life past in study and social intercourse.

CHAPTER XXII

The Story of George Marsh

Sunday, October 11th. Set sail this morning for the leeward, passed within sight of San Pedro, and to our great joy, did not come to anchor, but kept directly on to San Diego, where we arrived and moored ship on.

Thursday, October 15th. Found here the Italian ship *La Rosa*, from the windward, which reported the brig *Pilgrim* at San Francisco, all well. We discharged our hides, horns, and tallow, and were ready to sail again on the following Sunday. I went ashore to my old quarters, and found the gang at the hide-house going on in the even tenor of their way, and spent an hour or two after dark at the oven, taking a whiff with my old Kanaka friends, who really seemed glad to see me again, and saluted me as the *Aikane* of the Kanakas.

Sunday was again, as usual, our sailing day, and we got under way with a stiff breeze, which reminded us that it was the latter part of the autumn, and time to expect southeasters once more. We beat up against a strong head wind, under reefed topsails, as far as San Juan, where we came to anchor nearly three miles from the shore, with slip-ropes on our cables, in the old southeaster style of last winter.

Tuesday, October 20th. Having got everything ready, we set the agent ashore, who went up to the Mission to hasten down the hides for the next morning. This night we had the strictest orders to look out for southeasters; and the long, low clouds seemed rather threatening. But the night passed over without any trouble, and early the next morning we hove out the long-boat and pinnace, lowered away the quarter-boats, and went ashore to bring off our hides. The captain sent me, who was the only one of the crew that had ever been there before, to the top, to count the hides and pitch them down. There I stood again, as six months before, throwing off the hides, and watching them pitching and scaling to the bottom, while the men, dwarfed by the distance, were walking to and fro on the beach, carrying the hides, as they picked them up, to the distant boats upon the tops of their heads. Two or three boat-loads were sent off, until at last all were thrown down, and the boats nearly loaded again, when we were delayed by a dozen or twenty hides which had lodged in the recesses of the hill, and which we could not reach by any missiles, as the general line of the side was exactly perpendicular, and these places were caved in, and could not be seen or reached from the top. The captain sent on board for a pair of topgallant studding-sail halyards, and requested some one of the crew to go to the top and come down by the halyards. I offered my services, and went up, with one man to tend the rope, and prepared for the descent.

We found a stake fastened strongly into the ground, and apparently capable of holding my weight, to which we made one end of the halyards well fast, and taking the coil, threw it over the brink. Having nothing on but shirt, trousers, and hat, the common sea-rig of warm weather, I had no stripping to do, and began my descent by taking hold of the rope in each hand, and slipping down, sometimes with hands and feet round the rope, and sometimes breasting off with one hand and foot against the precipice and holding on the rope with the other. In this way I descended until I came to a place shelved in, and in which the hides were lodged. Keeping hold of the rope with one hand, I scrambled in, and by the other hand and feet succeeded in dislodging all the hides, and continued on my way. Just below this place the precipice projected again; and going over the projection I could see nothing below me but the sea, and the rocks upon which it broke, and a few gulls flying in mid air. I got down in safety pretty well covered with dirt; and for my pains was told, "What a fool you were to risk your life for a half dozen hides!"

While we were carrying the hides to the boat I perceived, what I had been too busy to observe before, that heavy black clouds were rolling up from seaward, a strong swell heaving in, and every sign of a southeaster. The captain hurried everything. The hides were pitched into the boats; and with some difficulty we got the boats through the surf and began pulling aboard. Our gig's crew towed the pinnace astern of the gig, and the launch was towed by six men in the jolly-boat. The ship was lying three miles off, pitching at her anchor, and the further we pulled the heavier grew the swell. We at length got alongside, our boats half full of water; and now came the greatest difficulty of all, — unloading the boats in a heavy sea. With great difficulty we got all the hides aboard and stowed under hatches, the yard and stay tackles hooked on, and the launch and pinnace hoisted, chocked and griped. The quarter-boats were then hoisted up, and we began heaving in on the chain. Getting the anchor was no easy work in such a sea, but as we were not coming back to this port, the captain determined not to slip. The ship's head pitched into the sea, and the water rushed through the hawse-holes, and the chain surged so as almost to unship the barrel of the windlass. "Hove short, sir!" said the mate. "Aye, aye! Weather-bit your chain and loose the topsails! Make sail on her, men — with a will!" A few moments served to loose the top-sails, which were furled with the reefs, to sheet them home and hoist them up. "Bear a hand!" was the order of the day; and everyone saw the necessity of it, for the gale was already upon us. The ship broke out her own anchor, which we catted and fished, after a fashion, and stood off from the lee shore against a heavy head sea, under reefed topsails, fore topmast staysail and spanker. The fore course was given to her, which helped her a little;

but as she hardly held her own against the sea, which was setting her to leeward — "Board the main tack!" shouted the captain; when the tack was carried forward and taken to the windlass, and all hands called to the handspikes. The great sail bellied out horizontally as though it would lift up the mainstay; the blocks rattled and flew about; but the force of machinery was too much for her. "Heave ho! Heave and pawl! Yo, heave, hearty, ho!" and, in time with the song, by the force of twenty strong arms, the windlass came slowly round, pawl after pawl, and the weather clew of the sail was brought down to the water-ways. The starboard watch hauled aft the sheet, and the ship tore through the water like a mad horse, quivering and shaking at every joint, and dashing from its head the foam, which flew off at every blow, yards and yards to leeward. A half hour of such sailing served our turn, when the clews of the sail were hauled up, the sail furled, and the ship, eased of her press, went more quietly on her way. Soon after the foresail was reefed, and we mizzen-top men were sent up to take another reef in the mizzen-top-sail.

Having cleared the point and got well out to sea, we squared away the yards, made more sail, and stood on, nearly before the wind, for San Pedro. It blew strong, with some rain, nearly all night, but fell calm toward morning, and the gale having gone over, we came to —

*Thursday, Octo*ber 22d, at San Pedro, in the old southeaster berth, a league from shore. Here we lay ten days, with the usual boating, hide-carrying, rolling of cargo up the steep hill, walking bare-footed over stones, and getting drenched in salt water.

The third day after our arrival the *Rosa* came in from San Juan, where she went the day after the southeaster.

While lying here we shipped one new hand, an Englishman of about two or three and twenty, who was quite an acquisition as he proved to be a good sailor, could sing tolerably, and what was of more importance to me, had a good education, and a somewhat remarkable history. He called himself George P. Marsh; professed to have been at sea from a small boy, and to have served his time in the smuggling trade between Germany and the coasts of France and England. Thus he accounted for his knowledge of the French language, which he spoke and read as well as he did English; but his cutter education would not account for his English, which was far too good to have been learned in a smuggler; for he wrote an uncommonly handsome hand, spoke with great correctness, and frequently, when in private talk with me, quoted from books, and showed a knowledge of the customs of society which surprised me. Still, he would give no other account of himself than that he was educated in a smuggler. A man whom we afterwards fell in with, who had been a shipmate of George's a few years before, said that he heard at the boarding-house from which they shipped, that George had been at a college, where he learned French and mathematics. After he had been a little while on board we learned from him his remarkable history for the last two years. He sailed from New York in the year 1833, if I mistake not, before the mast, in the brig *Lascar* for Canton. She was sold in the East Indies, and he shipped at Manila, in a small schooner bound on a trading voyage among the Ladrone and Pelew Islands. On one of the latter islands their schooner was wrecked on a reef and they were attacked by the natives, and, after a desperate resistance, in which all their number, except the captain, George, and a boy were killed or drowned, they surrendered, and were carried bound, in a canoe, to a neighboring island. In about a month after this an opportunity occurred by which one of their number might get away. They yielded to the captain upon his promising to send them aid if he escaped. He was successful in his attempt; got on board an American vessel, went back to Manila, and thence to America, without making any effort at their rescue. The boy that was with George died; and he, being alone, and there being no chance for his escape, the natives soon treated him with kindness, and even with attention. They painted him, tattooed his body, and, in fact, made quite a pet of him. In this way he lived for thirteen months, in a fine climate, with plenty to eat, half-naked, and nothing to do. One day he was out fishing in a small canoe with another man when he saw a large sail to windward, about a league and a half off, passing abreast of the island and standing westward. With some difficulty he persuaded the islander to go off with him to the ship, promising to return with a good supply of rum and tobacco. They paddled off in the track of the ship, and lay-to until she came down to them. George stepped on board the ship nearly naked, painted from head to foot, and in no way distinguishable from his companion until he began to speak. Upon this the people on board were not a little astonished, and having learned his story, the captain had him washed and clothed, and sending away the poor astonished native with a knife or two and some tobacco and calico, took George with him on the voyage. This was the ship *Cabot* of New York, Captain Low. She was bound to Manila from across the Pacific, and George did seaman's duty in her until her arrival in Manila, when he left her, and shipped in a brig bound to the Sandwich Islands. From Oahu he came, in the British brig *Clementine*, to Monterey, as second officer, where, having some difficulty with the captain, he left her, and coming down the coast joined us at San Pedro.

George had an interesting journal of his adventures in the Pelew Islands, which he had written out at length, in a handsome hand, and in correct English.

CHAPTER XXIII

A Gale

Sunday, November 1st. Sailed this day for Santa Barbara, where we arrived on the 5th. Coming round St. Buenaventura, and nearing the anchorage, we saw two vessels in port, a large full-rigged, and a small hermaphrodite brig. The former, the crew said, must be the *Pilgrim*; but a few minutes put it beyond a doubt, and we were lying by the side of the *Ayacucho*, which had sailed from San Diego about nine months before, while we were lying there in the *Pilgrim*.

The other vessel which we found in port was the hermaphrodite brig *Avon*, from the Sandwich Islands. She was fitted up in handsome style, and appeared rather like a pleasure yacht than a trader; yet, in connection with the *Loriotte*, *Clementine*, *Bolivar*, *Convoy*, and other small vessels, belonging to sundry Americans at Oahu, she carried on a great trade — legal and illegal — in otter skins, silks, teas, specie, etc.

The second day after our arrival a full-rigged brig came round the point from the northward, sailed leisurely through the bay, and stood off again for the southeast, in the direction of the large island of Catalina. The next day the *Avon* got under way, and stood in the same direction, bound for San Pedro. The brig was never again seen on the coast, and the *Avon* arrived at San Pedro in about a week, with a full cargo of Canton and American goods.

This was one of the means of escaping the heavy duties the Mexicans lay upon all imports. A vessel comes on the coast, enters a moderate cargo at Monterey, which is the only custom-house, and commences trading. In a month or more, having sold a large part of her cargo, she stretches over to Catalina, or other of the large uninhabited islands which lie off the coast, in a trip from port to port, and supplies herself with choice goods from a vessel from Oahu, which has been lying off and on the islands, waiting for her. Two days after the sailing of the *Avon*, the *Loriotte* came in from the leeward, and had without doubt also had a snatch at the brig's cargo.

Tuesday, November 10th. Going ashore, as usual, in the gig, just before sundown, to bring off the captain, we found, upon taking in the captain and pulling off again, that our ship, which lay the farthest out, had run up her ensign. This meant "Sail ho!" of course, but as we were within the point we could see nothing. "Give way, boys! Give way! Lay out on your oars, and long stroke!" said the captain; stretching to the whole length of our arms, bending back again, so that our backs touched the thwarts, we sent her through the water like a rocket. A few minutes of such pulling opened the islands, one after another, in range of the point, and gave us a view of the Canal, where was a ship, under top-gallant sails, standing in, with a light breeze, for the anchorage. Putting the boat's head in the direction of the ship, the captain told us to lay out again; and we needed no spurring for the prospect of boarding a new ship, perhaps from home. Hearing the news was excitement enough for us, and we gave way with a will. In the meantime it fell flat calm, and being within a couple of miles of the ship, we expected to board her in a few moments, when a sudden breeze sprung up, dead ahead for the ship, and she braced up and stood off toward the islands, sharp on the larboard tack, making good way through the water. This, of course, brought us up, and we had only to go aboard the *Alert*, with something very like a flea in the ear. There was a light land breeze all night, and the ship did not come to anchor until the next morning.

As soon as her anchor was down we went aboard, and found her to be the whale-ship, *Wilmington and Liverpool Packet* of New Bedford, last from the "off-shore ground," with nineteen hundred barrels of oil. A "spouter" we knew her to be as soon as we saw her, by her cranes and boats, and by her stump top-gallant masts, and a certain slovenly look to the sails, rigging, spars, and hull; and when we got on board, we found everything to correspond — spouter fashion. She had a false deck, which was rough and oily, and cut up in every direction by the chimes of oil-casks; her rigging was slack and turning white; no paint on the spars or blocks; clumsy seizings and straps without covers, and homeward-bound splices in every direction. Her crew, too, were not in much better order. Her captain was a Quaker, in a suit of brown, with a broad-brimmed hat, and sneaking about decks like a sheep, with his head down; and the men looked more like fishermen and farmers than they did like sailors.

We found they had been at sea six or eight months, and had no news to tell us; so we left them, and promised to get liberty to come on board in the evening, for some curiosities, etc. Accordingly, as soon as we were knocked off in the evening and had got supper, we obtained leave, took a boat, and went aboard and spent an hour or two.

Thursday, November 12th. This day was quite cool in the early part, and there were black clouds about; but as it was often so in the morning nothing was apprehended, and all the captains went ashore together to spend the day. Toward noon, the clouds hung heavily over the mountains, coming half-way down the hills that encircle the town of Santa Barbara, and a heavy swell rolled in from the southeast. The mate immediately ordered the gig's crew away, and, at the same time, we saw boats pulling ashore from the other vessels. Here was a grand chance for a rowing-match, and every one did his best. We passed the boats of the *Ayacucho* and *Loriotte*, but could gain nothing upon, and indeed, hardly hold our own with, the long six-oared boat of the whale-ship. They reached the breakers before us; but here we had the advantage of them, for, not being used to the surf, they were obliged to wait to see us beach our boat.

We had hardly got the boats beached, and their heads out, before our old friend, Bill Jackson, who steered the *Loriotte*'s boat, called out that the brig was adrift; and sure enough she was dragging her anchors, and drifting down into the bight of the bay. Without waiting for the captain, he sprang into the boat, called the Kanakas together, and tried to put off. But the Kanakas, though capital water-dogs, were frightened by their vessel's being adrift, and by the emergency of the case, and seemed to lose their faculty. Then we came forward, told the Kanakas to take their seats in the boat, and going two on each side, walked out with her till it was up to our shoulders, and gave them a shove, when, giving way with their oars, they got her safely into the long regular swell. In the meantime boats had put off from our ship and the whaler, and coming all on board the brig together, they let go the other anchor, paid out chain, braced the yards to the wind, and brought the vessel up.

In a few minutes the captains came hurrying down, on the run; and there was no time to be lost, for the gale promised to be a severe one, and the surf was breaking upon the beach, three deep, higher and higher every instant. The *Ayacucho*'s boat, pulled by four Kanakas, put off first, and as they had no rudder or steering-oar, would probably never have got off had we not waded out with them as far as the surf would permit. The next that made the attempt was the whaleboat, for we, being the most experienced "beachcombers," needed no help, and stayed till the last. Whalemen make the best boats' crews in the world for a long pull; but this landing was new to them, and notwithstanding the examples they had had, they slued round and were hove up — boat, oars, and men — all together, high and dry upon the sand. The second time they filled, and had to turn their boat over and set her off again. We could be of no help to them, for they were so many as to be in one another's way, without the addition of our numbers. The third time they got off, though not without shipping a sea which drenched them all, and half filled their boat, keeping them bailing until they reached their ship. We now got ready to go off, putting the boat's head out; English Ben and I, who were the largest, standing on each side of the bows to keep her "head on" to the sea, two more shipping and manning the two after oars, and the captain taking the steering oar. Two or three Spaniards, who stood upon the beach looking at us, wrapped their cloaks about them, shook their heads, and muttered, "Caramba!" They had no taste for such doings; in fact, the hydrophobia is a national malady, and shows itself in their persons as well as their actions.

Watching for a "smooth chance," we determined to show the other boats the way it should be done; and, as soon as ours floated, ran out with her, keeping her head on with all our strength and the help of the captain's oar, and the two after oarsmen giving way regularly and strongly, until our feet were off the ground, we tumbled into the bows, keeping perfectly still from fear of hindering the others. For some time it was doubtful how it would go. The boat stood nearly up and down in the water, and the sea, rolling from under her, let her fall upon the water with a force which seemed almost to stave her bottom in. By quietly sliding two oars forward along the thwarts, without impeding the rowers, we shipped two bow oars, and thus, by the help of four oars and the captain's strong arm, we got safely off, though we shipped several seas, which left us half full of water. We pulled alongside of the *Loriotte*, put her skipper on board and found her making preparations for slipping, and then pulled aboard our own ship. Here Mr. Brown, always "on hand," had got everything ready, so that we had only to hook on the gig and hoist it up, when the order was given to loose the sails. While we were on the yards, we saw the *Loriotte* under weigh, and before our yards were mast-headed, the *Ayacucho* had spread her wings, and, with yards braced sharp up, was standing athwart our hawse. There is no prettier sight in the world than a full-rigged, clipper-built brig, sailing sharp on the wind. In a moment our slip-rope was gone, the head-yards filled away, and we were off. Next came the whaler; and in half an hour from the time when four vessels were lying quietly at anchor, without a rag out, or a sign of motion, the bay was deserted, and four white clouds were standing off to sea. Being sure of clearing the point, we stood off with our yards a little braced in, while the *Ayacucho* went off with a taut bowline, which brought her to windward of us.

During all this day, and the greater part of the night, we had the usual southeaster entertainment. At daybreak, the clouds thinned off and rolled away, and the sun came up clear. The wind, instead of coming out from the northward, as is usual, blew steadily and freshly from the anchoring-ground. This was bad for us, for being "flying-light," with little more than ballast trim, we were in no condition for showing off on a taut bowline, and had depended upon a fair wind, with which, by the help of our light sails and studding-sails, we meant to have been the first at the anchoring-ground; but the *Ayacucho* was a good league to windward of us, and was standing in, in fine style, and when we reached the anchoring-ground, she had got her anchor, furled her sails, squared her yards, and was lying as quietly as if nothing had happened for the last twenty-four hours.

We had our usual good luck in getting our anchor without letting go another, and were all snug, with our boats at the boom-ends, in half an hour. In about two hours more the whaler came in, and made a clumsy piece of work in getting her anchor, being obliged to let go her best bower, and finally to get out a kedge and a hawser. They were heave-ho-ing, stopping and unstopping, pawling, catting, and fishing for three hours, and the sails hung from the yards all the afternoon, and were not furled until sundown. The *Loriotte* came in just after dark and let go her anchor, making no attempt to pick up the other until the next day.

This affair led to a great dispute as to the sailing of our ship and the *Ayacucho*. Bets were made between the captains, and the crews took it up in their own way; but as she was bound to leeward and we to windward, and merchant captains cannot deviate, a trial never took place; and perhaps it was well for us that it did not, for the *Ayacucho* had been eight years in the Pacific, in every part of it — Valparaiso, Sandwich Islands, Canton, California, and all, and was called the fastest merchantman that traded in the Pacific, unless it was the brig *John Gilpin*, and perhaps the ship *Anne McKim* of Baltimore.

Saturday, November 14th. This day we got under weigh, with the agent and several Spaniards of note, as passengers, bound up to Monterey. We went ashore in the gig to bring them off with their baggage, and found them waiting on the beach, and a little afraid about going off, as the surf was running very high. This was nuts to us; for we liked to have a Spaniard wet with salt water; and then the agent was very much disliked by the crew, one and all; and we hoped, as there was no officer in the boat, to have a chance to

199

duck them; for we knew that they were such "marines" that they would not know whether it was our fault or not. Accordingly, we kept the boat so far from shore as to oblige them to wet their feet in getting into her; and then waited for a good high comber, and letting the head slue a little round, sent the whole force of the sea into the stern-sheets, drenching them from head to feet. The Spaniards sprang out of the boat, swore, and shook themselves, and protested against trying it again; and it was with the greatest difficulty that the agent could prevail upon them to make another attempt. The next time we took care, and went off easily enough, and pulled aboard. The crew came to the side to hoist in their baggage, and we gave them the wink, and they heartily enjoyed the half-drowned looks of the company.

Everything being now ready, and the passengers aboard. we ran up the ensign and broad pennant, and the other vessels ran up their ensigns. Having hove short, cast off the gaskets, and made the bunt of each sail fast by the jigger, with a man on each yard; at the word, the whole canvas of the ship was loosed, and with the greatest rapidity possible, everything was sheeted home and hoisted up, the anchor tripped and cat-headed, and the ship under headway. The royal yards were all crossed at once, and royals and skysails set, and as we had the wind free, the booms were run out, and every one was aloft, active as cats, laying out on the yards and booms, reeving the studding-sail gear; and sail after sail the captain piled upon her, until she was covered with canvas, her sails looking like a great white cloud resting upon a black speck. The breeze died away at night, and we were becalmed all day on Sunday, about half-way between Santa Barbara and Point Conception. Sunday night we had a light fair wind, which set us up again; and having a fine sea-breeze on the first part of Monday, we had the prospect of passing without any trouble, Point Conception. Toward the latter part of the afternoon, however, the regular northwest wind, as usual, set in, which gave us the chance of beating round the Point, which we were now just abreast of. A capful of wind will be a bagful here; and before night our royals were furled, and the ship was laboring hard under her top-gallant sails. At eight bells our watch went below, leaving her with as much sail as she could stagger under, the water flying over the forecastle at every plunge.

We had been below but a short time before we had the usual premonitions of a coming gale, seas washing over the whole forward part of the vessel, and her bows beating against them with a force and sound like the driving of piles. In a short time we heard the top-gallant sails come in, one after another, and then the flying jib. This seemed to ease her a good deal, and we were fast going off to the land of Nod, when bang, bang, bang on the scuttle, and "All hands reef topsails, ahoy!" started us out of our berths, and, it not being very cold weather, we had nothing extra to put on, and were soon on deck. I shall never forget the fineness of the sight. It was a clear and rather a chilly night, the stars were twinkling with an intense brightness, and as far as the eye could reach there was not a cloud to be seen. Yet it was blowing great guns from the northwest. One reef after another we took in the top-sails, and before we could get them hoisted up we heard a sound like a short, quick rattling of thunder, and the jib was blown to atoms out of the bolt-rope. We got the topsails set, and the fragments of the jib stowed away, and the fore top-mast stay-sail set in its place, when the great main-sail gaped open and the sail ripped from head to foot. "Lay up on that main-yard and furl the sail before it blows to tatters!" shouted the captain; and in a moment we were up gathering the remains of it upon the yard. We got it wrapped round the yard, and passed gaskets over it as snugly as possible, and were just on deck again when, with another loud rent which was heard throughout the ship, the foretop-sail, which had been double-reefed, split in two athwart-ships, just below the reef-band, from earing to earing. Here again it was down yard, haul out reef-tackles, and lay out upon the yard for reefing. By hauling the reef-tackle chock-a-block we took the strain from the other earings, and passing the close-reef earing and knotting the points carefully we succeeded in setting the sail close-reefed.

We had but just got the rigging coiled up, and were waiting to hear "Go below the watch!" when the main-royal worked loose from the gaskets and blew directly out to leeward, flapping and shaking the mast like a wand. Here was a job for somebody. The royal must come in or be cut adrift, or the mast would be snapped short off. All the light hands in the starboard watch were sent up one after another, but they could do nothing with it. At length John, the tall Frenchman, sprang aloft, and, by the help of his long arms and legs, succeeded, after a hard struggle, in smothering it and frapping it with long pieces of sinnet. He came very near being blown or shaken from the yard several times, but he was a true sailor, every finger a fish-hook. Having made the sail snug, he prepared to send the yard down, which was a long and difficult job. The yard at length came down safe, and after it the fore and mizzen royal-yards were sent down. All hands were then sent aloft, and for an hour or two we were hard at work, making the booms well fast, unreeving the studding-sail and royal and sky-sail gear, getting rolling ropes on the yards, setting up the weather breast-back-stays, and making other preparations for a storm. It was a fine night for a gale, just cool and bracing enough for quick work without being cold, and as bright as day.

In a few minutes the man at the wheel struck four bells, and we found that the other watch was out and our own half out. Accordingly, the starboard watch went below, and left the ship to us for a couple of hours, yet with orders to stand by for a call.

Hardly had they got below before away went

the foretop-mast-staysail, blown to ribands. This was a small sail, which we could manage in the watch, so that we were not obliged to call up the other watch. We laid out upon the bowsprit, where we were under water half the time, and took in the fragments of the sail, and as she must have some head sail on her, prepared to bend another staysail. We got the new one out into the nettings, but before it was half-way up the stay it was blown all to pieces. When we belayed the halyards there was nothing left but the bolt-rope. Now large eyes began to show themselves in the foresail, and knowing that it must soon go, the mate ordered us upon the yard to furl it. Being unwilling to call up the watch who had been on deck all night, he roused out the carpenter, sail-maker, cook, steward, and other idlers, and with their help we manned the fore-yard, and, after nearly half an hour's struggle, mastered the sail and got it well furled round the yard. The force of the wind had never been greater than at this moment. In going up the rigging it seemed absolutely to pin us down to the shrouds, and on the yard there was no such thing as turning a face to windward. When we got on deck the man at the wheel struck eight bells (four o'clock in the morning), and "All starbowlines, ahoy!" brought the other watch up. But there was no going below for us. The gale was now at its height; the captain was on deck; the ship, which was light, rolling and pitching as though she would shake the long sticks out of her; and the sails gaping open and splitting in every direction. The mizzen-topsail, which was a comparatively new sail, and close-reefed, split from head to foot in the bunt; the fore-topsail went in one rent from clew to earing, and was blowing to tatters; one of the chain bob-stays parted; the sprit-sail yard sprung in the slings; the martingale had slued away off to lee-ward; and, owing to the long dry weather, the lee rigging hung in large bights at every lurch. One of the main-topgallant shrouds had parted, and, to crown all, the galley had got adrift and gone over to leeward, and the anchor on the lee bow had worked loose and was thumping the side. Here was work enough for all hands for half a day. Our gang laid out on the mizzen topsail-yard, and, after more than half an hour's hard work, furled the sail, though it bellied out over our heads, and again, by a slat of the wind, blew in under the yard with a fearful jerk, and almost threw us off from the foot-ropes.

Double gaskets were passed round the yards, rolling tackles and other gear bowsed taut, and everything made as secure as could be. Coming down, we found the rest of the crew just laying down the fore-rigging, having furled the tattered topsail, or rather swathed it round the yard, which looked like a broken limb bandaged. There was no sail now on the ship but the spanker and the close-reefed main-topsail, which still held good. But this was too much after-sail, and order was given to furl the spanker. The brails were hauled up, and all the light hands in the starboard watch sent out on the gaff to pass the gaskets, but they could do nothing with it. The second mate swore at them for a parcel of "sogers," and sent up a couple of the best men; but they could do no better, and the gaff was lowered down. All hands were now employed in setting up the lee rigging, fishing the sprit-sail-yard, lashing the galley, and getting tackles upon the martingale to bowse it to windward. Three of us were out on the martingale guys and back-ropes for more than half ans hour, carrying out, hooking and unhooking the tackles, several times buried in the seas, until the mate ordered us in from fear of our being washed off.

Having got everything secure again, we were promising ourselves some breakfast — for it was now nearly nine o'clock in the forenoon — when the main-topsail showed evident signs of giving way. Some sail must be kept on the ship, and the captain ordered the fore and main spencer-gaffs to be lowered down, and the two spencers to be got up and bent, leaving the main-topsail to blow away, with a blessing on it if it would only last until we could set the spencers. These we bent on very carefully, and making tackles fast to the clews, bowsed them down to the waterways. By this time the main-topsail was among the things that have been, and we went aloft to stow away the remnant of the last sail of all those which were on the ship twenty-four hours before. The spencers were now the only whole sails on the ship, and being strong and small and near the deck, presenting but little surface to the wind above the rail, promised to hold out well. Hove to under these, and eased by having no sail above the tops, the ship rose and fell and drifted off to leeward like a line-of-battle ship.

It was now eleven o'clock, and the watch was sent below to get breakfast, and at eight bells (noon), as everything was snug, although the gale had not in the least abated, the watch was set, and the other watch and idlers sent below. For three days and three nights the gale continued with unabated fury and with singular regularity. There were no lulls, and very little variation in its fierceness. Our ship, being light, rolled so as almost to send the fore-yard-arm under water, and drifted off bodily to leeward. All this time there was not a cloud to be seen in the sky, day or night. Every morning the sun rose cloudless from the sea, and set again at night in the sea, in a flood of light. The stars, too, came out of the blue, one after another, night after night, unobscured, and twinkled as clear as on a still frosty night at home, until the day came upon them. All this time the sea was rolling in immense surges, white with foam, as far as the eye could reach on every side, for we were now leagues and leagues from shore.

During these seventy-two hours we had nothing to do but to turn in and out, four hours on deck and four below, eat, sleep, and keep watch. Once the wheel-rope parted, which might have been fatal to us had not the chief mate sprung instantly with a relieving tackle to windward and kept the tiller up till a new one could be rove. On the morning of the 20th, at daybreak, the gale had evidently done its worst, and had somewhat abated — so much so that all hands were called to bend new sails, although it was still blowing as hard as two common gales. One at a time, and with great difficulty and labor, the old sails were unbent and sent down by the bunt-lines, and three new topsails made for the homeward passage round Cape Horn, and which had never been bent, were got up from the sail-room and fitted for bending, and sent up by the halyards into the tops, and, with stops and frapping lines, were bent to the yards, close-reefed, sheeted home, and hoisted. Two spare courses were got up and bent in the same manner and furled, and a storm-jib, with the bonnet off, bent and furled to the boom. Toward night a few clouds appeared in the horizon, and as the gale moderated the usual appearance of driving clouds relieved the face of the sky. The fifth day after the commencement of the storm we shook a reef out of each topsail, jib, and spanker; but it was not until after eight days of reefed topsails that we had a whole sail on the ship.

Friday, December 4th. After a passage of twenty days we arrived at the mouth of the bay of San Francisco.

CHAPTER XXIV

San Francisco

Our place of destination had been Monterey; but as we were to the northward of it when the wind hauled ahead, we made a fair wind for San Francisco. About thirty miles from the mouth of the bay, and on the southeast side, is a high point upon which the Presidio is built. Behind this is the harbor in which trading vessels anchor, and near it the Mission of San Francisco, and a newly-begun settlement, mostly of Yankee Californians, called Yerba Buena. Here, at anchor, and the only vessel, was a brig under Russian colors, from Asitka, in Russian America, which had come down to winter and to take in a supply of tallow and grain, great quantities of which latter article are raised in the missions at the head of the bay. The second day after our arrival, it being Sunday, we went on board the brig as a matter of curiosity; and there was enough there to gratify it. Though no larger than the *Pilgrim*, she had five or six officers, and a crew of between twenty and thirty; and such a stupid and greasy-looking set I certainly never saw before. Although it was quite comfortable weather, and we had nothing on but straw hats, shirts, and duck trousers, and were barefooted, they had, every man of them, double-soled boots, coming up to the knees, and well greased; thick woollen trousers, frocks, waist-coats, pea-jackets, woollen caps, and everything in true Nova Zembia rig; and in the warmest days they made no change. The clothing of one of these men would weigh nearly as much as that of half our crew. They had brutish faces, looked like the antipodes of sailors, and apparently dealt in nothing but grease. They lived upon grease — ate it, drank it, slept in the midst of it, and their clothes were covered with it. To a Russian grease is the greatest luxury. They looked with greedy eyes upon the tallow-bags as they were taken into the vessel, and no doubt would have eaten one up whole had not the officer kept watch over it. The grease seemed actually coming through their pores, and out in their hair, and on their faces. It seems as if it were this saturation which makes them stand cold and rain so well. If they were to go into a warm climate they would all die of the scurvy.

The vessel was no better than the crew. Everything was in the oldest and most inconvenient fashion possible; running trusses on the yards, and large hawser cables coiled all over the decks, and served and parcelled in all directions. The top-masts, top-gallant masts, and studding-sail booms were nearly black for want of scraping, and the decks would have turned the stomach of a man-of-war's man. The galley was down in the forecastle; and there the crew lived in the midst of the steam and grease of the cooking, in a place as hot as an oven and as dirty as a pig-stye. Five minutes in the forecastle was enough for us, and we were glad to get into the open air. We made some trade with them, buying Indian curiosities, of which they had a great number; such as bead-work, feathers of birds, fur moccasins, etc. I purchased a large robe, made of the skins of some animal, dried and sewed nicely together, and covered all over on the outside with thick downy feathers, taken from the breasts of various birds, and arranged with their different colors so as to make a brilliant show.

A few days after our arrival the rainy season set in, and for three weeks it rained almost every hour without cessation. This was bad for our trade, for the collecting of hides is managed differently in this port from what it is in any other on the coast. The Mission of San Francisco, near the anchorage, has no trade at all, but those of San José, Santa Clara, and others, situated on large creeks or rivers which run into the bay, and distant between fifteen and forty miles from the anchorage, do a greater business in hides than any in California. Large boats manned by Indians, and capable of carrying nearly a thousand hides a-piece, are attached to the missions, and sent down to the vessels with hides, to bring away goods in return.

One cold, rainy evening I received orders to get ready to start for San José at four the next morning, in one of these Indian boats, with four days' provisions. I turned into my hammock early, determined to get some sleep in advance, as the boat was to be alongside before daybreak. I slept on till all hands were called in the morning, for, fortunately for me, the Indians intentionally, or from mistaking their orders, had gone off alone in the night, and were far out of sight. Thus I escaped three or four days of very uncomfortable service.

Four of our men a few days afterwards went up in one of the quarter-boats to Santa Clara to carry the agent, and remained out all night in a drenching rain in the small boat, where there was not room for them to turn round; the agent having gone up to the mission and left the men to their fate, making no provision for their accommodation, and not even sending them anything to eat. After this they had to pull thirty miles, and when they got on board were so stiff that they could not come up the gangway ladder. This filled up the measure of the agent's unpopularity, and never after this could he get anything done by any of the crew; and many a delay and vexation, and many a good ducking in the surf, did he get to pay up old scores, or "square the yards with the dirty quill-driver."

Having collected nearly all the hides that were to be procured, we began our preparations for taking in a supply of wood and water, for both of which San Francisco is the best place on the coast. A small island, situated about two leagues from the anchorage, called by us "Wood Island,"

and by the Spaniards "Isla de los Angelos," was covered with trees to the water's edge; and to this, two of our crew, who were Kennebec men, and could handle an axe like a plaything, were sent every morning to cut wood, with two boys to pile it up for them. In about a week they had cut enough to last us a year; and the third mate, with myself and three others, were sent over in a large, schooner-rigged, open launch which we had hired of the mission, to take in the wood and bring it to the ship. We left the ship about noon, but, owing to a strong head-wind, and a tide which here runs four or five knots, did not go into the harbor formed by two points of the island, where the boats lie, until sundown. No sooner had we come-to than a strong southeaster, which had been threatening us all day, set in, with heavy rain and a chilly atmosphere. We were in rather a bad situation — an open boat, a heavy rain, and a long night — for in winter, in this latitude, it was dark nearly fifteen hours. Taking a small skiff which we had brought with us, we went ashore, but found no shelter, for everything was open to the rain, and collecting a little wood, which we found by lifting up the leaves and brush, and a few mussels, we put aboard again and made the best preparations in our power for passing the night. We unbent the mainsail, and formed an awning with it over the after-part of the boat, made a bed of wet logs of wood, and, with our jackets on, lay down about six o'clock to sleep. Finding the rain running down upon us, and our jackets getting wet through, and the rough, knotty logs rather indifferent couches, we turned out; and taking an iron pan which we brought with us, we wiped it out dry, put some stones around it, cut the wet bark from some sticks, and striking a light, made a small fire in the pan. Keeping some sticks near to dry, and covering the whole over with a roof of boards, we kept up a small fire, by which we cooked our mussels, and ate them, rather for an occupation than from hunger.

Toward morning the rain ceased, and the air became sensibly colder, so that we found sleep impossible, and sat up, watching for daybreak. No sooner was it light than we went ashore and began our preparations for loading our vessel. We were not mistaken in the coldness of the weather, for a white frost was on the ground, a thing we had never seen before in California, and one or two little puddles of fresh water were skimmed over with a thin coat of ice. In this state of the weather, and before sunrise, in the gray of the morning, we had to wade off, nearly up to our hips in water, to load the skiff with the wood by armfuls. We were all day at this work, and toward sundown, having loaded the vessel as deep as she would bear, we hove up our anchor and made sail, beating out of the bay. No sooner had we got into the large bay than we found a strong tide setting us out to seaward, a thick fog which prevented our seeing the ship, and a breeze too light to set us against the tide; for we were as deep as a sand-barge. By the utmost exertions we saved ourselves from being carried out to sea, and were glad to reach the leewardmost point of the island, where we came-to and prepared to pass another night, more uncomfortable than the first, for we were loaded up to the gunwale, and had only a choice among logs and sticks for a resting-place. The next morning we made sail at slack water, with a fair wind, and got on board by eleven o'clock, when all hands were turned out to unload and stow away the wood, which took till night.

Having now taken in all our wood, the next morning a water-party was ordered off with all the casks. From this we escaped, having had a pretty good siege with the wooding. The water-party were gone three days, during which time they narrowly escaped being carried out to sea, and passed one day on an island, where one of them shot a deer, great numbers of which overrun the islands and hills of San Francisco Bay.

While not off on these wood and water parties, or up the rivers to the missions, we had very easy times on board the ship. We were moored, stem and stern, within a cable's length of the shore, safe from southeasters, and with very little boating to do; and as it rained nearly all the time, awnings were put over the hatchways, and all hands sent down between decks, where we were at work day after day picking oakum, until we got enough to caulk the ship all over, and to last the whole voyage. Then we made a whole suit of gaskets for the voyage home, a pair of wheel-ropes from strips of green hide, great quantities of spun-yarn, and everything else that could be made between decks. It being now mid-winter and in high latitude, the nights were very long, so that we were not turned to until seven in the morning, and were obliged to knock off at five in the evening when we got supper, which gave us nearly three hours before eight bells, at which time the watch was set.

As we had now been about a year on the coast, it was time to think of the voyage home; and knowing that the last two or three months of our stay would be very busy ones, and that we should never have so good an opportunity to work for ourselves as the present, we all employed our evenings in making clothes for the passage home, and more especially for Cape Horn. Industry was the order of the day, and every one did something for himself; for we knew that as the season advanced, and we went further south, we should have no evenings to work in.

Friday, December 25th. This day was Christmas; and as it rained all day long, and there were no hides to take in, and nothing especial to do, the captain gave us a holiday and plum duff for dinner.

Sunday, December 27th. We had now finished all our business at this port, and it being Sunday, we unmoored ship and got under weigh.

We sailed down this magnificent bay with a light wind, the tide, which was running out, carrying us at the rate of four or five knots.

If California ever becomes a prosperous country this bay will be the center of its prosperity. The abundance of wood and water, the extreme fertility of its shores, the excellence of its climate, which is as near to being perfect as any in the world, and its facilities for navigation, affording the best anchoring-grounds in the whole western coast of America, all fit it for a place of great importance.

The tide leaving us, we came to anchor near the mouth of the bay, under a high and beautifully sloping hill, upon which herds of hundreds of red deer, and the stag, with his high-branching antlers, were bounding about, looking at us for a moment, and then starting off, affrighted at the noises which we made for the purpose of seeing the variety of their beautiful attitudes and motions.

At midnight, the tide having turned, we hove up our anchor and stood out of the bay, with a fine starry heaven above us. Before the light northerly winds, which blow here with the regularity of trades, we worked slowly along, and made point Año Nuevo, the northerly point of the bay of Monterey, on Monday afternoon. It was ten o'clock on Tuesday morning when we came to anchor.

CHAPTER XXV

A Wedding

The only other vessel in the harbor was a Russian government barque, from Asitka, mounting eight guns, and having on board the ex-governor, who was going in her to Mazatlan, and thence overland to Vera Cruz.

The brig *Pilgrim* had been lying in Monterey through the latter part of November, according to orders, waiting for us. Day after day Captain Faucon went up to the hill to look out for us, and at last gave us up, thinking we must have gone down in the gale which we experienced off Point Conception, and which had blown with great fury over the whole coast, driving ashore several vessels in the snuggest ports.

As we were to be here over Sunday, and we had had no liberty day for nearly three months, every one was for going ashore. On Sunday morning, as soon as the decks were washed and we had got breakfast, those who had obtained liberty began to clean themselves, as it is called, to go ashore. A bucket of fresh water apiece, a cake of soap, a large coarse towel, and we went to work scrubbing one another on the forecastle. Having gone through this, the next thing was to get into the head — one on each side — with a bucket apiece, and duck one another by drawing up water and heaving over each other, while we were stripped to a pair of trousers. Then came the rigging-up. The usual outfit of pumps, white stockings, loose white duck trousers, blue jackets, clean checked shirts, black kerchiefs, hats well varnished, with a fathom of black ribbon over the left eye, a silk handkerchief flying from the outside jacket pocket, and four or five dollars tied up in the back of the neckerchief, and we were "all right." One of the quarter-boats pulled us ashore, and we streamed up to the town. I tried to find the church, in order to see the worship, but was told that there was no service, except a mass early in the morning, so we went about the town, visiting the Americans and English, and the natives whom we had known when we were here before. Toward noon we procured horses, and rode out to the Carmel Mission, where we got something in the way of a dinner — beef, eggs, frijoles, tortillas, and some middling wine — from the mayordomo, who, of course, refused to make any charge, yet received our present as a gratuity.

After this repast we had a fine run, scouring the whole country on our fleet horses, and came into town soon after sundown. Here we found our companions who had refused to go to ride with us. They were moored, stem and stern in a grog-shop, making a great noise, with a crowd of Indians and hungry half-breeds about them, and with a fair prospect of being stripped and dirked, or left to pass the night in the calabozo. With a great deal of trouble we managed to get them down to the boats, though not without many angry looks and interferences from the Spaniards, who had marked them out for their prey. Nothing worthy of remark happened while we were here, except a little boxing-match on board our own ship, which gave us something to talk about. A broad-backed, big-headed Cape Cod boy, about sixteen years old, had been playing the bully for the whole voyage over a slender, delicate-looking boy from one of the Boston schools, and over whom he had much the advantage in strength, age, and experience in the ship's duty. The latter, however, had "picked up his crumbs," was learning his duty, and getting strength and confidence daily, and began to assert his rights against his oppressor. Still the other was his master, and always tackled with him and threw him down. One afternoon before we were turned-to, these boys got into a violent squabble in the between decks, when George (the Boston boy) said he would fight Nat, if he could have fair play. The chief mate heard the noise, dove down the hatchway, hauled them both up on deck, and told them to shake hands and have no more trouble for the voyage, or else they should fight till one gave in for beaten. Finding neither willing to make an offer of reconciliation, he called all hands up, ranged the crew in the waist, marked a line on the deck, brought the two boys up to it, making them "toe the mark." And there they stood, one on each side of it, face to face, and went at it like two game-cocks.

The Cape Cod boy, Nat, put in his double-fisters, starting the blood, and bringing the black and blue spots all over the face and arms of the other, whom we expected to see give in every moment, but the more he was hurt the better he fought. Time after time he was knocked nearly down, but up he came again and faced the mark, as bold as a lion, again to take the heavy blows, which sounded so as to make one's heart turn with pity for him. At length he came up to the mark the last time, his shirt torn from his body, his face covered with blood and bruises, and his eyes flashing fire, and swore he would stand there until the one or the other was killed and set to like a young fury. "Hurrah in the bow!" said the men, cheering him on. Nat tried to close with him, knowing his advantage, but the mate stopped that, saying there should be fair play and no fingering. Nat then came up to the mark, but looked white about the mouth, and his blows were not given with half the spirit of his first. He was evidently cowed. He had always been master, and had nothing to gain and everything to lose; while the other fought for honor and freedom, and under a sense of wrong. It would not do. It was soon over. Nat gave in, not so much beaten, as cowed and mortified, and never afterwards tried to act the bully on board. We took George forward, washed him in the deck-tub, compli-mented his pluck, and from this time he became somebody on board, having fought himself into notice.

Wednesday, January 6th. Set sail from Monterey with a number of Spaniards as passengers, and shaped our course for Santa Barbara. Among our passengers was a young man who was the best representation of a decayed gentleman I had ever seen. He was of the aristocracy of the country, his family being of pure Spanish blood, and once of great importance in Mexico. His father had been governor of the province, and having amassed a large property settled at San Diego, where he built a large house, kept a great retinue of Indians, and set up for the grandee of that part of the country. His son was sent to Mexico, where he received the best education, and went into the first society of the capital. Misfortune, extravagance, and the want of funds soon ate the estate up, and Don Juan Bandini returned from Mexico accomplished, poor, and proud, and without any office or occupation, to lead the life of most young men of the better families — dissolute and extravagant when the means are at hand. He had a slight and elegant figure, moved gracefully, danced and waltzed beautifully, spoke the best of Castilian, with a pleasant and refined voice and accent, and had throughout the bearing of a man of high birth and figure. Yet here he was, with his passage given him, for he had not the means of paying for it, and living upon the charity of our agent. I could not but feel a pity for him, especially when I saw him by the side of his fellow-passenger and townsman, a fat, coarse, vulgar, pretending fellow of a Yankee trader, who had made money in San Diego, and was eating out the very vitals of the Bandinis, fattening upon their extravagance, grinding them in their poverty; having mortgages on their lands, forestalling their cattle, and already making an inroad upon their jewels, which were their last hope.

Don Juan had with him a retainer, who was as much like many of the characters of Gil Blas as his master. He called himself a private secretary, though there was no writing for him to do, and he lived in the steerage with the carpenter and sailmaker. He was certainly a character; could read and write extremely well, spoke good Spanish, had been all over Spanish America, and lived in every possible situation, and served in every conceivable capacity, though generally in that of confidential servant to some man of figure.

The second morning after leaving Monterey we were off Point Conception. It was a bright, sunny day, and the wind, though strong, was fair; and everything was in striking contrast with our experience in the same place two months before, when we were drifting off from a northwester, under a fore and main spencer. "Sail ho!" cried a man who was rigging out a top-gallant studding-sail boom. "Where away?" — "Weather beam, sir!" — and in a few minutes a full-rigged brig was seen standing out from under Point Conception. The studding-sail halyards were let go and the yards boom-ended, the after-yards braced aback, and we waited her coming down. She rounded to, backed her main top-sail, and showed her decks full of men, four guns on a side, hammock nettings, and everything man-of-war fashion, except that there was no boatswain's whistle, and no uniforms on the quarter-deck. A short, square built man, in a rough gray jacket, with a speaking-trumpet in hand, stood in the weather hammock nettings. "Ship ahoy!" — "Hallo!" — "What ship is that, pray?" — "*Alert.*" — "Where are you from, pray?" etc., etc. She proved to be the brig *Convoy*, from the Sandwich Islands, engaged in otter-hunting among the islands which lie along the coast. Her armament was from her being an illegal trader. The otter are very numerous among these islands, and being of great value, the government require a heavy sum for a license to hunt them, and lay a high duty upon every one shot or carried out of the country. This vessel had no license, and paid no duty, besides being engaged in smuggling goods on board other vessels trading on the coast, and belonging to the same owners in Oahu. Our captain told him to look out for the Mexicans; but he said they had not an armed vessel of his size in the whole Pacific. This was, without doubt, the same vessel that showed herself off Santa Barbara a few months before. These vessels frequently remain on the coast for years without making port, except at the islands for wood and water, and an occasional visit to Oahu for a new outfit.

Sunday, January 10th. Arrived at Santa Barbara, and on the following Wednesday slipped our cable and went to sea, on account of a southeaster. Returned to our anchorage the next day. We were the only vessel in the port.

Great preparations were making on shore for the marriage of our agent, who was to marry Donna Anneta De G— De N—y C—, youngest daughter of Don Antonio N—, the grandee of the place, and the head of the first family in California. On the day appointed for the wedding we took the captain ashore in the gig, and had orders to come for him at night, with leave to go up to the house and see the fandango. At ten o'clock the bride went up with her sister to the confessional, dressed in deep black. Nearly an hour intervened, when the great doors of the mission-church opened, the bells rang out a loud, discordant peal, a private signal for us was run up by the captain ashore, the bride, dressed in complete white, came out of the church with the bridegroom, followed by a long procession. Just as she stepped from the church-door, a small white cloud issued from the bows of our ship, which was full in sight, a loud report echoed among the surrounding hills and over the bay, and instantly the ship was dressed in flags and pennants from stem to stern. Twenty-three guns followed in regular succession, with an interval of fifteen seconds between each, when the cloud cleared away, and the ship lay dressed in her colors all day. At sundown another salute of the same number of guns was fired, and all the flags run down.

After supper we rowed ashore, dressed in our uniform, beached the boat, and went up to the fandango. As we drew near we heard the accustomed sound of violins and guitars, and saw a great motion of the people within. Going in, we found nearly all the people of the town — men, women, and children — collected and crowded together, leaving barely room for the dancers; for on these occasions no invitations are given, but every one is expected to come, though there is always a private entertainment within the house for particular friends. The old women sat down in rows, clapping their hands to the music, and applauding the young ones.

In the dancing I was much disappointed. The women stood upright, with their hands down by their sides, their eyes fixed upon the ground before them, and slid about without any perceptible means of motion, for their feet were invisible, the hem of their dresses forming a perfect circle about them, reaching to the ground. They looked as grave as though they were going through some religious ceremony; and on the whole, instead of the spirited, fascinating Spanish dances which I had expected, I found the Californian fandango, on the part of the women at least, a lifeless affair. The men did better. They danced with grace and spirit, moving in circles round their nearly stationary partners, and showing their figures to great advantage.

A great deal was said about our friend Don

Juan Bandini; and when he did appear, which was toward the close of the evening, he certainly gave us the most graceful dancing that I had ever seen. He was dressed in white pantaloons, neatly made, a short jacket of dark silk gaily figured, white stockings and thin morocco slippers upon his very small feet. After the supper the waltzing began, which was confined to a very few of the "gente de razón," and was considered a high accomplishment and a mark of aristocracy. The great amusement of the evening — which I suppose was owing to its being carnival — was the breaking of eggs filled with cologne, or other essences, upon the heads of the company. One end of the egg is broken and the inside taken out, then it is partly filled with cologne, and the hole sealed up. The women bring a great number of these secretly about them, and the amusement is, to break one upon the head of a gentleman when his back is turned. He is bound in gallantry to find out the lady and return the compliment, though it must not be done if the person sees you. A tall, stately don with immense gray whiskers and a look of great importance was standing before me, when I felt a light hand on my shoulder, and turning round saw Donna Angustia (whom we all knew, as she had been up to Monterey and down again in the *Alert*), with her finger upon her lip, motioning me gently aside. I stepped back a little, when she went up behind the don, and with one hand knocked off his huge *sombrero*, and at the same instant, with the other, broke the egg upon his head, and springing behind me was out of sight in a moment. The don turned slowly round, the cologne running down his face and over his clothes, and a loud laugh breaking out from every quarter. He looked round in vain for some time, until the direction of so many laughing eyes showed him the fair offender. She was his niece, and a great favorite with him, so old Don Domingo had to join in the laugh. A great many such tricks were played, and many a war of sharp manœuvring was carried on between couples of the younger people; and at every successful exploit a general laugh was raised.

The captain sent for us about ten o'clock, and we went aboard in high spirits, having enjoyed the new scene much, and were of great importance among the crew, from having so much to tell, and from the prospect of going every night until it was over; for these fandangos generally last three days. The next day two of us were sent up to the town, and took care to come back by way of Captain Noriego's. The musicians were still there, upon their platform, scraping and twanging away, and a few people, apparently of the lower classes, were dancing. The dancing is kept up at intervals throughout the day, but the crowd, the spirit, and the *élite* come in at night. The next night, which was the last, we went ashore in the same manner, until we got almost tired of the monotonous twang of the instruments, and the drawling sounds which the women kept up as an accompaniment.

This last night they kept it up in great style, and were getting into a high-go, when the captain called us off to go aboard, for, it being southeaster season, he was afraid to remain on shore long; and it was well he did not, for that very night we slipped our cables, as a crowner to our fun ashore, and stood off before a southeaster, which lasted twelve hours.

CHAPTER XXVI

Preparing for the Home Voyage

Monday, February 1st. After having been in port twenty-one days we sailed for San Pedro, where we arrived on the following day. Here we found the *Ayacucho* and the *Pilgrim*, which last we had not seen since the 11th of September — nearly five months; and I really felt something like an affection for the old brig which had been my first home, and in which I had spent nearly a year, and got the first rough and tumble of a sea-life. I went on board the first night, after supper; found the old cook in the galley, playing upon the fife which I had given him as a parting present; and dove down into the forecastle, where were my old shipmates, the same as ever, glad to see me, for they had nearly given us up as lost. We both got under weigh on the 4th, she bound up to San Francisco again, and we to San Diego, where we arrived on the 6th.

We were always glad to see San Diego, it being the depôt, and a snug little place, and seeming quite like home, especially to me, who had spent a summer there. We discharged our hides, and in four days were ready to sail again for the windward, and, to our great joy, *for the last time!* Over thirty thousand hides had been already collected, cured, and stowed away in the house, which, together with what we should collect and the *Pilgrim* would bring down from San Francisco, would make out our cargo.

I spent one evening, as had been my custom, at the oven with the Sandwich Islanders; but it was far from being the usual noisy, laughing time. It has been said that the greatest curse to each of the South Sea Islands was the first man who discovered it. The white men, with their vices, have brought in diseases before unknown to the islanders, which are now sweeping off the native population of the Sandwich Islands at the rate of one-fortieth of the entire population annually. The curse of a people calling themselves Christian seems to follow them everywhere; and even here, in this obscure place, lay two young islanders, whom I had left strong, active young men, in the vigor of health, wasting away under a disease which they would never have known but for their intercourse with Christianized Mexico and people from Christian America. One of them was not so ill, and was moving about, smoking his pipe and talking, and trying to keep up his spirits; but the other who was my friend, and *aikane* — Hope — was the most dreadful object I had ever seen in my life; his eyes sunken and dead, his cheeks fallen in against his teeth, his hands looking like claws; a dreadful cough, which seemed to rack his whole shattered system, a hollow, whispering voice, and an entire inability to move himself.

There he lay, upon a mat on the ground, which was the only floor of the oven, with no medicine, no comforts, and no one to care for or help him but a few Kanakas, who were willing enough, but could do nothing. The sight of him made me sick and faint. Poor fellow! During the four months that I lived upon the beach we were continually together, both in work and in our excursions in the woods and upon the water. I really felt a strong affection for him, and preferred him to any of my own countrymen there. When I came into the oven he looked at me, held out his hand, and said in a low voice, but with a delightful smile, *"Aloha, Aikane! Aloha nui!"* I comforted him as well as I could, and promised to ask the captain to help him from the medicine-chest.

I could not get the thought of the poor fellow out of my head all night; his horrible suffering, and his apparently inevitable, horrible end.

The next day l told the captain of Hope's state, and asked him if he would be so kind as to go and see him.

"What! a Kanaka?"

"Yes, sir," said I; "but he has worked four years for our vessels."

The captain used a brutal expression and walked off.

This same man died afterwards of a fever on the deadly coast of Sumatra. God grant he had better care taken of him in his sufferings than he ever gave to anyone else!

Finding nothing was to be got from the captain,

I went to the mate and told him the case. Mr. Brown had been intrusted with the general care of the medicine-chest, and, although a driving fellow, he had good feelings, and was always inclined to be kind to the sick. He said that Hope was not strictly one of the crew; but as he was in our employ when taken sick he should have the necessary medicines, and he got them and gave them to me, with leave to go ashore at night. Nothing could exceed the delight of the Kanakas when I came bringing the medicines.

Poor Hope was so much revived at the bare thought of anything being done for him that he was already stronger and better. I knew he must die as he was, and he could but die under the medicines, and any chance was worth running. The applications, internal and external, were powerful, and I gave him strict directions to keep warm and sheltered, telling him it was his only chance for life. Twice after this I visited him, having only time to run up while waiting in the boat. He promised to take his medicines regularly until we returned, and insisted upon it that he was doing better.

We got under weigh on the 10th, bound up to San Pedro, and had three days of calm and head-winds, making but little progress. Arrived at San Pedro on the fourth day, and came-to in the old place a league from shore, with no other vessel in port, and the prospect of three weeks or more of dull life, rolling goods up a slippery hill, carrying hides on our heads over sharp stones, and perhaps slipping for a southeaster.

There was but one man in the only house here, and him I shall always remember as a good specimen of a California ranger. He had been a tailor in Philadelphia, and getting intemperate and in debt he joined a trapping party, and went to the Columbia River, and thence down to Monterey, where he spent everything, left his party, and came to the Pueblo de los Angelos to work at his trade. Here he went dead to leeward among the pulperias, gambling-rooms, etc., and came down to San Pedro to be moral by being out of temptation. He had been in the house several weeks, working hard at his trade upon orders which he had brought with him, and talked much of his resolution, and opened his heart to us about his past life.

After we had been here some time he started off one morning in fine spirits, well dressed, to carry the clothes which he had been making to the Pueblo, and saying he would bring back his money and some fresh orders the next day. The next day came, and a week passed, and nearly a fortnight, when one day, going ashore, we saw a tall man, who looked like our friend the tailor, getting out of the back of an Indian's cart, which had just come down from the Pueblo. He stood for the house, but we bore up after him, when, finding that we were overhauling him, he hove to and spoke to us. Such a sight I never saw before. Barefooted, with an old pair of trousers tied round his waist by a piece of green hide, a soiled cotton shirt, and a torn Indian hat — "cleaned out" to the last real, and completely "used up." He confessed the whole matter, acknowledged that he was on his back; and now he had a prospect of a fit of the horrors for a week, and of being worse than useless for months.

One of the same stamp was Russell, who was master of the hide-house at San Diego while I was there, and afterwards turned away for his misconduct. He spent his own money and nearly all the stores' among the half-bloods upon the beach, and, being turned away, went up to the Presidio, where he lived the life of a desperate "loafer," until some rascally deed sent him off "between two days," with men on horseback, dogs, and Indians in full cry after him among the hills. One night he burst into our room at the hide-house, breathless, pale as a ghost, covered with mud, and torn by thorns and briars, nearly naked, and begged for a crust of bread, saying he had neither eaten nor slept for three days. Here was the great Mr. Russell begging food and shelter of Kanakas and sailors. He stayed with us till he gave himself up and was dragged off to the calabozo.

Saturday, February 13th. Were called up at midnight to slip for a violent northeaster. We went off with a flowing sheet, and hove-to under the lee of Catalina Island, where we lay three days, and then returned to our anchorage.

Tuesday, February 23d. This afternoon a signal was made from the shore, and we went off in the gig, and found the agent's clerk, who had been up to the Pueblo, waiting at the landing-place, with a package under his arm, covered with brown paper, and tied carefully with twine. No sooner had we shoved off than he told us there was good news from Santa Barbara.

"What's that?" said one of the crew; "has the agent slipped off the hooks?" "No; better than that. The *California* has arrived." Letters, papers, news, and perhaps — friends, on board! Our hearts were all up in our mouths, and we pulled away like good fellows; for the precious packet could not be opened except by the captain. As we pulled under the stern the clerk held up the package, and called out to the mate who was leaning over the taffrail that the *California* had arrived.

"Hurrah!" said the mate so as to be heard fore and aft; "*California* come, and news from Boston!"

Instantly there was a confusion on board which no one could account for who has not been in the same situation. All discipline seemed for a moment relaxed.

The packet was sent down into the cabin, and every one waited to hear of the result. As nothing came up, the officers began to feel that they were acting rather a child's part, and turned the crew to again; and the same strict discipline was restored, which prohibits speech between man and man while at work on deck, so that when the steward came forward with letters for the crew, each man took his letters, carried them down to his chest, and came up again immediately; and not a letter was read until we had cleared up decks for the night.

An overstrained sense of manliness is the characteristic of seafaring men, or, rather, of life on board ship. This often gives an appearance of want of feeling, and even of cruelty. From this, if a man comes within an ace of breaking his neck, and escapes, it is made a joke of, and no notice must be taken of a bruise or a cut; and any expression of pity or any show of attention would look sisterly, and unbecoming to a man who has to face the rough and tumble of such a life. From this, too, the sick are neglected at sea, and whatever sailors may be ashore, a sick man finds little sympathy or attention, forward or aft. A man, too, can have nothing peculiar or sacred on board ship; for all the nicer feelings they take pride in disregarding, both in themselves and others. A thin-skinned man could not live an hour on shipboard. One would be torn raw unless he had the hide of an ox. A moment of natural feeling for home and friends, and then the frigid routine of sea-life returned. Jokes were made upon those who showed any interest in the expected news, and everything near and dear was made common stock for rude jokes and unfeeling coarseness, to which no exception could be taken by any one.

Supper, too, must be eaten before the letters were read; and when at last they were brought out, they all got round any one who had a letter, and expected to have it read aloud and have it all in common. If any one went by himself to read it was — "Fair play there; and no skulking!" I took mine and went into the sailmaker's berth, where I could read it without interruption.

Thursday, February 25th. Set sail for Santa Barbara, where we arrived on Sunday, the 28th. We just missed seeing the *California,* for she had sailed three days before bound to Monterey, to enter her cargo and procure her license, and thence to San Francisco, etc.

Saturday, March 5th. This was an important day in our almanac, for it was on this day that we were first assured that our voyage was really drawing to a close. The captain gave orders to have the ship ready for getting under weigh, and observed that there was a good breeze to take us down to San Pedro. Then we were not going up to windward. Thus much was certain, and was soon known fore and aft; and when we went in the gig to take him off, he shook hands with the people on the beach, and said that he never expected to see Santa Barbara again. This settled the matter and sent a thrill of pleasure through the heart of every one in the boat. We pulled off with a will, saying to ourselves, "Good-by, Santa Barbara! — this is the last pull here. No more duckings in your breakers, and slipping from your confounded southeasters!" The news was soon known aboard, and put life into everything when we were getting under weigh; and when all hands tallied on to the cat-fall the chorus of "Time for us to go!" was raised for the first time, and joined in with full swing by everybody.

We left here the young Englishman George Marsh, who left us to take the berth of second mate on board the *Ayacucho*, which was lying in port. I felt really sorry to part from him. The situation was offered him only a few hours before we sailed, and though he must give up returning to America, yet I have no doubt that the change from a dog's berth to an officer's was too agreeable to his feelings to be declined. Had I known an hour sooner that he was going to leave us, I would have made an effort to get from him the true history of his early life. He knew that I had no faith in the story, which he told the crew, and perhaps in the moment of parting from me, probably for ever, he would have given me the true account.

Two days brought us to San Pedro, and two days more, to our no small joy, gave us our last view of that place, which was universally called the hell of California, and seemed designed in every way for the wear and tear of sailors. Not even the last view could bring out one feeling of regret. Having kept close in-shore for the land breeze, we passed the Mission of San Juan Campestráno the same night, and saw distinctly by the bright moonlight the hill which I had gone down by a pair of halyards in search of a few paltry hides.

"Forsitan et hæc olim,"

thought I, and took my last look of that place too. And on the next morning we were under the high point of San Domingo. The flood-tide took us swiftly in, and we came-to opposite our hide-house, and prepared to get everything in trim for a long stay. This was our last port. Here we were to discharge everything from the ship, clean her out, smoke her, take in our hides, wood, water, etc., and set sail for Boston.

While all this was doing we were to lie still in one place, and the port was a safe one, and there was no fear of southeasters. Accordingly, having picked out a good berth in the stream, with a good smooth beach opposite for a landing-place, and within two cables' length of our hide-house, we moored ship, unbent all the sails, sent down the top-gallant-yards, and all the studding-sail-booms, and housed the top-gallant-masts. The boats were then hove out, and all the sails, the spare spars, the stores, the rigging not rove, and, in fact, everything which was not in daily use, sent ashore, and stowed away in the house. Then went all our hides and horns, and we left hardly anything in the ship but her ballast, and this we made preparation to heave out next day. Six weeks or two months of the hardest work we had yet seen was before us, and then — "Good-by to California!"

CHAPTER XXVII

Homeward Bound

We turned in early, knowing that we might expect an early call; and sure enough, before the stars had quite faded, "All hands ahoy!" and we were turned-to, heaving out ballast.

Friday, and a part of Saturday, we were engaged in this work, until we had thrown out all but what we wanted under our cargo on the passage home; when as the next day was Sunday, and a good day for smoking ship, we cleared everything out of the cabin and forecastle, made a slow fire of charcoal, birch bark, brimstone, and other matters, on the ballast in the bottom of the hold, caulked up the hatches and every open seam, and pasted over the cracks of the windows and the slides of the scuttles and companion-way. The captain and officers slept under the awning which was spread over the quarter-deck, and we stowed ourselves away under an old studding-sail, which we drew over one side of the forecastle. The next day, from fear that something might happen, orders were given for no one to leave the ship, and as the decks were lumbered up with everything we could not wash them down, so we had nothing to do all day long.

The next morning we took the battens from the hatches, and opened the ship. A few stifled rats were found, and what bugs, cockroaches, fleas, and other vermin there might have been on board must have unrove their life-lines before the hatches were opened. The ship being now ready, we covered the bottom of the hold over, fore and aft, with dried brush, for dunnage, and having levelled everything away, we were ready to take in our cargo. All the hides that had been collected since the *California* left the coast, amounting to about forty thousand, were cured, dried, and stowed away in the house, waiting for our good ship to take them to Boston.

Now began the operation of taking in our cargo, which kept us hard at work from the gray of the morning till starlight for six weeks, with the exception of Sundays. To carry the work on quicker a division of labor was made. Two men threw the hides down from the piles in the house, two more picked them up and put them on a long horizontal pole raised a few feet from the ground, where they were beaten by two more with flails, somewhat like those used in threshing wheat. When beaten, they were taken from this pole by two more, and placed upon a platform of boards; and ten or a dozen men, with their trousers rolled up, were constantly going backwards and for-wards from the platform to the boat, which was kept off where she would just float, with the hides upon their heads. The older men of the crew, whom it would have been dangerous to have kept in the water, remained on board with the mate to stow the hides away as fast as they were brought off by the boats.

Having filled the ship up, in this way, to within four feet of her beams, the process of steeving commenced, by which a hundred hides are got into a place where one could not be forced by hand, and which presses the hides to the utmost, sometimes starting the beams of the ship, resembling in its effects the jack-screws which are used in stowing cotton. Each morning we went ashore, and beat and brought off as many hides as we could steeve in the course of the day, and after breakfast went down into the hold, where we remained at work until night. The whole length of the hold, from stem to stern, was floored off level, and we began with raising a pile in the after part, hard against the bulkhead of the run, and filling it up to the beams, crowding in as many as we could by hand and pushing in with oars; when a large "book" was made of from twenty-five to fifty hides, doubled at the backs, and put into one another, like the leaves of a book. An opening was then made between two hides in the pile, and the back of the outside hide of the book inserted. Two long, heavy spars called steeves, made of the strongest wood and sharpened off like a wedge at one end, were placed with their wedge ends into the inside of the hide which was the center of the book, and to the other end of each straps were fitted, into which large tackles were hooked, composed each of two huge purchase-blocks, one hooked to the strap on the end of the steeve, and the other into a dog, fastened into one of the beams, as far aft as it could be got. When this was arranged, and the ways greased upon which the book was to slide, the falls of the tackle were stretched forward, and all hands tallied on, and bowsed away until the book was well entered; when these tackles were nippered, straps and toggles clapped upon the falls, and two more luff tackles hooked on, with dogs, in the same manner; and thus, by luff upon luff, the power was multiplied, until into a pile in which one hide more could not be crowded by hand, a hundred or a hundred and fifty were often driven in by this complication of purchases. When the last luff was hooked on, all hands were called to the rope — cook, steward, and all — and ranging ourselves at the falls, one behind the other, sitting down on the hides, with our heads just even with the beams, we set taut upon the tackles, and striking up a song, and all lying back at the chorus, we bowsed the tackles home, and drove the large books chock in out of sight.

The sailors' songs for capstans and falls are of a peculiar kind, having a chorus at the end of each line. The burden is usually sung by one alone, and at the chorus all hands join in, — and the louder the noise the better. With us the chorus seemed almost to raise the decks of the ship, and might be heard at a great distance ashore. A song is as necessary to sailors as the drum and fife to a soldier. They can't pull in time or pull with a will without it. Many a time, when a thing goes heavy, with one fellow yo-ho-ing, a lively song, like "Heave, to the girls!" "Nancy, oh," "Jack Crosstree," etc., has put life and strength into every arm. We often found a great difference in the effect of the different songs in the driving in the hides. Two or three songs would be tried, one after the other, with no effect; — not an inch could be got upon the tackles — when a new song struck up seemed to hit the humor of the moment, and drove the tackles "two blocks" at once. "Heave round, hearty!" "Captain gone ashore!" and the like might do for common pulls, but on an emergency, when we wanted a heavy, "raise-the-dead" pull, which should start the beams of the ship, there was nothing like "Time for us to go!" "Round the corner," or "Hurrah! hurrah! my hearty bullies!"

This was the most lively part of our work. A little boating and beach work in the morning; then twenty or thirty men down in a close hold, where we were obliged to sit down and slide about, passing hides, and rowsing about the great steeves, tackles, and dogs, singing out at the falls, and seeing the ship filling up every day. The work was as hard as it could well be. There was not a moment's cessation from Monday morning till Saturday night, when we were generally beaten out, and glad to have a full night's rest, a wash and shift of clothes, and a quiet Sunday. During all this time we lived upon almost nothing but fresh beef: fried beef-steaks, three times a day — morning, noon, and night. At morning and night we had a quart of tea to each man; and an allowance of about a pound of hard bread a day; but our chief article of food was the beef. A mess, consisting of six men, had a large wooden kid piled up with beef-steaks, cut thick, and fried in fat, with the grease poured over them. Round this we sat, attacking it with our jack-knives and teeth, and with the appetite of young lions, and sent back an empty kid to the galley. Whatever theories may be started by sedentary men, certainly no men could have gone through more hard work and exposure for sixteen months in more perfect health, and without ailings and failings, than our ship's crew, let them have lived upon Hygeia's own baking and dressing.

Friday, April 15th. Arrived, brig *Pilgrim,* from the windward. It was a sad sight for her crew to see us getting ready to go off the coast, while they, who had been longer on the coast than the *Alert,* were condemned to another year's hard service. I spent an evening on board, and found them making the best of the matter, and determined to rough it out as they might; but my friend S— was determined to go home in the ship, if money or interest could bring it to pass. After considerable negotiating and working, he succeeded in per-suading my English friend, Tom Harris, for thirty dollars some clothes, and an intimation from Captain Faucon that he should want a second mate before the voyage was up to take his place in the brig as soon as she was ready to go up to windward.

The first opportunity I could get to speak to Captain Faucon, I asked him to step up to the oven and look at Hope, whom he knew well, having had him on board his vessel. He went to see him, but said that he had so little medicine and expected to be so long on the coast, that he could do nothing for him, but that Captain Arthur would take care of him when he came down in the *California,* which would be in a week or more. I had been to see Hope the first night after we got into San Diego this last time, and had frequently since spent the early part of a night in the oven. I hardly expected, when I left him to go to windward, to find him alive upon my return. I was not a little rejoiced, therefore, and relieved to see him decidedly better. The medicines were strong, and took hold and gave a check to the disorder which was destroying him; and, more than that, they had begun the work of exterminating it. I shall never forget the gratitude that he expressed. My medicines, however, were gone, and no more could be got from the ship, so that his life was left to hang upon the arrival of the *California.*

Sunday, April 24th. We had now been nearly seven weeks in San Diego, and had taken in the greater part of our cargo, and were looking out every day for the arrival of the *California,* which had our agent on board, when, this afternoon, some Kanakas, who had been over the hill for rabbits, came running down the path, singing out "Sail ho!" with all their might. Mr. H., our third mate, was ashore, and asking them particularly about the size of the sail, etc., and learning that it was *"Moku — Nui Moku,"* hailed our ship, and said that the *California* was on the other side of the point. Instantly all hands were turned up, the bow guns run out and loaded, the ensign and broad pennant set, the yards squared by lifts and braces, and everything got ready to make a good appearance. The instant she showed her nose round the point we began our salute. She came in under top-gallant-sails, clewed up and furled her sails in good order and came-to within good swinging distance of us. It being Sunday, and nothing to do, all hands were on the forecastle criticising the new-comer.

At night some of us got a boat and went on board, and found a large, roomy forecastle, and a crew of a dozen or fifteen men and boys sitting around on their chests, smoking and talking, and ready to give a welcome to any of our ship's company. It was just seven months since they left Boston, which seemed but yesterday to us.

Among her crew were two English man-of-war's men, so that, of course, we soon had music. They sang in the true sailor's style, and the rest of the crew joined in the choruses. They had many of the latest sailor songs which had not yet got about among our merchantmen, and which they were very choice of. Battle songs, drinking songs, boat songs, love songs, and everything else, they seemed to have a complete assortment of; and I was glad to find that "All in the Downs," "Poor Tom Bowling," "The Bay of Biscay," "List, ye landsmen!" and all those classical songs of the sea, still held their places.

The next day the *California* commenced unloading her cargo; and her boats' crews, in coming and going, sang their boat-songs, keeping time with their oars. This they did all day long for several days, until their hides were all discharged, when a gang of them were sent on board the *Alert* to help us steeve our hides. This was a windfall for us; for they had a set of new songs for the capstan and fall, and ours had got nearly worn out by six weeks' constant use. I have no doubt that this timely reinforcement of songs hastened our work several days.

Our cargo was now nearly all taken in; and my old friend, the *Pilgrim*, having completed her discharge, unmoored, to set sail the next morning on another long trip to windward. I was just thinking of her hard lot, and congratulating myself upon my escape from her, when I received a summons into the cabin. I went aft, and there found seated round the cabin table my own captain, Captain Faucon of the *Pilgrim*, and Mr. R—, the agent. Captain T— turned to me, and asked abruptly —

"Dana, do you want to go home in the ship?"

"Certainly, sir," said I; "I expect to go home in the ship."

"Then," said he, "you must get some one to

go in your place on board the *Pilgrim*."

I was so completely "taken aback" by this sudden intimation, that for a moment I could make no reply. As soon as I had got my wits about me I put on a bold front, and told him plainly that I had a letter in my chest informing me that he had been written to by the owners in Boston to bring me home in the ship, and moreover, that he had told me that I was to go in the ship.

To have this told him, and to be opposed in such a manner, was more than my lord paramount had been used to. He turned fiercely upon me, and tried to look me down and face me out of my statement; but finding that that wouldn't do, and that I was entering upon my defense in such a way as would show to the other two that he was in the wrong, he changed his ground, and pointed to the shipping papers of the *Pilgrim*, from which my name had never been erased, and said that there was my name — that I belonged to her — that he had an absolute discretionary power, and, in short, that I must be on board the *Pilgrim* by the next morning with my chest and hammock, or have some one ready to go in my place, and that he would not hear another word from me. I saw the necessity of being determined. I repeated what I had said, and insisted on my right to return in the ship.

But it would have all availed me nothing, had I been "some poor body," before this absolute, domineering tribunal. But they saw that I would not go unless *"vi et armis,"* and they knew that I had friends and interest enough at home to make them suffer for any injustice they might do me. It was probably this that turned the matter; for the captain changed his tone entirely, and asked me if in case any one went in my place I would give him the same sum that S— gave Harris to exchange with him. I told him that if any one was sent on board the brig I should pity him, and be willing to help him to that or almost any amount; but would not speak of it as an exchange.

"Very well," said he. "Go forward about your business, and send English Ben here to me."

I went forward with a light heart, but feeling as angry and as much contempt as I could well contain between my teeth. English Ben was sent aft, and in a few moments came forward, looking as though he had received his sentence to be hung. The captain had told him to get his things ready to go on board the brig the next morning; and that I would give him thirty dollars and a suit of clothes. The hands had "knocked off" for dinner, and were standing about the forecastle, when Ben came forward and told his story. I could see plainly that it made a great excitement, and that unless I explained the matter to them the feeling would be turned against me. "Oh, yes!" said the crew, "the captain has let you off because you are a gentleman's son, and have got friends, and know the owners; and taken Ben because he is poor, and has got nobody to say a word for him!" I knew that this was too true to be answered; but

I excused myself from any blame, and told them that I had a right to go home at all events. This pacified them a little, but Jack had got a notion that a poor lad was to be imposed upon, and did not distinguish very clearly; and though I knew that I was in no fault, and in fact had barely escaped the grossest injustice, yet I felt that my berth was getting to be a disagreeable one. But far stronger than any feeling for myself was the pity I felt for the poor lad. He had depended upon going home in the ship; and from Boston was going immediately to Liverpool to see his friends.

From this consideration I did my best to get some one to go voluntarily. I offered to give an order upon the owners in Boston for six months' wages, and also all the clothes, books, and other matters which I should not want upon the voyage home. When this offer was published in the ship, several, who would not have dreamed of going themselves, were busy in talking it up to others, who they thought might be tempted to accept it; and, at length, a harum-scarum lad, who did not care what country or ship he was in if he had clothes enough and money enough, came forward, and offered to go and "sling his hammock in the hooker." I signed an order for the sum upon the owners in Boston, gave him all the clothes I could spare, and sent him aft to the captain to let him know what had been done. The skipper accepted the exchange. At the same time he cashed the order, which was endorsed to him, and the next morning the lad went aboard the brig, apparently in good spirits.

The same boat brought on board S—, my friend, who, like me, was going back to his family and to the society which we had been born and brought up in. None on board the ship were more glad than ourselves to see the old brig standing round the point under full sail. As she passed abreast of us we all collected in the waist and gave her three loud hearty cheers, waving our hats in the air. Her crew sprang into the rigging and chains and answered us with three as loud, to which we, after the nautical custom, gave one in return. The crew flew aloft to loose the top-gallant sails and royals; the two captains waved their hands to one another; and in ten minutes we saw the last inch of her white canvas as she rounded the point.

Relieved as I was to see her well off (and I felt like one who had just sprung from an iron trap which was closing upon him), I had yet a feeling of regret at taking the last look at the old craft in which I had spent a year, and the first year, of my sailor's life — which had been my first home in the new world into which I had entered — and with which I had associated so many things — my first leaving home, my first crossing the equator, Cape Horn, Juan Fernandez, death at sea, and other things, serious and common. Yet, with all this, and the feeling I had for my old shipmates, condemned to another term of Californian life, the thought that we were done with it, and that one week more would see us on our way to Boston, was a cure for everything.

Friday, May 6th, completed the taking in of our cargo, and was a memorable day in our calendar. The time when we were to take in our last hide we had looked forward to for sixteen months as the first bright spot. When the last hide was stowed away and the hatches caulked down, the tarpaulins battened on to them, the long-boat hoisted in and secured, and the decks swept down for the night, the chief mate sprang upon the top of the long-boat, called all hands into the waist, and giving us a signal by swinging his cap over his head, we gave three long, loud cheers which came from the bottom of our hearts, and made the hills and valleys ring again. In a moment we heard three, in answer, from the *California*'s crew, who had seen us taking in our long-boat.

The last week we had been occupied in taking in a supply of wood and water for the passage home, and in bringing on board the spare spars, sails, etc. This being all done with, we gave one day to bending our sails; and at night every sail, from the courses to the sky-sails, was bent, and every studding-sail ready for setting.

Soon after the arrival of the *California*, I spoke to Captain Arthur about Hope; and as he had known him on the voyage before, he immediately went to see him, and gave him proper medicines; and under such care he began rapidly to recover. The Saturday night before our sailing I spent an hour in the oven, and took leave of my Kanaka friends; and, really, this was the only thing connected with leaving California which was in any way unpleasant. Hope shook me by the hand; said he should soon be well again, and ready to work for me when I came upon the coast next voyage as officer of the ship; and told me not to forget, when I became captain, how to be kind to the sick.

Sunday, May 8th. This promised to be our last day in California. All our spare spars were taken on board and lashed; our water-casks secured, and our live stock, consisting of four bullocks, a dozen sheep, a dozen or more pigs,, and three or four dozen of poultry, were all stowed away in their different quarters — the bullocks in the long-boat, the sheep in a pen on the fore hatch, and the pigs in a sty under the bows of the long-boat, and the poultry in their proper coop; and the jolly-boat was full of hay for the sheep and bullocks. Our unusually large cargo, together with the stores for a five months' voyage, brought the ship's channels down into the water. In addition to this, she had been steeved so thoroughly, and was so bound by the compression of her cargo, forced into her by so powerful machinery, that she was like a man in a strait jacket, and would be but a dull sailer until she had worked herself loose.

The *California* had finished discharging her cargo, and was to get under weigh at the same time with us. Having washed down decks and got our breakfast, the two vessels lay side by side, in complete readiness for sea, our tall spars reflected from the glassy surface of the river, which, since sunrise, had been unbroken by a ripple. At length a few whiffs came across the water, and by eleven o'clock the regular northwest wind set steadily in. All eyes were aft upon the captain, who was walking the deck, with every now and then a look to windward. He made a sign to the mate, who came forward, took his station deliberately between the knight-heads, cast a glance aloft, and called out, "All hands lay aloft and loose the sails!" We were half in the rigging before the order came. "All ready forward, sir!" "All ready the main!" "Cross-jack yards all ready, sir!" "Lay down, all hands but one on each yard!" The yard-arm and bunt gaskets were cast off; and each sail hung by the jigger, with one man standing by the tie to let it go.

At the same moment that we sprang aloft a dozen hands sprang into the rigging of the *California*, and in an instant were all over her yards; and her sails, too, were ready to be dropped at the word. In the meantime our bow-gun had been loaded and run out, and its discharge was to be the signal for dropping the sails. A cloud of smoke came out of her bows; the echoes of the gun rattled our farewell among the hills of California; and the two ships were covered from head to foot with their white canvas. For a few minutes all was uproar and apparent confusion: men flying about like monkeys in the rigging; ropes and blocks flying; orders given and answered; and the confused noises of men singing out at the ropes. The top-sails came to the mast-heads with "Cheerily, men!" and in a few minutes every sail was set, for the wind was light. The head sails were backed, the windlass came round "slip — slap" to the cry of the sailors. "Hove short, sir," said the mate; "up with him!" "Aye, aye, sir." A few hearty and long heaves and the anchor showed its head. "Hook cat!" The fall was stretched along the decks; all hands laid hold. "Hurrah, for the last time!" said the mate, and the anchor came to the cathead to the tune of "Time for us to go," with a loud chorus. The head yards were filled away, and our ship began to move through the water on her homeward-bound course.

The *California* had got under weigh at the same moment; and we sailed down the narrow bay abreast, and were just off the mouth, and finding ourselves gradually shooting ahead of her, were on the point of giving her three parting cheers, when suddenly we found ourselves stopped short, and the *California* ranging fast ahead of us. A bar stretches across the mouth of the harbor, with water enough to float common vessels; but being low in the water, and having kept well to leeward, as we were bound to the southward, we had stuck fast, while the *California*, being light, had floated over.

We kept all sail on, in the hope of forcing over, but failing in this we hove aback, and lay waiting for the tide, which was on the flood, to take us back into the channel. This was somewhat of a damper to us, and the captain looked not a little mortified and vexed. In a few minutes the force of the wind and the rising of the tide backed us into the stream, and we were on our way to our old anchoring-place, the tide setting swiftly up, and the ship barely manageable in the breeze. We came-to in our old berth, opposite the hide-house, whose inmates were not a little surprised to see us return.

In about half an hour, which was near high-water, the order was given to man the windlass, and again the anchor was catted. The *California* had come back on finding that we had returned, and was hove-to, waiting for us, off the point. This time we passed the bar safely, and were soon up with the *California*, who filled away, and kept us company. She seemed desirous of a trial of speed, and our captain accepted the challenge, although we were bound so taut with our cargo that we were no more fit for a race than a man in fetters. Being clear of the point the breeze became stiff, and the royal masts bent under our sails; but we would not take them in until we saw three boys spring aloft into the rigging of the *California*, when they were all furled at once, but with orders to stay aloft at the top-gallant mast-heads and loose them again at the word. The *California* was to windward of us, and had every advantage, yet, while the breeze was stiff, we held our own. As soon as it began to slacken she ranged a little ahead, and the order was given to loose the royals. In an instant the gaskets were off and the bunt dropped. "Sheet home the fore-royal! Weather sheet's home!" "Lee sheet's home!" "Hoist away, sir!" is bawled from aloft. "Overhaul your clewlines!" shouts the mate. "Aye, aye, sir! all clear!" "Taut leech! belay! Well the lee-brace; haul taut to windward" — and the royals are set. These brought us up again; but the wind continuing light the *California* set hers, and it was soon evident that she was walking away from us. Our captain then hailed and said that he should keep off to his course, adding, "She isn't the *Alert* now. If I had her in your trim she would have been out of sight by this time." This was good-naturedly answered from the *California*, and she braced sharp up, and stood close upon the wind up the coast; while we squared our yards and stood before the wind to the south-south-west.

As soon as we parted company with the *California* all hands were sent aloft to set the studding-sails. Booms were rigged out, tacks and halyards rove, sail after sail packed upon her, until every available inch of canvas was spread that we might not lose a breath of the fair wind. We could now see how much she was cramped and deadened by her cargo, for, with a good breeze on her quarter, and every stitch of canvas spread, we could not get more than six knots out of her. We had hardly patience with her, but the older sailors said, "Stand by; you'll see her work herself loose in a week or two, and then she'll walk up to Cape Horn like a race-horse."

When all sail had been set and the decks cleared up the *California* was a speck in the horizon, and the coast lay like a low cloud along the northeast. At sunset they were both out of sight, and we were once more upon the ocean, where sky and water meet.

CHAPTER XXVIII

The Voyage

At eight o'clock all hands were called aft and the watches set for the voyage. Some changes were made, but I was glad to find myself still in the larboard watch. Our crew was somewhat diminished, and we were short-handed for a voyage round Cape Horn in the dead of winter. Beside S— and myself, there were only five in the forecastle, who, together with four boys in the steerage, the sailmaker, carpenter, etc., composed the whole crew. In addition to this, we were only three or four days out, when the sailmaker, who was the oldest and best seaman on board, was taken with the palsy and was useless for the rest of the voyage. By the loss of the sailmaker our watch was reduced to five, of whom two were boys, who never steered but in fine weather, so that the other two and myself had to stand at the wheel four hours apiece out of every twenty-four; and the other watch had only four helmsmen. "Never mind, we're homeward bound!" was the answer to everything, and we should not have minded this were it not for the thought that we should be off Cape Horn in the very dead of winter.

During our watches below we overhauled our clothes, and made and mended everything for bad weather. Thus we took advantage of the warm sun and fine weather of the Pacific to prepare for its other face. In the forenoon watches below our forecastle looked like the workshop of what a sailor is — a Jack at all trades. Even the cobbler's art was not out of place.

There was one difficulty, however, which nothing that we could do would remedy, and that was the leaking of the forecastle, which made it very uncomfortable in bad weather, and rendered half the berths tenantless. The tightest ships, on a long voyage, from the constant strain which is upon the bowsprit, will leak more or less round the heel of the bowsprit and the bitts, which come down into the forecastle; but in addition to this, we had an unaccountable leak on the starboard bow, near the cathead, which drove us from the forward berths on that side, and indeed, when she was on the starboard tack, from all the forward berths. One of the after berths, too, leaked in very bad weather; so that in a ship which was in other respects as tight as a bottle, and brought her cargo to Boston perfectly dry, we had, after every effort made to prevent it in the way of caulking and leading, a forecastle with only three dry berths for seven of us. However, as there is never but one watch below at a time, by "turning in and out" we did pretty well; and there being in our watch but three of us who lived forward, we generally had a dry berth apiece in bad weather.

All this, however, was but anticipation. We were still in fine weather in the North Pacific, running down the northeast trades, which we took on the second day after leaving San Diego.

Sunday, May 15th, one week out, we were in lat. 14° 56′ N., long. 116° 14′ W., having gone, by reckoning, over thirteen hundred miles in seven days. In fact, ever since leaving San Diego, we had had a fair wind, and as much as we wanted of it. For seven days our lower and topmast studding-sails were set all the time, and our royals and top-gallant studding-sails whenever she could stagger under them. In this way we frequently made three degrees of latitude, besides something in longitude, in the course of twenty-four hours. Every wave that we threw aside brought us nearer home, and every day's observation at noon showed a progress which, if it continued, would in less than five months take us into Boston Bay. This is the pleasure of life at sea — fine weather, day after day, without interruption, fair wind and a plenty of it, and homeward bound. Every one was in good humor, things went right, and all was done with a will.

Every night, after the kids and pots were put away, and we had lighted our pipes and cigars at the galley, and gathered about the windlass, the first question was —

"Well, Tom, what was the latitude to-day?"

"Why, fourteen north, and she has been going

seven knots ever since."

"Well, this will bring us up to the line in five days?"

"Yes, but these trades won't last twenty-four hours longer," says an old salt; "I know that by the look of the clouds."

Then came all manner of calculations and conjectures as to the continuance of the wind, the weather under the line, the southeast trades, etc., and rough guesses as to the time the ship would be up with the Horn.

Rumors also of what had been said in the cabin, as usual, found their way forward. The steward had heard the captain say something about the Straits of Magellan; and the man at the wheel fancied he had heard him tell the "passenger" that, if he found the wind ahead and the weather very bad off the Cape, he should stick her off for New Holland, and come home round the Cape of Good Hope.

This passenger was no one else than a gentleman whom I had known in my better days, and the last person I should have expected to have seen on the coast of California — Professor N—, of Cambridge. I had left him quietly seated in the chair of botany and ornithology in Harvard University, and the next I saw of him was strolling about San Diego beach, in a sailor's pea-jacket, with a wide straw hat, and barefooted, picking up stones and shells. He had traveled overland to the Northwest Coast, and come down in a small vessel to Monterey. There he learned that there was a ship at the leeward, about to sail for Boston; and, taking passage in the *Pilgrim*, which was then at Monterey, he came slowly down, visiting the immediate ports, and examining the trees, plants, earths, birds, etc., and joined us at San Diego shortly before we sailed. I was often amused to see the sailors puzzled to know what to make of him, and to hear their conjectures about him and his business. They were as much puzzled as our old sailmaker was with the captain's instruments in the cabin. He said there were three: — the *chro*-nometer, the *chre*-nometer and the *the*-nometer. (Chronometer, barometer, and thermometer.) The *Pilgrim*'s crew christened Mr. N. "Old Curious," from his zeal for curiosities; and some of them said that he was crazy, and that his friends let him go about and amuse himself in this way. Why else a rich man should leave a Christian country and come to such a place as California, to pick up shells and stones, they could not understand.

Wednesday, May 18th. Lat. 9° 54′ N., long. 113° 7′ W. The northeast trades had now left us, and we had the usual variable winds which prevail near the line, together with some rain. So long as we were in these latitudes we had but little rest in our watch on deck at night; for, as the winds were light and variable, and we could not lose a breath, we were all the watch bracing the yards, and taking in and making sail, and "humbugging" with our flying kites. A little puff of wind on the larboard quarter, and then — "Larboard fore braces!" and studding-booms were rigged out, studding-sails set alow and aloft, the yards trimmed and jibs and spanker in; when it would come as calm as a duck-pond, and the man at the wheel stand with the palm of his hand up, feeling for the wind. "Keep her off a little!" "All aback forward, sir!" cries a man from the forecastle. Down go the braces again; in come the studding-sails all in a mess, which half an hour won't set right; yards braced sharp up, and she's on the starboard tack, close-hauled. The studding-sails must now be cleared away, and sent up in the tops and on the booms. By the time this is done, and you are looking out for a soft plank for a nap, — "Lay aft here, and square in the head yards!" and the studding-sails are all set again on the starboard side. So it goes until it is eight bells, — call the watch, — heave the log, — relieve the wheel, and go below the larboard watch.

Sunday, May 22d. Lat. 5° 14′ N., long. 166° 45′ W. We were now a fortnight out, and within five degrees of the line, to which two days of good breeze would take us; but we had for the most part what the sailors call "an Irishman's hurricane, — right up and down." This day it rained nearly all day, and being Sunday, and nothing to do, we stopped up the scuppers and filled the decks with rain-water, and bringing all on deck, had a grand wash fore and aft. When this was through we stripped to our drawers, and taking pieces of soap, with strips of canvas for towels, we turned to, and soaped, washed, and scrubbed one another down, to get off, as we said, the Californian dust; for the common wash in salt water, which is all that Jack can get, being on an allowance of fresh, had little efficacy, and was more for taste than utility. The next day, the sun rising, the ship was covered fore and aft with clothes of all sorts, hanging out to dry.

As we approached the line the wind became more easterly and the weather clearer, and in twenty days from San Diego, —

Saturday, May 28th, at about three P.M., with a fine breeze from the east-southeast, we crossed the equator. In twenty-four hours after crossing the line, which was very unusual, we took the regular southeast trades. With us they blew directly from the east-southeast, which was fortunate for us, for our course was south-by-west, and we could go thus one point free. For twelve days this breeze blew steadily, not varying a point, and just so fresh that we could carry our royals; and, during the whole time, we hardly started a brace. Such progress did we make, that at the end of seven days from the time we took the breeze, on

Sunday, June 5th, we were in lat. 19° 29′ S., and long. 118° 10′ W., having made twelve hundred miles in seven days. very nearly on a taut bowline. Our good ship had increased her rate of sailing more than one-third since leaving San Diego. The crew ceased complaining of her, and the officers hove the log every two hours with evident satisfaction. This was glorious sailing. Already we had sunk the north star and the Great Bear in the northern horizon, and all hands looked out sharp to the southward for the Magellan Clouds, which, each succeeding night, we expected to make. "The next time we see the north star," said one, "we shall be standing to the northward, the other side of the Horn."

These trades were the same that, in the passage out in the *Pilgrim*, lasted nearly all the way from Juan Fernandez to the line, blowing steadily on our starboard quarter for three weeks, without our starting a brace or even brailing down the sky-sails. Though we had now the same wind, and were in the same latitude with the *Pilgrim* on her passage out, yet we were nearly twelve hundred miles to the westward of her course; for the captain, depending upon the strong southwest winds which prevail in high southern latitudes during the winter months, took the full advantage of the trades and stood well to the westward, so far that we passed within about two hundred miles of Ducie's Island.

It was this weather and sailing that brought to my mind a little incident that occurred on board the *Pilgrim* while we were in the same latitude. We were going along at a great rate, dead before the wind, with studding-sails out on both sides, alow and aloft, on a dark night, just after midnight, and everything as still as the grave, except the washing of the water by the vessel's side; for, being before the wind, with a smooth sea, the little brig, covered with canvas, was doing great business with very little noise. The other watch was below, and all our watch, except myself and the man at the wheel, were asleep under the lee of the boat. The second mate, who came out before the mast, and was always very *thick* with me, had been holding a yarn with me, and just gone aft to his place on the quarter-deck, and I had resumed my usual walk to and from the windlass-end, when suddenly we heard a loud scream coming from ahead, apparently directly from under the bows. The darkness and complete stillness of the night, and the solitude of the ocean, gave to the sound a dreadful and almost supernatural effect. I stood perfectly still, and my heart beat quick. The sound woke up the rest of the watch, who stood looking at one another fearfully. "What in thunder is that?" said the second mate, coming slowly forward. The first thought I had was that it might be a boat, with the crew of some wrecked vessel, or perhaps the boat of some whale-ship out overnight, and we had run them down in the darkness. Another scream, but less loud than the first. This started us, and we ran forward and looked over the bows, and over the sides to leeward, but nothing was to be seen or heard. What was to be done? Call the captain, and heave the ship aback? Just at this moment, in crossing the forecastle one of the men saw a light below, and looking down into the scuttle, saw the watch all out of their berths, and afoul of one poor fellow, dragging him out of his berth, and shaking him to wake him out of a nightmare.

They had been waked out of their sleep, and as much alarmed at the scream as we were, and were hesitating whether to come on deck, when the second sound, coming directly from one of the berths, revealed the cause of the alarm. The fellow got a good shaking for the trouble he had given. We made a joke of the matter, and we could well laugh, for our minds were not a little relieved by its ridiculous termination.

We were now close upon the southern tropical line, and with so fine a breeze, were daily leaving the sun behind us, and drawing nearer to Cape Horn, for which it behoved us to make every preparation. Our rigging was all examined and overhauled and mended, or replaced with new where it was necessary, new and strong bobstays fitted in the place of the chain ones, which were worn out; and other preparations made, in good season, that the ropes might have time to stretch and become limber before we got into cold weather.

Sunday, June 12th. Lat. 26° 04′ S., long. 116° 31′ W. We had now lost the regular trades, and had the winds variable, principally from the westward, and kept on, in a southerly course, sailing very nearly upon a meridian, and at the end of the week —

Sunday, June 19th, were in lat. 34° 15′ S., and long. 116° 38′ W.

CHAPTER XXIX

Bad Prospects

There began now to be a decided change in the appearance of things. The days became shorter and shorter, the sun running lower in its course each day, and giving less and less heat, and the nights so cold as to prevent our sleeping on deck; the Magellan Clouds in sight of a clear night, the skies looking cold and angry; and at times a long, heavy, ugly sea, setting in from the southward, told us what we were coming to. Toward the middle of the week, the wind hauled to the southward, which brought us upon a taut bowline, made the ship meet, nearly head-on, the heavy swell which rolled from that direction; and there was something not at all encouraging in the manner in which she met it. Being so deep and heavy, she wanted the buoyancy which should have carried her over the seas, and she dropped heavily into them, the water washing over the decks; and every now and then, when an unusually large sea met her fairly upon the bows, she struck it with a sound as dead and heavy as that with which a sledge-hammer falls upon the pile, and took the whole of it in upon the forecastle and, rising, carried it aft in the scuppers, washing the rigging off the pins, and carrying along with it everything which was loose on deck. She had been acting in this way all of our forenoon watch below, as we could tell by the washing of the water over our heads. At eight bells the watch was called, and we came on deck, one hand going aft to take the wheel, and another going to the galley to get the *grub* for dinner. I stood on the forecastle, looking at the seas, which were rolling high, as far as the eye could reach, their tops white with foam, and the body of them of a deep indigo blue, reflecting the bright rays of the sun. Our ship rose slowly over a few of the largest of them, until one immense fellow came rolling on, threatening to cover her. I sprang upon the knight-heads, and seizing hold of the forestay with my hands, drew myself up upon it. My feet were just off the stanchion, when she struck fairly into the middle of the sea, and it washed her fore and aft, burying her in the water. As soon as she rose out of it I looked aft, and everything forward of the mainmast, except the longboat, which was griped and double-lashed down to the ringbolts, was swept off clear. The galley, the pigsty, the hen-coop, and a large sheep-pen which had been built upon the fore-hatch, were all gone, in the twinkling of an eye, leaving the deck as clean as a chin new reaped, and not a stick left to show where they had stood. In the scuppers lay the galley, bottom up, and a few boards floating about — the wreck of the sheep-pen — and half a dozen miserable sheep floating among them, wet through, and not a little frightened at the sudden change that had come upon them. As soon as the sea had washed by, all hands sprung up out of the forecastle to see what had become of the ship; and in a few moments the cook and old Bill crawled out from under the galley, where they had been lying in the water, nearly smothered, with the galley over them. When the water ran off, we picked the sheep up, and put them in the long-boat, got the galley back in its place, and set things a little to rights; but, had not our ship had uncommonly high bulwarks and rail, everything must have been washed overboard. "This will never do!" was what some said, and every one felt. Here we were, not yet within a thousand miles of the latitude of Cape Horn, and our decks swept by a sea not one-half so high as we must expect to find there. Some blamed the captain for loading his ship so deep, when he knew what he must expect; while others said that the wind was always southwest off the Cape in the winter, and that, running before it, we should not mind the seas so much. At two bells all hands were called and set to work, getting lashings upon everything on deck; and the captain talked of sending down the long top-gallant-mast; but as the sea went down toward night, and the wind hauled abeam, we left them standing, and set the studding-sails.

Through the rest of the week we continued on with a fair wind, gradually, as we got more to the southward, keeping a more easterly course, and bringing the wind on our larboard quarter, until —

Sunday, June 26th, when, having a fine, clear day, the captain got a lunar observation as well as his meridian altitude, which made us in lat. 47° 50′ S., long. 113° 49′ W.; Cape Horn bearing, according to my calculation, E.S.E. ½ E., and distant eighteen hundred miles.

Monday, June 27th. During the first part of this day the wind continued fair, and, as we were going before it, it did not feel very cold, so that we kept at work on deck in our common clothes and round jackets. Our watch had an afternoon watch below, for the first time since leaving San Diego, and having inquired of the third mate what the latitude was at noon, and made our usual guesses as to the time she would need to be up with the Horn, we turned in for a nap. We were sleeping away "at the rate of knots," when three knocks on the scuttle, and "All hands ahoy!" started us from our berths. What could be the matter? It did not appear to be blowing hard, and looking up through the scuttle, we could see that it was a clear day overhead; yet the watch were taking in sail. We thought there must be a sail in sight, and that we were about to heave-to and speak her; and were just congratulating ourselves upon it, when we heard the mate's voice on deck, singing out to the men who were taking in the studding-sails, and asking where his watch were. We did not wait for a second call, but tumbled up the ladder; and there, on the starboard bow, was a bank of mist, covering sea and sky, and driving directly for us. I had seen the same before, in my passage round in the *Pilgrim*, and knew what it meant, and that there was no time to be lost. We had nothing on but thin clothes, yet there was not a moment to spare, and at it we went.

The boys of the other watch were in the tops, taking in the top-gallant studding-sails, and the lower and topmast studding-sails were coming down by the run. It was nothing but "haul down and clew up," until we got all the studding-sails in, and the royals, flying-jib, and mizzen top-gallant-sail furled, and the ship kept off a little to take the squall. The fore and main top-gallant-sails were still on her, for the "old man" did not mean to be frightened in broad daylight, and was determined to carry sail till the last minute. We all stood waiting for its coming, when the first blast showed us that it was not to be trifled with. Rain, sleet, snow, and wind, enough to take our breath from us, and make the toughest turn his back to windward! The ship lay nearly over upon her beam-ends; the spars and rigging snapped and cracked, and her top-gallant-masts bent like whipsticks. "Clew up the fore and main top-gallant-sails!" shouted the captain, and all hands sprang to the clew-lines. The decks were standing nearly at an angle of forty-five degrees, and the ship going like a mad steed through the water, the whole forward part of her in a smother of foam. The halyards were let go, and the yard clewed down, and the sheets started, and, in a few minutes, the sails smothered and kept in by clewlines and buntlines. "Furl 'em, sir?" asked the mate. "Let go the topsail-halyards, fore and aft!" shouted the captain, in answer, at the top of his voice. Down came the topsail-yards, the reef-tackles were manned and hauled out, and we climbed up to windward, and sprang into the weather-rigging.

The violence of the wind, and the hail and sleet, driving nearly horizontally across the ocean, seemed actually to pin us down to the rigging. It was hard work making head against them. One after another we got out upon the yards. And here we had work to do, for our new sails, which had hardly been bent long enough to get the starch out of them, were as stiff as boards, and the new earings and reef-points, stiffened with the sleet, knotted like pieces of iron-wire. Having only our round jackets and straw hats on, we were soon wet through, and it was every moment growing colder. Our hands were soon stiffened and numbed, which, added to the stiffness of every-thing else, kept us a good while on the yard. After we had got the sail hauled upon the yard, we had to wait a long time for the weather earing to be passed; but there was no fault to be found, for French John was at the earing, and a better sailor never laid out on a yard; so we leaned over the yard, and beat our hands upon the sail, to keep them from freezing. At length the word came — "Haul out to leeward!" — and we seized the reef-points and hauled the band taut for the lee earing. "Taut band — knot away!" and we got the first reef fast, and were just going to lay down, when — "Two reefs — two reefs!" shouted the mate, and we had a second reef to take in the same way. When this was fast, we went down on deck, manned the halyards to leeward, nearly up to our knees in water, set the topsail, and then laid aloft on the main topsail-yard, and reefed that sail in the same manner. From the main topsail-yard, we went upon the main yard, and took a reef in the mainsail. No sooner had we got on deck than — "Lay aloft there, mizzen-topmen, and close-reef the mizzen topsail!" This called me; and being nearest to the rigging, I got first aloft, and out to the weather earing. English Ben was on the yard just after me, and took the lee earing, and the rest of our gang were soon on the yard, and began to fist the sail, when the mate considerately sent up the cook and steward to help us. I could now account for the long time it took to pass the other earings, for, to do my best, with a strong hand to help me at the dog's ear, I could not get it passed until I heard them beginning to complain in the bunt. One reef after another we took in, until the sail was close-reefed, when we went down and hoisted away at the halyards. In the meantime the jib had been furled and the staysail set, and the ship, under her reduced sail, had got more upright, and was under management; but the two top-gallant-sails were still hanging in the buntlines, and slatting and jerking as though they would take the masts out of her. We gave a look aloft, and knew that our work was not done yet; and sure enough, no sooner did the mate see that we were on deck, than — "Lay aloft there, four of you, and furl the top-gallant-sails!" Two of us went aloft, up the fore-rigging, and two more up the main, upon the top-gallant-yards. When we got upon the yard, my hands were so numb that I could not have cast off the knot of the gasket to have saved my life. We both lay over the yard for a few seconds, beating our hands upon the sail, until we started the blood into our fingers' ends, and at the next moment our hands were in a burning heat. We fisted the sail together, and after six or eight minutes of hard hauling and pulling and beating down the sail, which was as stiff as sheet iron, we managed to get it furled.

I had been on the look-out for a moment to jump below and clap on a thick jacket and south-wester; but when we got on deck we found that eight bells had been struck and the other watch gone below, so that there were two hours of dog watch for us and plenty of work to do. The decks were covered with snow, and there was a constant driving of sleet. In fact, Cape Horn had set in with good earnest. In the midst of all this, and before it became dark, we had all the studding-sails to make up and stow away, and then to lay aloft and rig in all the booms, fore and aft, and coil away the tacks, sheets, and halyards. It was after dark when we got through, and we were not a little pleased to hear four bells struck, which sent us below two hours, and gave us each a pot of hot tea with our cold beef and bread, and, what was better yet, a suit of thick, dry clothing fitted for the weather in place of our thin clothes, which were wet through and now frozen stiff.

This sudden turn, for which we were so little prepared, was as unacceptable to me as to any of the rest; for I had been troubled for several days with a slight toothache, and this cold weather, and wetting and freezing, were not the best things in the world for it. I soon found that it was getting strong hold and running over all parts of my face; and before the watch was out I went aft to the mate, who had charge of the medicine-chest, to get something for it. But the chest showed like the end of a long voyage, for there was nothing that would answer but a few drops of laudanum, which must be saved for any emergency; so I had only to bear the pain as well as I could.

When we went on deck at eight bells, it had stopped snowing, and there were a few stars out, but the clouds were still black and it was blowing a steady gale. The next four hours below were but little relief to me, for I lay awake in my berth the whole time, from the pain in my face, and heard every bell strike, and at four o'clock turned out with the watch, feeling little spirit for the hard duties of the day. There was, however, too much to do to allow time to think; for the gale of yesterday, and the heavy seas we met with a few days before, while we had yet ten degrees more southing to make, had convinced the captain that we had something before us which was not to be trifled with; and orders were given to send down the long top-gallant-masts. The top-gallant and royal yards were accordingly struck, the flying jib-boom rigged in, and the top-gallant-masts sent down on deck, and all lashed together by the side of the long-boat. The rigging was then sent down and coiled away below, and everything made snug aloft.

Friday, July 1st. We were now nearly up to the latitude of Cape Horn, and having over forty degrees of casting to make, we squared away the yards before a strong westerly gale, shook a reef out of the fore topsail, and stood on our way east-by-south, with the prospect of being up with the Cape in a week or ten days. As for myself, I had had no sleep for forty-eight hours; and the want of rest, together with constant wet and cold, had increased the swelling so that my face was nearly as large as two, and I found it impossible to get my mouth open wide enough to eat. In this state, the steward applied to the captain for some rice to boil for me, but he only got a —. "Tell him to eat salt junk and hard bread like the rest of them!" For this, of course, I was much obliged to him; and in truth it was just what I expected. However, I did not starve; for the mate, who was a man as well as a sailor, and had always been a good friend to me, smuggled a pan of rice into the galley, and told the cook to boil it for me, and not let the "old man" see it.

Saturday, July 2d. This day the sun rose fair, but it ran too low in the heavens to give any heat, or thaw out our sails and rigging; yet the sight of it was pleasant, and we had a steady "reef-topsail breeze" from the westward. The atmosphere, which had previously been clear and cold, for the last few hours grew damp, and had a disagreeable wet chilliness in it; and the man who came from the wheel said he heard the captain tell "the passenger" that the thermometer had fallen several degrees since morning, which he could not account for in any other way than by supposing that there must be ice near us, though such a thing had never been heard of in this latitude at this season of the year. At twelve o'clock we went below, and had just got through dinner, when the cook put his head down the scuttle, and told us to come on deck and see the finest sight that we had ever seen. "Where away, cook?" asked the first man who was up. "On the larboard bow." And there lay, floating in the ocean, several miles off, an immense irregular mass, its top and points covered with snow, and its center of a deep indigo color. This was an iceberg, and of the largest size. As far as the eye could reach the sea in every direction was of a deep blue color, the waves running high and fresh, and sparkling in the light; and in the midst lay this immense mountain-island, its cavities and valleys thrown into deep shade, and its points and pinnacles glittering in the sun. But no description can give any idea of the strangeness, splendor, and really, the sublimity of the sight. Its great size — for it must have been from two to three miles in circumference, and several hundred feet in height; its slow motion, as its base rose and sank in the water, and its high points nodded against the clouds; the dashing of the waves upon it, which, breaking high with foam, lined its base with a white crust; and the thundering sound of the cracking of the mass, and the breaking and tumbling down of huge pieces; together with its nearness and approach, which added a slight element of fear — all combined to give it the character of true sublimity. The main body of the mass was, as I have said, of an indigo color, its base crusted with frozen foam; and as it grew thin and transparent toward the edges and top, its color shaded off from a deep blue to the whiteness of snow. Toward morning a strong breeze sprang up, and we filled away and left it astern, and at daylight it was out of sight. The next day, which was

Sunday, July 3d, the breeze continued strong, the air exceedingly chilly, and the thermometer low. In the course of the day we saw several icebergs of different sizes, but none so near as the one which we saw the day before. Toward night the wind hauled to the southward, and headed us off our course a little and blew a tremendous gale; but this we did not mind, as there was no rain nor snow, and we were already under close sail.

Monday, July 4th. This was "Independence Day" in Boston. This, to be sure, was no place to keep the 4th of July. To keep ourselves warm and the ship out of ice was as much as we could do. Yet no one forgot the day; and many were the wishes, and conjectures, and comparisons, both serious and ludicrous, which were made among all hands. The sun shone bright as long as it was up, only that a scud of black clouds was ever and anon driving across it. At noon we were in lat. 54° 57′ S., and long. 85° 5′ W., having made a good deal of casting, but having lost in our latitude by the heading of the wind. Between daylight and dark we saw thirty-four ice-islands of various sizes, some no bigger than the hull of our vessel, and others apparently nearly as large as the one that we first saw; though as we went on the islands became smaller and more numerous; and at sundown of this day a man at the mast-head saw large fields of floating ice at the southeast. A constant look-out was necessary; for any of these pieces coming with the heave of the sea was large enough to have knocked a hole in the ship, and that would have been the end of us; for no boat could have lived in such a sea. To make our condition still worse, the wind came out due east just after sundown, and it blew a gale dead ahead, with hail and sleet and a thick fog, so that we could not see half the length of the ship. Our chief reliance, the prevailing westerly gales, was thus cut off; and here we were, nearly seven hundred miles to the westward of the Cape, with a gale dead from the eastward, and the weather so thick that we could not see the ice with which we were surrounded until it was directly under our bows. At four P.M. all hands were called and sent aloft, in a violent squall of hail and rain, to take in sail. Our ship was now all cased with ice, and the running rigging so stiff that we could hardly bend it so as to belay it, or, still worse, make a knot with it, and the sails nearly as stiff as sheet iron. One at a time we furled the courses, mizzen topsail, and fore topmast staysail, and close-reefed the fore and main topsails, and hove the ship to under the fore, with the main hauled up by the clewlines and buntlines, and ready to be sheeted home, if we found it necessary to make sail to get to windward of an island. A regular look-out was then set, and kept by each watch in turn, until the morning. The captain was on deck nearly the whole night, and kept the cook in the galley, with a roaring fire, to make coffee for him, which he took every few hours, and once or twice gave a little to his officers; but not a drop of anything was there for the crew. The captain, who sleeps all the daytime, and comes and goes at night as he chooses, can have his hot coffee at the galley while Jack, who has to stand through everything and work in wet and cold, can have nothing to wet his lips or warm his stomach. This was a "temperance ship"; and, like too many such ships, the temperance was all in the forecastle.

I never knew a sailor in my life who would not prefer a pot of hot coffee or chocolate in a cold night to all the rum afloat. They all say that rum only warms them for a time; yet if they can get nothing better, they will miss what they have lost.

On my passage round Cape Horn before, the vessel I was in was not under temperance articles, and grog was served out every middle and morning watch, and after every reefing of topsails; and though I had never drunk rum before, and never intend to again, I took my allowance then at the capstan, as the rest did, merely for the momentary warmth it gave the system, and the change in our feelings and aspect of our duties on the watch. At the same time, as I have stated, there was not a man on board who would not have pitched the rum to the dogs for a pot of coffee or chocolate, or even for our common beverage — "water bewitched and tea begrudged" as it was.

Eight hours of the night our watch was on deck; and during the whole of that time we kept a bright look-out. The chief mate was everywhere, and commanded the ship when the captain was below.

In the meantime the wet and cold had brought my face into such a state that I could neither eat nor sleep; and though I stood it out all night, yet when it became light I was in such a state that all hands told me I must go below, and lie by for a day or two, or I should be laid up for a long time, and perhaps have the lock-jaw. When the watch was changed I went into the steerage, and took off my hat and comforter, and showed my face to the mate, who told me to go below at once, and stay in my berth until the swelling went down, and gave the cook orders to make a poultice for me, and said he would speak to the captain.

I went below and turned in, covering myself over with blankets and jackets, and lay in my berth nearly twenty-four hours, half-asleep and half-awake, stupid from the dull pain. At the end of twenty-four hours the pain went down, and I had a long sleep, which brought me back to my proper state; yet my face was so swollen and tender that I was obliged to keep to my berth for two or three days longer. At the end of the third day, the ice was very thick; a complete fog-bank covered the ship. It blew a tremendous gale from the eastward, with sleet and snow, and there was every promise of a dangerous and fatiguing night. At dark, the captain called all hands aft, and told them that not a man was to leave the deck that night; that the ship was in the greatest danger; any cake of ice might knock a hole in her, or she might run on an island and go to pieces. The look-outs were then set, and every man was put in his station. When I heard what was the state of things, I began to put on my clothes to stand it out with the rest of them, when the mate came below, and looking at my face ordered me back to my berth, saying that if we went down we should all go down together, but if I went on deck I might lay myself up for life.

In obedience to the mate's orders, I went back to my berth; but a more miserable night I never wish to spend. Several times in the course of the night I got up, determined to go on deck, but the silence which showed that there was nothing do-ing, and the knowledge that I might make myself seriously ill for nothing, kept me back. It was a dreadful night for those on deck. A watch of eighteen hours, with wet and cold, and constant anxiety, nearly wore them out; and when they came below at nine o'clock for breakfast, they almost dropped asleep on their chests; and some of them were so stiff that they could with difficulty sit down. By a constant look-out, and a quick shifting of the helm, as the islands and pieces came in sight, the ship went clear of everything but a few small pieces, though daylight showed the ocean covered for miles. At daybreak it fell a dead calm, and with the sun the fog cleared a little, and a breeze sprang up from the westward, which soon grew into a gale. We had now a fair wind, daylight, and comparatively clear weather; yet to the surprise of everyone, the ship continued hove-to. Why does not he run? What is the captain about? was asked by everyone; and from questions it soon grew into complaints and murmurings. As hour followed hour, and the captain showed no sign of making sail, the crew became impatient; and there was a good deal of talking and consultation together on the forecastle. They had been beaten out with the exposure and hardship, and impatient to get out of it; and this unaccountable delay was more than they could bear in quietness in their excited and restless state. Some said that the captain was frightened, completely cowed by the dangers and difficulties that surrounded us — and was afraid to make sail; while others said that in his anxiety and suspense he had made a free use of brandy and opium, and was unfit for his duty. The carpenter, who was an intelligent man, and a thorough seaman, and had great influence with the crew, came down into the forecastle, and tried to induce the crew to go aft and ask the captain why he did not run, or request him, in the name of all hands, to make sail. This appeared to be a very reasonable request, and the crew agreed that if he did not make sail before noon, they would go aft. Noon came, and no sail was made. A consultation was held again, and it was proposed to take the ship from the captain and give the command of her to the mate. And so irritated and impatient had the crew become, that even this proposition, which was open mutiny, was entertained, and the carpenter went to his berth, leaving it tacitly understood that something serious would be done if things remained as they were many hours longer. When the carpenter left, we talked it all over, and I gave my advice strongly against it. S——, who soon came down, joined us, and we determined to have nothing to do with it. By these means, they were soon induced to give it up for the present, though they said they would not lie where they were much longer without knowing the reason.

The affair remained in this state until four o'clock, when an order came forward for all hands to come aft upon the quarter-deck. In about ten minutes they came forward again, and the whole affair had been blown. The carpenter, very prematurely, and without any authority from the crew, had sounded the mate as to whether he would take command of the ship, and intimated an intention to displace the captain, and the mate, as in duty bound, had told the whole to the captain, who immediately sent for all hands aft. Instead of violent measures, or, at least, an outbreak of quarter-deck bravado, threats, and abuse, which they had every reason to expect, a sense of common danger and common suffering seemed to have tamed his spirit, and begotten something like a humane fellow-feeling; for he received the crew in a manner quiet, and even almost kind. He told them what he had heard, and said that he did not believe that they would try to do any such thing as was intimated; that they had always been good men, obedient, and knew their duty, and he had no fault to find with them; and asked them what they had to complain of — said that no one could say that he was slow to carry sail (which was true enough), and that, as soon as he thought it was safe and proper, he should make sail.

For two days more the wind blew from the southward and eastward; or in the short intervals when it was fair, the ice was too thick to run; yet the weather was not so dreadfully bad, and the crew had watch and watch. I still remained in my berth, fast recovering, yet still not well enough to go safely on deck. And I should have been perfectly useless; for, from having eaten nothing for nearly a week except a little rice which I forced into my mouth the last day or two, I was as weak as an infant. Fortunately, I needed no help from any one, and no medicine; and if I had needed help, I don't know where I should have found it.

Accordingly, as soon as I could possibly go back to my duty, I put on my thick clothes and boots, and southwester, and made my appearance on deck. The ship was cased in ice — decks, sides, masts, yards, and rigging. Two close-reefed top-sails were all the sail she had on, and every sail and rope was frozen so stiff in its place that it seemed as though it would be impossible to start anything. The sun had come up brightly; the snow was swept off the decks, and ashes thrown upon them, so that we could walk. The wind was still ahead, and the whole ocean, to the eastward, covered with islands and field-ice. At four bells, the order was given to square away the yards; and the man who came from the helm said that the captain had kept her off to N.N.E. What could this mean? Soon it leaked out, and we found that we were running for the Straits of Magellan. Having made a fair wind of it, we were going off at a good rate, and leaving the thickest of the ice behind us. This, at least, was something.

Sunday, July 10th. Lat. 54° 10′, long. 79° 07′. This was our position at noon. The sun was out bright; the ice was all left behind, and things had quite a cheering appearance. After dinner, all hands were turned-to to get the anchors over the bows, bend on the chains, etc. The fish-tackle was got up, fish-davit rigged out; and, after two or three hours of hard and cold work, both the anchors were ready for instant use, a hawser coiled away upon the fore hatch, and the deep-sea leadline overhauled and got ready. Our spirits returned with having something to do; and when the tackle was manned to bowse the anchor home, notwithstanding the desolation of the scene, we struck up "Cheerily ho!" in full chorus. This pleased the mate, who rubbed his hands and cried out — "That's right, my boys! That sounds like the old crew!"

This preparation of the cable and anchors was for the passage of the straits; for, being very crooked, and with a variety of currents, it is necessary to come frequently to anchor. This was not by any means a pleasant prospect, for of all the work that a sailor is called upon to do in cold weather, there is none so bad as working the ground-tackle. The heavy chain cables to be hauled and pulled about decks with bare hands; wet hawsers, slip-ropes, and buoy-ropes to be hauled aboard, dripping in water; clearing hawse under the bows; getting under weigh and coming-to, at all hours of the night and day; and a constant look-out for rocks and sands and turns of tides; — these are some of the disagreeables of such a navigation to a common sailor. The next day, when we must have been near the Cape of Pillars, which is the southwest point of the mouth of the straits, a gale set in from the eastward, with a heavy fog, so that we could not see half of the ship's length ahead. This, of course, put an end to the project for the present; for a thick fog, and a gale blowing dead ahead, are not the most favorable circumstances for the passage of difficult and dangerous straits; so we braced up on the larboard tack, put the ship's head due south, and stuck her off for Cape Horn again.

CHAPTER XXX

Doubling Cape Horn

In our first attempt to double the Cape, when we came up to the latitude of it, we were nearly seventeen hundred miles to the westward; but, in running for the Straits of Magellan, we stood so far to the eastward, that we made our second attempt at a distance of not more than four or five hundred miles; and we had great hopes, by this means, to run clear of the ice; thinking that the easterly gales, which had prevailed for a long time, would have driven it to the westward. With the wind about two points free, we made great way toward the southward; and, almost every watch, when we came on deck, the air seemed to grow colder, and the sea to run higher. Still we saw no ice, and had great hopes of going clear of it altogether, when, one afternoon, about three o'clock, "All hands!" was called in a loud and fearful voice. We sprang out of our berths and hurried upon deck. The loud, sharp voice of the captain was heard giving orders, as though for life or death, and we ran aft to the braces, not waiting to look ahead, for not a moment was to be lost. The helm was hard up, the after yards shaking, and the ship in the act of wearing. Slowly, with the stiff ropes and iced rigging, we swung the yards round, everything coming hard. The ship wore round fairly, the yards were steadied, and we stood off on the other tack, leaving behind us, directly under our larboard quarter, a large ice island, peering out of the mist, and reaching high above our tops, while astern, and on either side of the island, large tracts of field-ice were dimly seen, heaving and rolling in the sea. We were now safe, and standing to the northward; but, in a few minutes more, had it not been for the sharp look-out of the watch, we should have been fairly upon the ice, and left our ship's old bones adrift in the Southern Ocean. After standing to the northward a few hours, we wore ship, and the wind having hauled, we stood to the southward and eastward. During our watch on deck, which was from twelve to four, the wind came out ahead, with a pelting storm of hail and sleet, and we lay hove-to, under a close-reefed fore topsail, the whole watch. During the next watch it fell calm, with a drenching rain, until daybreak, when the wind came out to the westward, and the weather cleared up, and showed us the whole ocean, in the course which we should have steered had it not been for the head wind and calm, completely blocked up with ice. Here then our progress was stopped; and we wore ship, and once more stood to the northward and eastward, not for the Straits of Magellan, but to make another attempt to double the Cape, still farther to the eastward.

With a fair wind we soon ran clear of the field-ice, and by noon had only the stray islands floating far and near upon the ocean. The sun was out bright, the sea of a deep blue, fringed with the white foam of the waves, which ran high before a strong southwester; our solitary ship tore on through the water as though glad to be out of her confinement; and the ice islands lay scattered upon the ocean here and there, of various sizes and shapes, reflecting the bright rays of the sun, and drifting slowly northward before the gale. It was a contrast to much that we had lately seen, and a spectacle not only of beauty, but of life.

From a northeast course we gradually hauled to the eastward; and after sailing about two hundred miles, which brought us as near to the western coast of Terra del Fuego as was safe, and having lost sight of the ice altogether, for the third time we put the ship's head to the southward, to try the passage of the Cape. The weather continued clear and cold, and we were fast getting up with the latitude of the Cape, with a prospect of soon being round. One fine afternoon, a man who had gone into the fore-top to shift the rolling tackles sung out, at the top of his voice, — "Sail ho!" Any one who has traversed the length of a whole ocean alone, can imagine what an excitement such an announcement produced on board. Beside the pleasure of seeing a ship and human beings in so desolate a place, it was important for us to speak a vessel to learn whether there was ice to the eastward, and to ascertain the longitude; for we had no chronometer, and had been drifting about so long that we had nearly lost our reckoning. For these various reasons, the excitement in our little community was running high, when the man aloft sung out — "Another sail, large on the weather bow!" At length the man in the top hailed, and said he believed it was land after all. "Land in your eye!" said the mate, who was looking through the telescope; "they are ice islands"; and a few moments showed the mate to be right, and instead of what we most wished to see, we had what we most dreaded. We soon, however, left these astern, and at sundown the horizon was clear in all directions.

Having a fine wind, we were soon up with and passed the latitude of the Cape; and having stood far enough to the southward to give it a wide berth, we began to stand to the eastward, with a good prospect of being round, and steering to the northward on the other side in a very few days. But not four hours had we been standing on in this course before it fell dead calm; and in an hour more we lay hove-to under a close-reefed main topsail, drifting bodily off to leeward before the fiercest storm that we had yet felt, blowing dead ahead from the eastward. It seemed as though the genius of the place had been roused at finding that we had nearly slipped through his fingers, and had come down upon us with tenfold fury.

For eight days we lay drifting about in this manner. Sometimes — generally toward noon — it fell calm; once or twice a round copper ball showed itself for a few moments in the place where the sun ought to have been; and a puff or two came from the westward, giving some hope that a fair wind had come at last. During the first two days we made sail for these puffs, shaking the reefs out of the topsails, and boarding the tacks of the courses; but finding that it only made work for us when the gale set in again, it was soon given up, and we lay-to under our close-reefs. We had less snow and hail than when we were farther to the westward; but we had an abundance of what is worse to a sailor in cold weather — drenching rain. Snow is blinding, and very bad when coming upon a coast, but for genuine discomfort give me rain with freezing weather. A snowstorm is exciting, and it does not wet through the clothes (which is important to a sailor), but a constant rain there is no escaping from. It wets to the skin, and makes all protection vain. We had long ago run through all our dry clothes, and as sailors have no other way of drying them than by the sun, we had nothing to do but to put on those which were the least wet. At the end of each watch, when we came below, we took off our clothes and wrung them out, two taking hold of a pair of trousers, one at each end, and jackets in the same way. Stockings, mittens, and all were wrung out also, and then hung up to drain and chafe dry against the bulkheads. Then, feeling all our clothes, we picked out those which were the least wet, and put them on, so as to be ready for a call, and turned in, covered ourselves up with blankets, and slept until three knocks on the scuttle, and the dismal sound of "All star-bowlines ahoy! Eight bells, there below! Do you hear the news?" drawled out from on deck, and the sulky answer of "Aye, aye!" from below, sent us up again.

On deck all was as dark as pitch, and either a dead calm with the rain pouring steadily down, or more generally a violent gale dead ahead, with rain pelting horizontally, and occasional variations of hail and sleet; and constantly wet feet — for boots could not be wrung out like drawers, and no composition could stand the constant soaking. Few words were spoken between the watches as they shifted, the wheel was relieved, the mate took his place on the quarter-deck, the look-outs in the bows, and each man had his narrow space to swing himself forward and back in, from one belaying-pin to another — for the decks were too slippery with ice and water to allow of much walking. The bells seemed to be an hour or two apart, instead of half an hour, and an age to elapse before the welcome sound of eight bells.

I commenced a deliberate system of time-killing, which united some profit with a cheering up of the heavy hours. As soon as I came on deck, and took my place and regular walk, I began with repeating over to myself a string of matters which I had in my memory, in regular order. In this way, with an occasional break by relieving the wheel, heaving the log, and going to the scuttlebutt for a drink of water, the longest watch was passed away; and I was so regular in my silent recitations, that if there was no interruption by ship's duty, I could tell very nearly the number of bells by my progress.

Our watches below were no more varied than the watch on deck. All washing, sewing, and reading was given up, and we did nothing but eat, sleep, and stand our watch, leading what might be called a Cape-Horn life. At every watch, when we came below, before turning-in, the bread-barge and beef-kid were overhauled. Each man drank his quart of hot tea night and morning: and glad enough we were to get it, for no nectar and ambrosia were sweeter to the lazy immortals than was a pot of hot tea, a hard biscuit, and a slice of cold salt beef, to us, after a watch on deck.

After about eight days of constant easterly gales, the wind hauled occasionally a little to the southward, and blew hard, which, as we were well to the southward, allowed us to brace in a little and stand on, under all the sail we could carry. These turns lasted but a short while, and sooner or later it set in again from the old quarter. One night, after one of these shifts of the wind, and when all hands had been up a great part of the time, our watch was left on deck, with the main-sail hanging in the buntlines, ready to be set, if necessary. It came on to blow worse and worse, with hail and snow beating like so many furies upon the ship. The mainsail was blowing and slatting with a noise like thunder, when the captain came on deck and ordered it to be furled. The mate was about to call all hands, when the captain stopped him, and said that the men would be beaten out if they were called up so often; that as our watch must stay on deck, it might as well be doing that as anything else. Accordingly we went upon the yard; and never shall I forget that piece of work. Our watch had been so reduced by sickness, that, with one man at the wheel, we had only the third mate and three beside myself to go aloft; so that, at most, we could only attempt to furl one yard-arm at a time. We manned the weather yard-arm, and set to work to make a furl of it. Our lower masts being short, and our yards very square, the sail had a head of nearly fifty feet, and a short leach made still shorter by the deep reef which was in it, which brought the clew away out on the quarters of the yard, and made a bunt nearly as square as the mizzen royal-yard. Besides this difficulty, the yard over which we lay was cased with ice, the gaskets and rope of the foot and leach of the sail as stiff and hard as a piece of suction-hose, and the sail itself about as pliable as though it had been made of sheets of sheathing-copper. It blew a perfect hurricane, with alternate blasts of snow, hail, and rain. Several times we got the sail upon the yard, but it blew away again before we could secure it. Frequently we were obliged to leave off altogether, and take to beating our hands upon the sail, to keep them from freezing.

After some time we got the weather side stowed

after a fashion, and went over to leeward for another trial. This was still worse, for the body of the sail had been blown over to leeward; and as the yard was a cock-bill by the lying over of the vessel, we had to light it all up to windward. When the yard-arms were furled, the bunt was all adrift again, which made more work for us. We got all secure at last; but we had been nearly an hour and a half upon the yard, and it seemed an age. We were glad enough to get on deck, and still more to go below.

During the greater part of the next two days the wind was pretty steady from the southward. We had evidently made great progress, and had good hope of being soon up with the Cape, if we were not there already. We could put but little confidence in our reckoning, as there had been no opportunities for an observation, and we had drifted too much to allow of our dead reckoning being anywhere near the mark. If it would clear off enough to give a chance for an observation, or if we could make land, we should know where we were; and upon these, and the chances of falling in with a sail from the eastward, we depended almost entirely.

Friday, July 22d. This day we had a steady gale from the southward, and stood on under close sail, with the yards eased a little by the weather braces, the clouds lifting a little, and showing signs of breaking away. In the afternoon I was below with the third mate, and two others, filling the bread-locker in the steerage from the casks, when a bright gleam of sunshine broke out and shone down the companion-way and through the skylight, lighting up everything below, and sending a warm glow through the heart of every one. It was a sight we had not seen for weeks. Even the roughest and hardest face acknowledged its influence. Just at that moment we heard a loud shout from all parts of the deck, and the mate called out down the companion-way to the captain, who was sitting in the cabin. What he said we could not distinguish; but the captain kicked over his chair, and was on deck at one jump. We could not tell what it was; and, anxious as we were to know, the discipline of the ship would not allow of our leaving our places. Yet, as we were not called, we knew there was no danger. We hurried to get through with our job, when seeing the steward's black face peering out of the pantry, Mr. H— hailed him, to know what was the matter. "Lan' o, to be sure, sir! De cap'em say 'im Cape Horn!"

This gave us a new start, and we were soon through our work, and on deck; and there lay the land, fair upon the larboard beam, and slowly edging away upon the quarter.

The land was the island of Staten Land, just to the eastward of Cape Horn; and a more desolate-looking spot I never wish to set eyes upon. Yet, dismal as it was, it was a pleasant sight to us; not only as being the first land we had seen, but because it told us that we had passed the Cape, were in the Atlantic, and that, with twenty-four hours of this breeze, might bid defiance to the Southern Ocean. It told us, too, our latitude and longitude better than any observation.

We left the land gradually astern; and at sun-down had the Atlantic Ocean clear before us.

CHAPTER XXXI

Sailing Northward

It is usual in voyages round the Cape from the Pacific to keep to the eastward of the Falkland Islands, but as it had now set in a strong, steady, and clear southwester, with every prospect of its lasting, and we had had enough of high latitudes, the captain determined to stand immediately to the northward, running inside the Falkland Islands. Accordingly, when the wheel was relieved at eight o'clock, the order was given to keep her due north, and all hands were turned up to square away the yards and make sail. The wind was now due southwest, and blowing a gale to which a vessel close-hauled could have shown no more than a single close-reefed sail, but as we were going before it, we could carry on. Accordingly, hands were sent aloft, and a reef shaken out of the topsails, and the reefed foresail set. When we came to masthead the topsail-yards, with all hands at the halyards, we struck up "Cheerily, men," with a chorus which might have been heard half-way to Staten Land. Under her increased sail, the ship drove on through the water. Yet she could bear it well, and the captain sang out from the quarter-deck, "Another reef out of that fore topsail!" Two hands sprang aloft; the frozen reef-points and earings were cast adrift, the halyards manned, and the sail gave out her increased canvas to the gale. It was as much as she could well carry, and with a heavy sea astern, it took two men at the wheel to steer her. Still everything held.

The captain walked the deck at a rapid stride, looked aloft at the sails, and then to windward; the mate stood in the gangway rubbing his hands, and talking aloud to the ship — "Hurrah, old bucket! the Boston girls have got hold of the tow-rope!" and the like; and we were on the forecastle, looking to see how the spars stood it, and guessing the rate at which she was going, when the captain called out — "Mr. Brown, get up the top-mast studding-sail! what she can't carry she may drag!" The mate looked a moment; but he would let no one be before him in daring. He sprang forward — "Hurrah, men! rig out the top-mast studding-sail boom! lay aloft, and I'll send the rigging up to you!"

We sprang aloft into the top; lowered a girt-line down, by which we hauled up the rigging; rove the tacks and halyards; ran out the boom and lashed it fast; and sent down the lower halyards as a preventer. It was a clear starlight night, cold and blowing; but everybody worked with a will.

While we were aloft the sail had been got out, bent to the yard, reefed, and ready for hoisting. Waiting for a good opportunity, the halyards were manned and the yard hoisted fairly up to the block; but when the mate came to shake the catspaw out of the downhaul, and we began to boom-end the sail, it shook the ship to her center. The boom buckled up and bent like a whip-stick, and we looked every moment to see something go; but, being of the short, tough, upland spruce, it bent like whalebone, and nothing could break it. The strength of all hands soon brought the tack to the boom-end, and the sheet was trimmed down, and the preventer and the weather-brace hauled taut to take off the strain. Every rope-yarn seemed stretched to the utmost and every thread of canvas; and with this sail added to her the ship sprang through the water like a thing possessed. The sail being nearly all forward, it lifted her out of the water, and she seemed actually to jump from sea to sea.

Finding that she would bear the sail the hands were sent below and our watch remained on deck. Two men at the wheel had as much as they could do to keep her within three points of her course, for she steered as wild as a young colt. At four bells we hove the log, and she was going eleven knots fairly; and had it not been for the sea from aft which sent the log-ship home, and threw her continually off her course, the log would have shown her to have been going much faster. I went to the wheel with a young fellow from the Kennebec, who was a good helmsman; and for two hours we had our hands full. A few minutes showed us that our monkey-jackets must come off; and cold as it was, we stood in our shirt-sleeves, in a perspiration, and were glad enough to have it eight bells and the wheel relieved.

At four o'clock we were called again. The same sail was still on the vessel, and the gale, if there was any change, had increased a little. No attempt was made to take the studding-sail in, and, indeed, it was too late now. If we had started anything toward taking it in, either tack or halyards, it would have blown to pieces and carried something away with it. For more than an hour she was driven on at such a rate that she seemed actually to crowd the sea into a heap before her; and the water poured over the sprit-sail yard as it would over a dam. Toward daybreak the gale abated a little, and she was just beginning to go more easily along, relieved of the pressure, when Mr. Brown determined to give her no respite, and depending upon the wind's subsiding as the sun rose told us to get along the lower studding-sail. This was an immense sail, and held wind enough to last a Dutchman a week — hove-to. It was soon ready, the boom topped up, preventer guys rove, and the idlers called up to man the halyards; yet such was still the force of the gale that we were nearly an hour setting the sail. No sooner was it set than the ship tore on again like one that was mad, and began to steer as wild as a hawk. The men at the wheel were puffing and blowing at their work, and the helm was going hard up and hard down constantly. Add to this, the gale did not lessen as the day came on, but the sun rose in clouds. A sudden lurch threw the man from the weather wheel across the deck and against the side. The mate sprang to the wheel, and the man, regaining his feet, seized the spokes, and they hove the wheel up just in time to save her from broaching-to, though nearly half the studding-sail went under water; and as she came-to, the boom stood up at an angle of forty-five degrees. She had evidently more on her than she could bear; yet it was in vain to try to take it in — the clewline was not strong enough; and they were thinking of cutting away when another wide yaw and a come-to snapped the guys, and the swinging boom came in with a crash against the lower rigging. The outhaul block gave way, and the topmast studding-sail boom bent in a manner which I never before supposed a stick could bend. The clewline gave way at the first pull; the cleat to which the halyards were belayed was wrenched off, and the sail blew round the sprit-sail yard and head guys, which gave us a bad job to get it in.

Sunday, July 24th, we were in latitude 50° 27′ S., longitude 62° 13′ W., having made four degrees of latitude in the last twenty-four hours. Being now to the northward of the Falkland Islands, the ship was kept off, northeast, for the equator; and with her head for the equator, and Cape Horn over her taffrail, she went gloriously on. Everyone was in the highest spirits, and the ship seemed as glad as any of us at getting out of her confinement. Each day the sun rose higher in the horizon, and the nights grew shorter; and at coming on deck each morning there was a sensible change in the temperature. As we left the gale behind us the reefs were shaken out of the topsails and sail made as fast as she could bear it; and every time all hands were sent to the halyards a song was called for, and we hoisted away with a will.

Sail after sail was added as we drew into fine weather; and in one week after leaving Cape Horn the long top-gallant-masts were got up, top-gallant and royal yards crossed, and the ship restored to her fair proportions.

Sunday, July 31st. At noon we were in lat. 36° 41′ S., long. 38° 08′ W., having traversed the distance of two thousand miles, allowing for changes of course, in nine days.

Soon after eight o'clock the appearance of the ship gave evidence that this was the first Sunday we had yet had in fine weather. As the sun came up clear, with the promise of a fair, warm day, and, as usual on Sunday, there was no work going on, all hands turned-to upon clearing out the forecastle. The wet and soiled clothes which had accumulated there during the past month were brought up on deck; the chests moved; brooms, buckets of water, swabs, scrubbing-brushes and scrapers carried down and applied until the forecastle floor was as white as chalk and everything neat and in order. The bedding from the berths was then spread on deck and dried and aired; the deck-tub filled with water, and a grand washing begun of all the clothes which were brought up. After we had done with our clothes we began upon our own persons. A little fresh water, which we had saved from our allowance, was put in buckets, and with soap and towels, we had what sailors call a fresh-water wash. After this came shaving and combing and brushing; and when, having spent the first part of the day in this way, we sat down on the forecastle, in the afternoon, with clean duck trousers and shirts on, washed, shaved, and combed, and looking a dozen shades lighter for it, reading, sewing, and talking at our ease, with a clear sky and warm sun over our heads, a steady breeze over the larboard quarter, studding-sails out alow and aloft, and all the flying kites abroad — we felt that we had got back into the pleasantest part of a sailor's life.

One night, while we were in these tropics, I went out to the end of the flying jib-boom upon some duty, and having finished it turned round and lay over the boom for a long time, admiring the beauty of the sight before me. Being so far out from the deck I could look at the ship as at a separate vessel, and there rose up from the water, supported only by the small black hull, a pyramid of canvas, spreading out far beyond the hull, and towering up almost, as it seemed in the indistinct night air, to the clouds. The sea was as still as an inland lake; the light trade-wind was gently and steadily breathing from astern; there was no sound but the rippling of the water under the stem; and the sails were spread out wide and high — the two lower studding-sails stretching, on each side, far beyond the deck; the top-mast studding-sails, like wings to the topsails; the top-gallant studding-sails spreading fearlessly out above them; still higher, the two royal studding-sails, looking like two kites flying from the same string; and, highest of all, the little skysail, the apex of the pyramid, seeming actually to touch the stars and to be out of reach of human hand. Not a ripple upon the surface of the canvas, not even a quivering of the extreme edges of the sail, so perfectly were they distended by the breeze.

The fine weather brought work with it, as the ship was to be put in order for coming into port. The new, strong sails, which we had up off Cape Horn, were to be sent down, and the old set, which were still serviceable in fine weather, to be bent in their place; all the rigging to be set up, fore and aft; the masts stayed; the standing rigging to be tarred down; lower and top-mast rigging rattled down, fore and aft; the ship scraped, inside and out, and painted; decks varnished; new and neat knots, seizings, and coverings to be fitted; and every part put in order, to look well to the owner's eye on coming into Boston.

In merchant vessels the captain gives his orders, as to the ship's work, to the mate, in a general way, and leaves the execution of them, with the particular ordering to him. This has become so fixed a custom that it is like a law, and is never infringed upon by a wise master unless his mate is no seaman. This, however, could not be said of our chief mate; and he was very jealous of any encroachment upon the borders of his authority.

On Monday morning the captain told him to stay the fore top-mast plumb. He accordingly came forward, turned all hands to, with tackles on the stays and backstays, coming up with the seizings, hauling here, belaying there, and full of business, standing between the knight-heads to sight the mast, when the captain came forward, and also began to give orders. This made confusion, and the mate, finding that he was all aback, left his place and went aft, saying to the captain:

"If you come forward, sir, I'll go aft. One is enough on the forecastle."

This produced a reply and another fierce answer; and the words flew, fists were doubled up, and things looked threateningly.

"I'm master of this ship."

"Yes, sir, and I'm mate of her, and know my place! My place is forward, and yours is aft!"

"My place is where I choose! I command the *whole* ship and you are mate only so long as I choose!"

"Say the word, Captain T., and I'm done! I can do a man's work aboard! I didn't come through the cabin windows! If I'm not mate I can be man."

This was all fun for us, who stood by, winking at each other, and enjoying the contest between the higher powers. The captain took the mate aft; and they had a long talk, which ended in the mate's returning to his duty. The captain had broken through a custom, which is a part of the common law of a ship, and without reason, for he knew that his mate was a sailor, and the mate was excusable for being angry. Yet he was wrong, and the captain right.

CHAPTER XXXII

A Tropical Thunderstorm

The same day I met with one of those narrow escapes which are so often happening in a sailor's life. I had been aloft nearly all the afternoon at work, standing for as much as an hour on the fore top-gallant-yard, which was hoisted up, and hung only by the tie, when, having got through my work, laid hold deliberately of the top-gallant rigging, took one foot from the yard, and was just lifting the other when the tie parted and down the yard fell. I was safe, by my hold upon the rigging, but it made my heart beat quick.

Had the tie parted one instant sooner, I should inevitably have been thrown ninety or a hundred feet overboard, or, what is worse, upon the deck. An escape is always a joke on board ship. A man would be ridiculed who should make a serious matter of it. One of our boys, when off Cape Horn, reefing topsails of a dark night, and when there were no boats to be lowered away, and where, if a man fell overboard, he must be left behind, lost his hold of the reef-point, slipped from the foot-rope, and would have been in the water in a moment, when the man who was next to him on the yard caught him by the collar of his jacket and hauled him up upon the yard, with, "Hold on another time, you young monkey," and that was all that was heard about it.

Sunday, August 7th. Lat. 25° 59′ S., long. 27° 0′ W. Spoke the English barque stark *Mary Catherine* from Bahia, bound to Calcutta. This was the first sail we had fallen in with. She was an old, damaged-looking craft, with a high poop and top-gallant forecastle, and sawed off square, stem and stern, like a true English "tea-waggon," and with a run like a sugar-box. She had studding-sails out alow and aloft with a light but steady breeze; and her captain said he could not get more than four knots out of her. We were going six on an easy bowline.

The next day we passed a large corvette-built ship, close upon the wind, with royals and skysails set fore and aft, under English colors. She had men in her tops, and black mast-heads, heavily sparred, with sails cut to a *t*, and other marks of a man-of-war. She sailed well, and presented a fine appearance, the proud, aristocratic banner of St. George — the cross on a blood-red field — waving from the mizzen.

Friday, August 12th. At daylight made the island of Trinidad, situated in lat. 20° 28′ S., long. 29° 08′ W. It was a beautiful day, the sea hardly ruffled by the light trades, and the island looking like a small blue mound rising from a field of glass.

Thursday, August 18th. At three P.M. made the island of Fernando Noronha, lying in lat. 3° 55′

S., long. 32° 35′ W.; and between twelve o'clock Friday night and one o'clock Saturday morning crossed the equator, in long. 35° W., having been twenty-seven days from Staten Land — a distance by the course we had made of more than four thousand miles.

For a week or ten days after we had the usual variety of headwinds, and fair winds; at one time braced sharp upon the wind, with a taut bowline, and in an hour after slipping quietly along with a light breeze over the taffrail, and studding-sails out on both sides, until we fell in with the northeast trade-winds, which we did on the afternoon of

Sunday, August 28th, in lat. 12° N. The trade-wind clouds had been in sight for a day or two previously. The light southerly breeze, which had been blowing languidly during the first part of the day, died away toward noon, and in its place came puffs from the northeast, which caused us to take our studding-sails in and brace up; and in a couple of hours more we were bowling gloriously along, with the cool, steady, northeasterly trades freshening up the sea, and giving us as much as we could carry our royals to.

Sunday, September 4th, they left us, in lat. 22° N., long. 51° W., directly under the tropic of Cancer.

For several days we lay "humbugging about" in the Horse latitudes, with all sorts of winds and weather, and occasionally, a thunderstorm. The first night after the trade-winds left us, while we were in the latitude of the island of Cuba, we had a specimen of a true tropical thunderstorm. Before midnight it was dead calm, and a heavy black cloud had shrouded the whole sky. When our watch came on deck at twelve o'clock it was as black as Erebus; not a breath was stirring; the sails hung heavy and motionless from the yards; and the perfect stillness, and the darkness, which was almost palpable, were truly appalling. Not a word was spoken, but everyone stood as though waiting for something to happen. In a few minutes the mate came forward, and in a low tone, which was almost a whisper, told us to haul down the jib. The fore and mizzen top-gallant-sails were taken in, in the same silent manner; and we lay motionless upon the water, with an uneasy expectation, which, from the long suspense, became actually painful. Soon the mate came forward again and gave an order to clew up the main top-gallant-sail; and so infectious was the awe and silence that the clewlines and buntlines were hauled up without any of the customary singing out at the ropes. An English lad and myself went up to furl it; and we had just got the bunt up when the mate called out to us something, we did not hear what; but, supposing it to be an order to bear a hand, we hurried, and made all fast, and came down, feeling our way among the rigging. When we got down we found all hands looking aloft, and there, directly over where we had been standing, upon the main top-gallant mast-head, was a ball of light, which the sailors name a corposant (*corpus sancti*). They were all watching it carefully, for sailors have a notion that if the corposant rises in the rigging it is a sign of fair weather, but if it comes lower down there will be a storm. Unfortunately, as an omen, it came down, and showed itself on the top-gallant yard-arm.

In a few minutes it disappeared and showed itself again on the fore top-gallant-yard, and, after playing about, disappeared again, when the man on the forecastle pointed to it upon the flying jib-boom-end. In a few minutes low grumbling thunder was heard, and some random flashes of lightning came from the southwest. Every sail was taken in but the topsail. A few puffs lifted the topsails, but they fell again to the mast, and all was as still as ever. A moment more and a terrific flash and peal broke simultaneously upon us, and a cloud appeared to open directly over our heads, and let down the water in one body like a falling ocean. Peal after peal rattled over our heads with a sound which actually seemed to stop the breath in the body. The violent fall of the rain lasted but a few minutes, but the lightning continued incessant for several hours, breaking the midnight darkness with irregular and blinding flashes.

During this time hardly a word was spoken, no bells were struck, and the wheel was silently relieved. The rain fell in heavy showers, and we stood drenched through, and blinded by the flashes, which broke the darkness with a brightness which seemed almost malignant; while the thunder rolled in peals, the concussion of which appeared to shake the very ocean. A ship is not often injured by lightning for the electricity is separated by the great number of points she presents and the quantity of iron which she has scattered in various parts. The electric fluid ran over our anchors, topsail-sheets, and ties; yet no harm was done. We went below at four o'clock, leaving things in the same state. It is not easy to sleep when the very next flash may tear the ship in two or set her on fire; or where the death-like calm may be broken by the blast of a hurricane taking the masts out of the ship. But a man is no sailor if he cannot sleep when he turns-in, and turn out when he's called. And when, at seven bells, the customary "All the larboard watch, ahoy!" brought us on deck, it was a clear, sunny morning, the ship going leisurely, with a good breeze, and all sail set.

CHAPTER XXXIII

In the Gulf Stream

From the latitude of the West Indies, until we got inside the Bermudas, where we took the westerly and southwesterly winds, which blow steadily off the coast of the United States early in the autumn, we had two or three moderate gales, which came on in the usual manner, of which one is a specimen of all. — A fine afternoon; all hands at work, some in the rigging, and others on deck; a stiff breeze, and ship close upon the wind, and skysails brailed down. Latter part of the afternoon, breeze increases, ship lies over to it, and clouds look windy. Spray begins to fly over the forecastle, and wets the yarns the boys are knotting; — ball them up and put them below. — Mate knocks off work, and orders a man aloft to send the royal halyards over to windward, as he comes down. One of the boys furls the mizzen royal. — Mate gives orders to get supper by the watch, instead of all hands, as usual. — While eating supper, hear the watch on deck taking in the royals. — Coming on deck, find it is blowing harder, and an ugly head sea is running. — Instead of having all hands on the forecastle in the dog-watch, one watch goes below and turns-in.

320

Clouds look black and wild; wind rising, and ship working hard against a heavy head sea, which breaks over the forecastle, and washes aft through the scuppers. Still no more sail is taken in. At eight bells the watch go below, with orders to "stand by for a call." We turn in "all standing," and keep awake; there is no use going to sleep to be waked again. — Wind whistles on deck, and ship works hard, groaning and creaking, and pitching into a heavy head sea, which strikes against the bows with a noise like knocking upon a rock. — By and by, an order is given: — "Aye, aye, sir!" from the forecastle; rigging is heaved down on deck; — the noise of a sail is heard fluttering aloft, and the short, quick cry which sailors make when hauling upon clewlines. — "Here comes his fore top-gallant-sail in!" — We are wide awake, and know all that's going on as well as if we were on deck. — A well-known voice is heard from the mast-head singing out to the officer of the watch to haul taut the weather brace. — Next thing, rigging is heaved down directly over our heads, and a long-drawn cry and a rattling of hanks announce that the flying-jib has come in. — The second mate holds on to the main top-gallant-sail until a heavy sea is shipped, and washes over the forecastle; when a noise further aft shows that sail, too, is taking in. — By and by, — bang, bang, bang, on the scuttle — "All ha-a-ands aho-o-y!" — We spring out of our berths, clap on a monkey-jacket and southwester, and tumble up the ladder. — Mate up before us, and on the forecastle, singing out like a roaring bull; the captain singing out on the quarter-deck; and the second mate yelling, like a hyena, in the waist. The ship is lying over half upon her beam ends; lee scuppers under water, and forecastle all in a smother of foam. — Rigging all let go, and washing about decks; topsail-yards down upon the caps, and sails flapping and beating against the masts; and starboard watch hauling out the reef-tackles of the main topsail. Our watch haul out the fore, and lay aloft and put two reefs into it, and reef the foresail, and race with the starboard watch, to see which will mast-head its topsail first. All hands tally-on to the main tack, and while some are furling the jib and hoisting the staysail, we mizzen topmen double-reef the mizzen topsail and hoist it up. All being made fast — "Go below, the watch!" and we turn in to sleep out the rest of the time, which is an hour and a half.

Beside the natural desire to get home, we had another reason for urging the ship on. The scurvy had begun to show itself on board. One man had it so badly as to be disabled and off duty; and the English lad, Ben, was in a dreadful state. His legs swelled and pained him so he could not walk; his flesh lost its elasticity; if it was pressed in it would not return to its shape; and his gums swelled until he could not open his mouth. His breath, too, became offensive; he lost all strength and spirit; could eat nothing; grew worse every day; and, unless something was done for him, would be a dead man in a week. The medicines were nearly all gone; and if we had had a chest-full, they would have been of no use; for nothing but fresh provisions and *terra firma* has any effect upon the scurvy.

Depending upon the westerly winds, which prevail off the coast in the autumn, the captain stood well to the westward, to run inside of the Bermudas in hope of falling in with some vessel bound to the West Indies or the Southern States. The scurvy had spread no farther among the crew, but there was danger it might; and these cases were bad ones.

Sunday, September 11th. Lat. 30° 04′ N., long. 63° 23′ W.; the Bermudas bearing north-north-west, distant one hundred and fifty miles. The next morning, about ten o'clock, "Sail ho!" was cried on deck, and all hands turned up to see the stranger. As she drew nearer, she proved to be an ordinary-looking hermaphrodite brig, standing south-southeast. She hove-to, seeing we wished to speak to her; and we ran down to her, boom-ended our studding-sails, backed our main top-sail, and hailed her — "Brig, ahoy!" — "Hallo!" — "Where are you from?" — "From New York, bound to Curaçoa." — "Have you any fresh provisions to spare?" — "Aye, aye! plenty of them!" We lowered away the quarter-boat instantly; the captain and four hands sprang in, and were soon dancing over the water, and alongside the brig. In half an hour they returned with half a boat-load of potatoes and onions, and each vessel filled away, and kept on her course. She proved to be the brig *Solon*, of Plymouth, from the Connecticut river, and last from New York, bound to this Spanish Main, with a cargo of fresh provisions, mules, tin bake-pans, and other *notions*.

It was just dinner-time when we filled away; and the steward, taking a few bunches of onions for the cabin, gave the rest to us, with a bottle of vinegar. We stowed them away in the forecastle, refusing to have them cooked, and ate them raw, with our beef and bread. And a glorious treat they were. The freshness and crispness of the raw onion, with the earthy taste, give it a great relish to one who has been a long time on salt provisions. We ate them at every meal, and filled our pockets with them, to eat in our watch on deck. The chief use, however, of the fresh provisions was for the men with the scurvy. One of them was able to eat, and he soon brought himself to by gnawing upon raw potatoes; but the other, by this time, was hardly able to open his mouth; and the cook took the potatoes raw, pounded them in a mortar, and gave him the juice to drink. The strong earthy taste and smell of this extract of the raw potato at first produced a shuddering through his whole frame, and after drinking it, an acute pain, which ran through all parts of his body; but knowing by this that it was taking strong hold, he persevered, drinking a spoonful every hour or so, until, by the effect of this drink, and of his own restored hope, he became so well as to be able to move about, and open his mouth enough to eat the raw potatoes and onions pounded into a soft pulp. This course soon restored his appetite and strength; and ten days after we spoke the *Solon*, that, from lying helpless and almost hopeless in his berth, he was at the mast-head, furling a royal.

With a fine southwest wind we passed inside of the Bermudas; and notwithstanding the old couplet —

"If the Bermudas let you pass,
    You must beware of Hatteras —"

we were to the northward of Hatteras, with good weather and beginning to count the hours, to the time when we should be at anchor in Boston harbor.

Thursday, September 15th. This morning the temperature and appearance of the water, the gulf-weed floating about, and a bank of clouds lying directly before us, showed that we were on the border of the Gulf Stream. This remarkable current, running northeast, nearly across the ocean, is almost constantly shrouded in clouds, and is the region of storms and heavy seas. Vessels often run from a clear sky and light wind, with all sail, at once into a heavy sea and cloudy sky, with double-reefed topsails. As we drew into it the sky became cloudy, the sea high, and everything had the appearance of the going off, or the coming on, of a storm. It was blowing no more than a stiff breeze; yet the wind, being northeast, which is directly against the course of the current, made an ugly, chopping sea, which heaved and pitched the vessel about, so that we were obliged to send down the royal-yards, and to take in our light sails. At noon the thermometer showed the temperature to be seventy, which was considerably above that of the air — as is always the case in the center of the Stream. A few hours more carried us through; and when we saw the sun go down we had left the bank of dark, stormy clouds astern in the twilight.

CHAPTER XXXIV

In Harbor

Friday, September 16th. Lat. 38° N.; long. 69° 00′ W. A fine southwest wind, carrying us nearer in toward the land. All hands on deck at the dog-watch, and nothing talked about but our getting in. Everyone was in the best spirits; and the voyage being nearly at an end, the strictness of discipline was relaxed. The little differences and quarrels which a long voyage breeds on board a ship were forgotten, and everyone was friendly. When the mate came forward he talked to the men, and said we should be on George's Bank before to-morrow noon; and joked with the boys, promising to go and see them, and to take them down to Marblehead in a coach.

Saturday, 17th. The wind was light all day, which kept us back somewhat; but a fine breeze springing up at nightfall, we were running fast in toward the land. At six o'clock we expected to have the ship hove-to for soundings, as a thick fog coming up showed we were near them; but no order was given, and we kept on our way. Eight o'clock came, and the watch went below; and, for the whole of the first hour, the ship was tearing on with studding-sails out, alow and aloft, and the night as dark as a pocket. At two bells the captain came on deck, and said a word to the mate, when the studding-sails were hauled into the tops, or boom-ended, the after-yards backed, the deep-sea lead carried forward, and everything got ready for sounding. A man on the sprit-sail yard with the lead, another on the cat-head with a handful of the line coiled up, another in the fore-chains, another in the waist, and another in the main-chains — each with a quantity of the line coiled away in his hand. "All ready there, forward?" "Aye, aye, sir!" "He-e-ave!" "Watch! ho! watch!" sings out the man on the sprit-sail yard, and the heavy lead drops in the water. "Watch! ho! watch!" bawls the man on the cat-head, as the last fake of the coil drops from his hand; and "Watch! ho! watch!" is shouted by each one as the line falls from his hold, until it comes to the mate, who tends the lead, and has the line in coils on the quarter-deck. Eighty fathoms, and no bottom! The line is snatched in a block upon the swifter, and three or four men haul it in and coil it away. The after-yards are braced full, the studding-sails hauled out again, and in a few minutes more the ship has her whole way upon her. At four bells, backed again, hove the lead, and — soundings! at sixty fathoms! Hurrah for Yankee land! Hand over hand we hauled the lead in, and the captain, taking it to the light, found black mud on the bottom. Studding-sails taken in; after-yards filled, and ship kept on under easy sail all night, the wind dying away.

Being off Block Island, our course was due east to Nantucket Shoals and the South Channel; but the wind died away, and left us becalmed in a thick fog, in which we lay all Sunday. At noon, *Sunday, 18th,* Block Island bore, by calculation, N.W. ¼ W. fifteen miles; but the fog was so thick all day that we could see nothing.

Having got through the ship's duty, and washed and shaved, we went below, and had a fine time overhauling our chests, laying aside the clothes we meant to go ashore in, and throwing overboard all that were worn out and good for nothing. We got our chests all ready for going ashore; ate the last "duff" we expected to have on board the ship *Alert*; and talked as confidently about matters on shore as though our anchor were on the bottom.

Toward night a moderate breeze sprang up, the fog, however, continuing as thick as before. About the middle of the first watch a man on the forecastle sung out, in a tone which showed that there was not a moment to be lost, "Hard up the helm!" and a great ship loomed up out of the fog, coming directly down upon us. She luffed at the same moment, and we just passed one another — our spanker-boom grazing over her quarter. The fog continued through the night, with a very light breeze, before which we ran to the eastward, literally feeling our way along. The lead was hove every two hours, and the gradual change from black mud to sand showed that we were approaching Nantucket South Shoals.

On Monday morning the increased depth and deep blue color of the water, and the mixture of shells and white sand which we brought up, upon sounding, showed that we were in the channel and nearing George's. Accordingly, the ship's head was put directly to the northward, and we stood on, with perfect confidence in the soundings, though we had not taken an observation for two days, nor seen land. Throughout the day a provokingly light wind prevailed, and at eight o'clock a small fishing schooner, which we passed, told us we were nearly abreast of Chatham lights. Just before midnight a light land-breeze sprang up, which carried us well along; and at four o'clock, thinking ourselves to the northward of Race Point, we hauled upon the wind, and stood into the bay, north-northwest, for Boston light, and commenced firing guns for a pilot. Our watch went below at four o'clock, but could not sleep, for the watch on deck were banging away at the guns every few minutes.

We turned out at daybreak to get a sight of land. In the gray of the morning, one or two small fishing smacks peered out of the mist; and when the broad day broke upon us, there lay the low sand-hills of Cape Cod over our larboard quarter, and before us the wide waters of Massachusetts Bay, with here and there a sail gliding over its smooth surface. As we drew in toward the mouth of the harbor the vessels began to multiply, until the bay seemed actually alive with sails gliding about in every direction — some on the wind, others before it, as they were bound to or from the emporium of trade and center of the bay. It was a stirring sight for us who had been months on the ocean without seeing anything but two solitary sails, and over two years without seeing more than the three or four traders on an almost desolate coast. About ten o'clock a little boat came bobbing over the water, and put a pilot on board. Being now within the scope of the telegraph stations, our signals were run up at the fore; and in half an hour afterwards the owner on 'Change, or in his counting-room, knew that his ship was below.

The wind continuing very light, all hands were sent aloft to strip off the chafing gear; and battens, parcellings, roundings, hoops, mats, and leathers came flying from aloft, and left the rigging neat and clean, stripped of all its sea bandaging. The last touch was put to the vessel by painting the skysail poles, and I was sent up to the fore, with a bucket of white paint and a brush, and touched her off, from the truck to the eyes of the royal rigging. At noon we lay becalmed off the lower lighthouse, and it being about slack water, we made little progress. About two o'clock a breeze sprang up ahead, from the westward, and we began beating up against it. A full-rigged brig was beating in at the same time, and we passed one another in our tacks, sometimes one and sometimes the other working to windward, as the wind and tide favored or opposed. It was my trick at the wheel from two till four, and I stood my last helm, making between nine hundred and a thousand hours which I had spent at the helms of our two vessels. The tide beginning to set against us, we made slow work; and the afternoon was nearly spent before we got abreast of the inner light. Toward sundown the wind came off in flaws, sometimes blowing very stiff, so that the pilot took in the royals, and then it died away — when, in order to get us in before the tide became too strong, the royals were set again. As this kept us running up and down the rigging all the time, one hand was sent aloft at each mast-head, to stand by to loose and furl the sails at the moment of the order.

We had all set our hearts upon getting up to town before night, and going ashore; but the tide, beginning to run strong against us, and the wind being ahead, we made but little by weather-bowing the tide, and the pilot gave orders to cockbill the anchor and overhaul the chain. Making two long stretches, which brought us into the roads, under the lee of the Castle, he clewed up the topsails and let go the anchor; and for the first time since leaving San Diego — one hundred and thirty-five days — our anchor was upon bottom. In half an hour more we were lying snugly, with all sails furled, safe in Boston harbor, our long voyage ended.

We had just done furling the sails, when a beautiful little pleasure-boat luffed up into the wind, under our quarter, and the junior partner of the firm, to which our ship belonged, jumped on board. I saw him from the mizzen topsail-yard, and knew him well. He shook the captain by the hand, and went down into the cabin, and in a few moments came up and inquired of the mate for me. The last time I had seen him I was in the uniform of an under-graduate of Harvard College, and now, to his astonishment, there came down from aloft a "rough alley" looking fellow, with duck trousers and red shirt, long hair, and face burnt as black as an Indian's. He shook me by the hand, congratulated me upon my return, and my appearance of health and strength, and said my friends were all well.

The captain went up to town in the boat with Mr. H—, and left us to pass another night on board ship, and to come up with the morning's tide under command of the pilot.

So much did we feel ourselves to be already at home, that our plain supper was barely touched; and many on board, to whom this was the first voyage, could scarcely sleep.

About ten o'clock a sea-breeze sprang up, and the pilot gave orders to get the ship under weigh. All hands manned the windlass; and the long-drawn "Yo, heave, ho!" which we had last heard dying away among the desolate hills of San Diego, soon brought the anchor to the bows; and, with a fair wind and tide, a bright sunny morning, royals and skysails set ensign, streamer, signals, and pennant flying, and with our guns firing, we came swiftly and handsomely up to the city. Off the end of the wharf, we rounded-to and let go our anchor; and no sooner was it on the bottom than the decks were filled with people — custom house officers; Topliff's agent, to inquire for news; others inquiring for friends on board, or left upon the coast; and last and chief, boarding-house runners, to secure their men. The city bells were just ringing one when the last turn was made fast, and the crew dismissed; and in five minutes more, not a soul was left on board the good ship *Alert* but the old ship-keeper, who had come down from the counting-house to take charge of her.